WHITE WATER SKIPPERS
OF THE NORTH

DEDICATION

To all those captains, steamboat men and
families who lost their lives on the
Princess Sophia during the wreck in 1918.

WHITE WATER SKIPPERS
OF THE NORTH

THE BARRINGTONS

Nancy Warren Ferrell

hancock

house

ISBN 978-0-88839-616-7
Copyright © 2008 Nancy Warren Ferrell   2nd printing 2010

Cataloging in Publication Data

Ferrell, Nancy Warren
    White water skippers of the north : the Barringtons /
Nancy Warren Ferrell.

Includes bibliographical references and index.
ISBN 978-0-88839-616-7

    1. Barrington family. 2. River boats—British Columbia,
Northern—History. 3. River boats—Yukon Territory—History.
4. River boats—Alaska—History. 5. River boats—Washington
(State)—Puget Sound—History. 6. Klondike River Valley
(Yukon)—Gold discoveries. 7. Ship captains—United States—
Biography. I. Title.

VK140.B36F47 2008   386'.30922   C2008-907826-8

Printed in South Korea — PACOM

Editor: Nancy Miller, Theresa Laviolette
Indexing: Ann Chandonnet
Production: Mia Hancock
Cover Design: Ingrid Luters
Front cover images: *SS Clifford Sifton,* Yukon Archives, MacBride Museum Coll.,
Whitehorse; Barrington children, courtesy Island County Historical Society, Washington State

Published simultaneously in Canada and the United States by

HANCOCK HOUSE PUBLISHERS LTD.
19313 Zero Avenue, Surrey, B.C. Canada V3S 9R9
(604) 538-1114 Fax (604) 538-2262

HANCOCK HOUSE PUBLISHERS
1431 Harrison Avenue, Blaine, WA U.S.A. 98230-5005
(604) 538-1114 Fax (604) 538-2262

Website: **www.hancockhouse.com**
Email: **sales@hancockhouse.com**

CONTENTS

ACKNOWLEDGMENTS

This book is given richness by the kindnesses of contributors. Special thanks go to Bill and Elna Barrington (now passed away) and Peggy Darst Townsdin of Coupeville, Washington, who spoke with me over and over. Peggy Darst Townsdin is credited for most of the personal photographs in the book, as well as many of the memories. Bill and Elna, too, contributed photographs and helped me with fleshing out the sections on the Barrington brothers and their families. My heartfelt appreciation goes to Liisa Barrington Johnson, now the custodian of Bill and Elna's photos, and Ed Barrington, Anchorage. Thanks also to Marlene and Hill Barrington, III of Tacoma, Washington, who shared memories, taped and otherwise.

Thank you to those who gave interviews: Ed Arola, Charles "Jim" Binkley, Amos Burg, Daisy Callbreath, Edwin Callbreath, Leonard Campbell, Edith Carter, Robert DeArmond, David and Jean Ellis, Darlynne Gendreau, Betty Henning, Bob Henning, Kay Jabusch, Cathy Kaer, Verna Kaer, Lael Morgan, Ken Mason, Patricia Neal, Dorothy Otteson, Ed Rasmuson, Margaret Rose Seimears and Theresa Thibault.

Thank you to agencies who provided a great deal of information, services and photographs: KTOO Broadcasting (Jeff Brown) of Juneau, Alaska; Yukon Archives, Whitehorse, Yukon Territory; Dawson City Museum & Historical Society, Whitehorse; Suselow Library, University of Washington Libraries, Seattle, Washington; Alaska Historical Library (Gladi Culp and Jim Simard), Juneau; Juneau Public Library, Juneau; University of Alaska, Fairbanks,

Alaska; Irene Ingle Public Library, Wrangell, Alaska; Columbia River Maritime Museum, Astoria, Oregon; Jefferson County Historical Society, Port Townsend, Washington; National Archives and Records Administration (Pacific Alaska Region), Seattle, Washington; Seattle Public Library, Seattle; San Francisco Maritime National Historical Park, San Francisco, California; Island County Historical Society, Coupeville, Washinton; *Wrangell Sentinel* newspaper, Wrangell, Alaska; *Alaska* magazine, Anchorage, Alaska.

A sincere appreciation goes to my husband, Ed Ferrell, who offered comments, information and encouragement along the journey. Not to be forgotten is my writing group—Bridget Smith, Jean Rogers and Susi Gregg Fowler—for their full writing view and strong support.

PREFACE

Years ago I was researching Barrett Willoughby for my book *Barrett Willoughby: Alaska's Forgotten Lady*. In her own book, *Gentlemen Unafraid,* I came across the feature she had done on Sydney Barrington. My curiosity found Barrington's adventures fascinating, and I wanted to know more about him. I checked to find a book on the family. None. The Alaska State Library had a few bits about Syd on its international research network. The scattered references only challenged me. The more I talked to people, the chains of information led from Dawson City, Juneau, Fairbanks, Anchorage and Wrangell on to Washington's Whidbey Island and Tacoma, and even to Ottawa, Canada. Trails continued into newspapers, archives, homes and libraries. The most meaningful excursions took me to meet with several important and helpful people who knew or knew of this daring steamboat family of the Pacific Northwest.

Along the way I learned that the Barringtons not only ran their lives on steamboats, but also that gambling and gold drove their lives as well. And, oh, what adventures they had.

INTRODUCTION

Occasionally in time, a family and its place in history are right for each other. Two family generations of mariners, both fueled by gambling blood and gold, wove their own unique stories. Such were the Barrington captains during the full journey of commercial riverboating in the Northwest.

Father Edward Barrington, Sr., a tall, fiery redhead, pioneered river travel in the mid-1850s.[1]

Lured west from the Cape Breton area of Nova Scotia in Canada to the California goldfields in the United States, Barrington soon found his way north. From canoe to rowboat to schooner, the determined businessman carved a livelihood from the wilds of Whidbey Island, Washington. Native Indians proved a danger then, but they grew both to fear and respect the skipper—Red Devil they called him.

Edward Sr. eventually married Christina McCrohan in 1865,[2] and a crew of offspring soon followed. The family, sons Eddie, Harry, Sydney, Yorke and Hill, also included a half-sister Olivia, and another sister, Sibella. All prospered on Whidbey, the island becoming a home for future generations.

The senior Barrington died in 1883.[3]

Historians labeled him the "Father of Captains," boat captains who earned a strong reputation in the Northwest. Carrying on in their father's tradition, it was only natural the sons looked to the sea. In the late 1880s and into the '90s, the boys, one after another, hired on ships plying the waters of Puget Sound. Four of the boys eventually made their livelihood running boats in Washington, British Columbia, the Yukon Territory and Alaska. Storytellers, gamblers, men of reckless daring, these adventurers, like their vessels, experienced a lusty existence marked with triumph and tragedy.

The Klondike Gold Rush in Canada began it all. When news burst upon the world in 1897, the boys—in the right place at the right time, with the right personalities—grabbed their gear and headed north. Like their parents, the young men would need fortitude and humor as they faced, and embraced, the most exciting frontier of a decade.

• • •

1. E.W. Wright (Editor), *Lewis and Dryden's Marine History of the Pacific Northwest.* Seattle: Antiquarian Press, 1961.
2. Lucile McDonald, "The Barringtons of Oak Harbor." *Seattle Times,* Nov. 29, 1964.
3. Ibid.

First store in Oak Harbor, Washington, built by Ed Barrington Sr. in the 1860s.
Credit: Courtesy of Peggy Darst Townsdin.

Edward Barrington Sr. and Christina McCrohan on their wedding day in 1865.
Credit: Courtesy of Peggy Darst Townsdin.

Barrington Children. Ed (16) sitting on left, Yorke (7), Harry (11) standing behind, Syd (5) sitting in front, Sibella (13), Hill (3) far right.
Credit: Courtesy of the Island County Historical Society, Washington.

1: THE CALL NORTH

Growing up in a mariner's household, it seemed natural for the Barrington brothers to step into the wheelhouse. After Edward Sr.'s death in 1883, there was, too, a livelihood to be made. In his teens, Ed Jr. took up steamboating, followed by Harry and Sydney after their schooling. For their eagerness to be out on the water, the boys earned their unlimited master's licenses when they were only twenty-one years old.[1] (Being the highest license level, that meant the boys could operate a ship of any size with unlimited passengers aboard.) All the Barringtons made good money with their ability. Eddie managed to buy a small boat of his own, the *Cricket*. Only brother Yorke opted for a landlubber's life and went into the drugstore business in Seattle.

With their father's head for business, the brothers kept up with national news. For a number of reasons—poor Wall Street investments and too much railroad building, to mention two—the United States fell into an economic depression in the 1890s. Seattle experienced the decline too. Jobs were scarce.

News of gold discoveries in Alaska's wilderness drifted south in mid-decade. Birch Creek near Circle City in eastern Alaska was one of the discovery locations, the Cook Inlet area of Southcentral Alaska another. Gamblers and risk-takers at heart, the Barrington brothers yearned to go. But they had no money to grubstake a trip north, until one day a boat fire offered the opportunity.

In February of 1896, Ed's small passenger steamer, *Cricket*, broke from her moorings in Everett and burned. With the $1,325 insurance

Ed Barrington, Jr. mastered on the *Wasco* in the late 1880s and early 1890s in the Puget Sound area. Here the *Wasco* is making a run to Anacortes.
Credit: Courtesy of Peggy Darst Townsdin.

proceeds from the wreck,[2] Ed and Syd bought outdoor gear and hired on with a company headed north to Cook Inlet. As soon as northern grounds could be worked, the prospecting party took off. The crew sailed to the Sunrise City area on the Kenai Peninsula[3] in 1896. All the men dug into hard work for the summer.

Young Hill longed to join his brothers, but he was still a teenage boy, just out of high school. Besides, the family thought one in their number should be college educated. The family sent Hill to study at San Francisco's Cooper Medical School in 1896.

Hill's high energy, fun-loving style persisted in the California school setting. Very soon after arriving there Hill, along with several pranksters in his chemistry class, concocted a foam mercury mixture. Secretly, they poured it on a section of street trolley tracks running downtown. When the trolley car rolled over the rails, the foam burst like exploding firecrackers.[4] Imagine the students' glee as the trolley riders jumped and screamed. Yet, no harm done.

Meanwhile Ed and Syd prospected in the Cook Inlet area.

Young Eddie Barrington, Jr. Photo taken in Seattle possibly before 1890.
Credit: Courtesy of Peggy Darst Townsdin.

Syd Barrington and cousin Allie Nunan, Whidbey Island, circa 1890–95.
Credit: Island Country Historical Society.

Most of the Barrington brothers captained on the steamer *Fairhaven* at one time or another.
Credit: Courtesy of Peggy Darst Townsdin.

On the steamer *Greyhound,* Puget Sound in the early 1890s.
Eddie Jr. as captain, with Harry to his left and relative Tom
Nunan on the far left of the photo.
Credit: Courtesy of Peggy Darst Townsdin.

The smaller *Cricket* was one of the boats Harry and Eddie mastered
on the inland sea of Puget Sound.
Credit: Courtesy of Peggy Darst Townsdin.

Relative Al Nunan on the left, Hill Barrington on the right. Photo taken in Washington in the early 1890s.
Credit: Courtesy of Peggy Darst Townsdin.

"Our party left Seattle on June 2," Ed told a *Seattle Times* reporter, "and arrived at Tyonook, in Cook inlet, about 120 miles above the mouth on the 13th."[5] The crew labored hard all summer. Yet even into late August the weather turned cold. "Already the miners are getting out by the hundreds," Ed wrote in a letter home to his mother. "There are a few good claims here, but they are all owned and it gives the outsiders no show at all. Syd is cook for the 12 of us."[6]

The first lengthy time away from home proved a crushing blow for men from a warm family. Homesickness hit them both. "I was sorry and much disappointed mail day," Ed went on in the same letter, "as I walked 19 miles over the rainyist mountain trail to get mail and I wanted one [letter] from you more than anything. And I waited 3 days for the mail boat and there was no mail from you or York and I never felt so bad in my life to think that I had to walk back home without any letters."[7]

Finally, the miners gave up hope of hitting pay streak. After working one side of the claim and pulling out $850 (roughly $36,000 in today's money), they decided to abandon the diggings.[8] The Cook Inlet venture, Ed told a reporter after returning in the fall of 1896, proved a disappointment, but he finished the season. After all, he had earned wages over his expenses and was not out anything.[9]

Perhaps as the Barringtons worked their Cook Inlet claim, they heard talk of rich diggings east in the Yukon area of Canada. The air, however, often hung heavy with rumors, and with the bright hope of Cook Inlet fizzling out, the experience left them discouraged.

As Syd told a Seattle reporter, the trip south across the Gulf of Alaska to Washington proved harrowing: "We left for home on the 26th of September [1896], about 40 passengers taking passage in the schooner. On the second day out we encountered a terrific gale, in which we lost our rudder and narrowly escaped being shipwrecked. The wind blew 80 or 90 knots, and if our schooner had not been an uncommonly staunch sea boat, she never would have weathered it."[10]

Returning from Cook Inlet, Edward took positions, in turn, on the Seattle fire boats *Snoqualmie* and *Fairhaven*. Then, like so many others, the Barringtons' lives dramatically changed when the Klondike steamer, *Portland*, docked in Seattle on July 17, 1897. The blast from its horn trumpeted a fantastic gold strike in Canada.

Newspaper headlines electrified the Puget Sound area. Riches! Gold! A Ton of It! Adventure! Here was the distraction from hard times. Here was the last great adventure. "Come to Seattle, the Gateway to Alaska and the Yukon," the Chamber of Commerce advertised.[11] Forget everything. Just go. Get there fast, before all the claims are staked![12]

In a blink, minds switched from everyday survival to dreams of wealth. News bulletins flashed around the world.

The trip Syd and Ed made to Cook Inlet in 1896 might have been the itch, but arrival of the *Portland* steamer in Seattle the following July, 1897, demanded action. For adventurers like the Barringtons and thousands of others, such an explosive shout of "Gold!" could not be denied.

It was at this time Syd thought of Hill in San Francisco, missing all the excitement. Closest in age to Syd—Hill almost twenty, Syd just twenty-two—the two had forged a strong brother-bond that lasted all their lives. Syd sent a telegram.

Hill's medical ambitions could not have been intense, for when Syd's wire arrived telling him to steer for the Klondike gold rush,[13] the younger brother bolted back to Seattle. "I figured I'd kill the first 50 patients I operated on when I became a doctor," Hill said, "and I didn't want it on my conscience…I closed the books and headed north."[14]

And so the adventure began.

• • •

1. "Capt. Sydney Barrington Services Set." *Seattle Post-Intelligencer*, June 29 [?], 1963.
2. Gordon Newell (Ed), *The H.W. McCurdy Marine History of the Pacific Northwest*. Seattle: Superior Publishing Company, 1966, p. 7.
3. R.M. Patterson, *Trail to the Interior*. NY: William Morrow and Co., 1966, p. 37.
4. Seattle phone conversation with grandson, Hill Barrington, III in Tacoma, Feb. 18, 1998.
5. "From Cook Inlet" *Seattle Times*, undated, sometime in 1896. Courtesy of Peggy Darst Townsdin, Coupeville, WA.
6. Letter from Ed Barrington Jr. to his mother, Aug. 7, 1896. Courtesy of Peggy Darst Townsdin.
7. Ibid., courtesy of Peggy Darst Townsdin.
8. "From Cook Inlet." *Seattle Times*, undated, sometime in 1896. Courtesy of Peggy Townsdin, Coupeville.
9. "Obituary." *Island County Times*, specific date not available, Sept. 1898. Courtesy of Peggy Darst Townsdin.
10. "From Cook Inlet." *Seattle Times*, undated, probably 1896. Courtesy of Peggy Darst Townsdin, Coupeville.
11. www.washington.edu/unwired/outreach/cspn Center for the Study of the Pacific Northwest, July, 2003.
12. Lisa Mighetto and Marcia Montgomery, *Hard Drive to the Klondike*. Seattle: Northwest Interpretive Assoc. with the University of Washington Press, 2002, p. 10.
13. Conversation with Elna Barrington, Anchorage, August 29, 1998.
14. Peggy Darst Townsdin, *History of a Whidbey Island Family*. Clipping from an Oak Harbor newspaper, Dec. 29, 1966, titled: "Captain Born Here in 1877."

2: THE FIRST ADVENTURE

The 1897 Klondike Gold Rush was on. Swarms of stampeders hiked through Canada, or rushed to gateways via Skagway, St. Michael, Wrangell, or Dyea crammed upon yachts, scows, sloops, steamers and barges. As author Pierre Berton wrote, "many of them little more than floating coffins."[1] Everyone longed to get there fast.

Living in the Seattle area proved the right place at the right time. The brothers, along with cousin, George Nunan, packed themselves aboard the little Pacific Coast steamer *Al-ki*. Of the many ships preparing to go, the *Al-ki* was the first to set off the day after the *Portland* arrived in July of 1897.[2] The Barringtons found themselves only a few among the 9,000 hopefuls who charged north by the end of summer.[3] To the stampeders, the boats could not speed fast enough.

The men sailed to Skagway up the Inside Passage, then tramped to Dyea, three miles away. After a grueling sixteen-mile hike, they packed into Canada over the Chilkoot Pass, a dauntingly precipitous climb. On their backs, pounds and pounds of supplies weighted them down. Syd later remembered the struggle to the top where, exhausted, he gazed down at the long line of stampeders. "I often looked back down at the hundreds of men with packs, and wondered what the hell we were all doing it for."[4]

On to thirty-two-mile-long Lake Bennett which, by then, was more a boat building hub than a vast, serene wilderness. A litter of tents crowded back from the shoreline. Like feverish insects, stampeders busied themselves, saws scraping, hammers pounding, the air dense with smoke and noise. In a period of two months, stampeder

Dyea, Alaska — Route to the Klondike goldfields
through Chilkoot Pass.
Credit: University of Alaska: Moore; 76-35-43 N

Angelo Heilprin recalled that about 3,000 craft "—sailboats, scows, and canoes, many of the lighter ones brought bodily over the passes— were launched upon the still icy waters of Lake Bennett."[5] Stampeders, wild to make Dawson, but with no transportation, booked on dog sleds, horse sleds, horses, canoes and steamers. Some used kayaks, arks or skiffs; some fashioned boats from hollowed tree trunks, even floating packing boxes—any mode to get there fast.[6] Everyone was crazy to reach the crude town of Dawson in the Klondike.

No record exists of the Barrington's trip to Dawson that fall. Likely they constructed or bought a boat. Down the Yukon River they floated, past Caribou Crossing, perhaps portaging around Miles Canyon and Whitehorse Rapids, and on to a new community springing up—Whitehorse.[7] Still a 400-mile journey to go, from there they would have gone through Five Finger Rapids, down Lake Lebarge, passing tributaries, the Teslin, the Big Salmon, the Ross, the Pelly, the Stewart, the White, and on to the Klondike. And there was Dawson, a tent and log town that was a hive of people and activity. The

A long line of humans extends from the steep stretch of the Chilkoot Pass out of Alaska and British Columbia during the late 1890s gold rush.
Credit: Stereographic Coll. UAF 1975-0178-27

Barringtons survived the run, making it through before freeze-up that brutal winter.

The young men prospected the Klondike a few months. They staked several claims[8] of different sizes as close to the main discovery claim as they could. The boys experienced good and bad luck. After working five or six days, the brothers dug out about $70,000 worth of gold. A sum to excite any prospector, and roughly equivalent to more than $3 million in today's gold market.[9] An agent for the rich American Guggenheim organization heard of this success, and offered to buy them out. Sell out on a good claim? No, they answered. Figuring they could take out more than offered, the Barringtons turned it down, only to see their pay streak run out against a rock wall a few days later.[10]

If the Barringtons had not learned from Cook Inlet, they certainly discovered it now: King Midas proved a fickle ruler. The claim above theirs owned by someone else pulled out $700,000, while the claim below hauled out over a million dollars in gold. Although the Barrington party sank twenty-one holes on their property, Hill said, they only found one $5 rock.[11]

In nearby Dawson, provisions dwindled to a frightening level.

Mining crew. Hill Barrington sitting on big rock in center.
(Location and date unknown.)
Credit: Bill and Elna Barrington Collection

Some stampeders, their pockets heavy with gold, had to kill their dogs because there was no food to feed them. As with supply and demand, prices tripled. Salt was literally worth its weight in gold.[13]

Hard and disappointing times faced the Barringtons, too. As food quickly disappeared, and with little hope of restocking over the winter, the brothers decided to head for Seattle that December of 1897. No record of the journey exists, but the trek proved a fight for survival. Braving temperatures well below zero, and being last to cross the snow and ice, the journey[12] took twenty-three brutal days to complete.

Forget the horrors, however. The brothers were hooked. The gold was there! They would keep searching.

And until the gamble with gold succeeded, they would make their fortune by another route. They would pilot the Yukon River sternwheelers, hauling the hundreds of fortune-seekers to the gold fields. The Barringtons had the skills and hard work would provide the way.

The main headwaters of the Yukon River itself burst from an ice cave in the Llewellyn Glacier of northwestern B.C. Each day about a thousand *tons* of silt pour out, and more in the peak of summer. Silt was a major concern for steamer captains—or for any person who accidentally fell in the water.

At the time of the original strike in 1896, only four large sternwheelers navigated up and down the 2000-mile Yukon River,[14] far too few to carry the hordes coming later. Frantic boat building along the Pacific Coast brought more and more vessels to the river, but still not enough, and not fast enough. Those on sternwheelers crammed themselves in, often taking turns sleeping. Passengers "slept in relays," Syd told author Barrett Willoughby, "and the berths never had a chance to get cold."[15]

Others, like the White Pass and Yukon Company, saw the transportation demand, too. Already they had begun an "impossible" railway building job that would ease the way from saltwater into the interior.

This mammoth plan proved a three-year project building a 110-mile railroad from Skagway to Whitehorse. The first shovel turned over in May of 1898, under the experienced eye of Irish engineer Michael J. Heney. Without modern machinery, workers literally began hacking their way with pick, shovel and blasting powder, up, through and over the White Pass trail.[16] In effect then, this Skagway route could remain open longer, and would prove shorter, faster and easier for railway shipping.

The brothers, with their background, already had a jump on river traffic. Ed and Syd both carried Washington State master boat licenses. With a Canadian skipper on board they could pilot through either American or Canadian inland waters[17] and still be legal. Yukon companies valued these captains for their skill and knowledge. They paid them monthly all year around, even though they plied the river only during the open season.[18]

Eddie, the oldest Barrington brother, saw the Yukon River transportation possibilities right away. When the Barringtons returned south, Ed was aflame with plans, writing his mother in San de Fuca, Washington, from Seattle in February 1898: "A New York Co. wants me to go to work for them while I am in town building 2 boats. I have no work to do, only superintending the work and I get $250 per month so I may work a month and then [they may] offer me $100 a month to take charge of their interests in Alaska."[19]

Later in the spring after several profitable runs on the Yukon, Eddie wrote home: "The ACCo [Alaska Commercial Company] offered me $750 or $25.00 a day since I have made 3 successful trips."[20] Ed had proven himself. His steamboating skills were in demand. But he knew the sure "pay streak" of the Yukon lay in becoming an independent boat owner.

Before the gold rush, Ed Barrington, along with Syd, had run a small passenger and freight boat, the *Aquila*, between Tacoma and Seattle in Puget Sound.[21] Now, understanding how desperately stampeders needed transportation up north, Ed planned on shipping his boat to the Yukon. Ordinarily, if a captain did not actually sail a boat from Seattle, it was knocked down there and then shipped north in segments. After carting sections over the mountains, the owner would then reassemble it somewhere along the Yukon River where it began its journeys.

During his stay in Seattle that winter, Ed contracted to have the *Aquila* shipped over the mountains from Dyea, the motive simple and daring: he determined to be the first man to shoot the impossible downstream waters of Miles Canyon and Whitehorse Rapids under steam that spring when the ice broke on the Yukon River. He would wager money, of course, and prove his skill at the same time.

Closing out business interests in Seattle and saying goodbye to relatives, Syd, Hill and Ed sailed back to Dyea in April. What money they pocketed, the brothers invested in the steamboat business.

Such were the hectic conditions and setting as the Barringtons began steamboating on the Upper Yukon. They transported loads of stampeders and supplies to Dawson. Then back to Whitehorse for another quick run. Back and forth, back and forth. During the next two years, 100,000 people, on all modes of transportation, from all over the world, flooded through the Yukon area.[22]

For the Barrington brothers, what started as a one-time Klondike adventure running stampeders on the river, turned into a colorful, wild career. They were just getting started.

• • •

1. Pierre Berton, *The Klondike Fever*. NY: Alfred A. Knopf, 1960, p. 137.
2. "Capt. Barrington is Dead," *Seattle Post-Intelligencer*, Sept. 17, 1898.
3. Ibid, p. 123.
4. R.M. Patterson, *Trail to the Interior*. NY: William Morrow and Co., Inc., 1966, p. 37.
5. Angelo Heilprin, *Alaska and the Klondike*. NY: D. Appleton and Co., 1899, p. 25.

6. Ibid., Berton, p. 277.
7. Helene Dobrowolsky and Rob Ingram, *Edge of the River; Heart of the City*. Whitehorse, Canada: Lost Moose Publishing, 1994, p. 8.
8 ."Filson's Pan for Gold Database." Dawson City Museum. Internet. 1/8/98.
9. John J. McCusker, "Comparing the Purchasing Power of Money in the United States (or Colonies) from 1665 to Any Other Year Including the Present" Economic History Services, 2004, www.en.net/hmlt/ppowerusd/.
10. Ibid., Patterson, p. 38.
11. "Captain Born in 1877." *Whidbey News-Times*, Dec. 29, 1966.
12. Ibid., Berton, p. 75.
13. Ibid., map.
14. Barry C. Anderson, *Lifeline to the Yukon*. Seattle: Superior Publishing Co., 1983, p. 40.
15. Barrett Willoughby, "Champion White Water Pilot of the North." *American Magazine*, Oct. 1928, p. 30. A steamer of early Klondike days, the *Portus B. Weare*, tried to tout itself as having fancy fittings. To draw passengers, owners of the *Portus* declared in advertising the ship's "luxurious accommodations." Sourdoughs knew better. As to accommodations, old-timers said, "Of the *Portus*, beware." Burlingame, Virginia, "John J. Healy's Alaskan Adventure," *Alaska Journal*, Autumn, 1978, p. 313.
16. Howard Clifford, *Rails North*. Seattle, WA: Superior Publishing Co., 1981.
17. Letter to author from Angela Wheelock, Yukon Archives, Whitehorse, Yukon, dated Dec. 1, 1998.
18. "Off for the South." *Dawson Daily News*, October 14, 1903.
19. Letter from Ed Barrington to his mother, Seattle, WA, Seattle Athletic Club, Feb. 11, 1898. Courtesy of Peggy Darst Townsdin.
20. Letter from Ed Barrington to his mother, June 25, 1898. Courtesy of Peggy Darst Townsdin.
21. "Story of Steamboats." *Dawson Daily News*, May 19, 1900.
22. Michael Parfit, "The Untamed Yukon River." *National Geographic Magazine*, July, 1998, p. 110.

3: MAKING THEIR MARK

The 1898 spring atmosphere in the Yukon throbbed with life. The new Klondike gold find shifted prospecting focus from Circle City, Alaska, east to the booming Dawson area.

The Barrington boys accepted jobs piloting with the Alaska Commercial Company, whose ships plied the length of the Yukon River in Alaska and the Yukon Territory. They were assigned the sternwheeler, *Victoria*, recently built at St. Michaels[1] on the Bering Sea coast. Impatiently Eddie waited upriver on the Circle City waterfront for the Yukon River ice to break. The *Victoria* poised there, ready to strike for Dawson, and arrive as first boat of the season. Heavy betting marked the outcome.

To steam into Dawson leading the pack was a skipper's glory. The first boat after the ice breakup—racing from upriver or down—announced its captain "champion of the spring." Sailing in on the heels of ice meant you had "swept everyone else aside" and your boat could sprout proud brooms from the flagstaff.

That first real spring stampede set a pattern that grew in years to come. Clear weather or rough, day or night, no one could predict the exact time of a winning boat's arrival with certainty.[2] Dawson residents kept their ears tuned for the thunder of moving ice and their eyes peeled for smoke from a steamboat stack. And when the ice broke, the eager fleet would not be far behind.[3]

To greet the first boat, cheering townspeople stood on shore, docks, buildings, streets and on every empty spot. Released from their eight-month ice-bound freezer, they were anxious to bite into a fresh

A young Dawson City, four months old. (Undated)
Credit: Charles F. Metcalfe/Alaska Sate Library/ Charles Horton Metcalfe Coll./PCA 34-84.

Ice, during spring break-up at Dawson waterfront, makes the rules. Right foreground is the steamer *Schwatka*.
Credit: Dawson City Museum and Historical Society. Edna Sherbeck Coll. #991.42.13.

The power of ice can crush a boat. Here the *General Jeff C. Davis* is caught in Yukon River ice.
Credit: The Anchorage Museum of History and Art. B 64.1.722.

orange while reading a letter from home. Everyone wagered heavily on their favorite vessel; on occasion, as much as $150,000 changed pockets.[4] The Barringtons, ace gamblers, could practically hear the swish of the bills dropping into their hands.

Alas, the *Victoria* would not sail into Dawson a proud "first" the spring of 1898. When the river did break at Circle, ice chunks heaved the boat on land like some child playing with blocks. And that was that. There was no chance to make Dawson first. The sternwheeler *May West*, built at St. Michaels in 1896[5] did the honors. Workers repaired the *Victoria*, and she began making runs to Fort Yukon, Alaska, and later between Whitehorse and Dawson.[6] And as the pulse of the rush intensified, brother Harry and other relatives streamed north to search for gold.

With stampeders now steadily flooding in through the Skagway port, the Barringtons preferred wintering boats at the foot of Lake Lebarge. Gambling was the core reason. The lake was closer to Dawson, and the river below Lebarge often broke first. The odds were better for charging into Dawson first in the spring. When possible, a Lebarge wintering became a pattern the Barringtons followed every season.

DAWSON TO
SALT WATER

IN 14 DAYS

Take the fast, neat and comfortable
steamer

"WILLIE IRVING"

E. M. BARRINGTON, Master

Connecting at Rink Rapids with

DAULTON TRAIL

STOPPING AT ALL WAY POINTS

At Rink Rapids good Saddle Horses will be provided and the journey
made overland to Haines' Mission, connecting with Seattle steamers.
Meals Furnished and a Place to Sleep Provided from Rink Rapids out.

—— FARE ——

Dawson to Rink Rapids	$ 60
Dawson to Salt Water	2

Eddie Barrington Jr.'s flyer while he was captaining the *Willie Irving* on the
Yukon. Barringtons took the *Willie* upstream through Five Finger Rapids in 1898.
Credit: Courtesy of Peggy Darst Townsdin.

The *Willie Irving* in the process of being repaired.
Credit: The Yukon Archives, National Museum of Canada, #709.

Besides losing the race that spring of '98, Ed Barrington felt frustrated for another reason. He was anxious for his little *Aquila* to arrive so he could put the steamboating profits in his own pocket rather than working for someone else. In June Ed Barrington learned the contractors had failed to haul the *Aquila* up the mountain pass outside Dyea as contracted. Terribly disappointed, Ed changed his plans. Since he could no longer be first to defeat the rapids as hoped, he ordered the shippers to take the *Aquila* the long way around — from Dyea across the Gulf of Alaska to St. Michael, and then up the Yukon to Dawson. He could still make his packet when the boat arrived — if the contractors would only hurry!

Ed's irritation shows through in a June 25, 1898 letter home, writing from the steamer *Victoria*: "I am working for the ACCo. I am running this old box just to learn the channel...I am half crazy worrying about the *Aquila*. I am losing just $1,000 a day by her not being here. This old box I am on now has made $21,000 in the 3 trips.

I have run her 13 days work. She can only go upstream 2 miles an hour so if the *Aquila* gets here she will make good."[7] The Barringtons knew, the more boats, the better.

Without the *Aquila* available, another steamer caught the Barringtons' eye. Purchased for $20,000 by Syd and Ed at the end of June that summer, the *Willie Irving* proved a favorite of the brothers. Boasting powerful machinery for the era, the ship had a ninety-foot length with a thirty-foot beam. Made of California redwood, packers originally carted the parts over the White and Chilkoot Passes, finally assembling it at Lake Bennett.[8] A trim craft, the *Willie Irving* made the trip from Lake Bennett to Dawson in four days' traveling time.[9]

Reversing the run, plowing upstream to Whitehorse against the Yukon's current, especially the murderous Five Finger Rapids, tested the stamina of the *Willie*.

In rough areas like the Rapids, where upriver vessels could not conquer the downriver current, boats "lined" up by hand or "winched" up from shore by cable. Using this method, a man on land helped pull the boat upstream, or a crew hooked a tow line cable to the shore above the rapids. A winch attached to the bow of the boat reeled in the cable while the paddle and engines thrashed full steam ahead, pushing from the rear.[10]

Five Finger Rapids proved a near impossible obstacle. The Rapids themselves funneled into five channels between steep, jagged rock walls about 80-feet wide, the length of the rapids running about a quarter mile. In the middle of the river, four rocks, like fingers, thrust above the surging water.[11] Sailing downstream, travelers took the right-hand passage, which was free of obstacles. The water streamed onward calm enough at this point, until an underwater rock surface dropped off, forcing the rapids to plunge along at terrific speed. No one had taken a boat *upriver* through the Rapids by sheer vessel power alone. The words "no one" drew the gambling Barringtons like a magnet.

Why not, Ed and Syd asked themselves, see if the *Willie* could plough upstream through the Rapids, against the brutal current, without lining or winching? Could the stalwart *Willie* fight through? It was the kind of challenge the brothers relished. Hence, the Barringtons mapped their strategy—and placed their bets. Finally the day of the attempt arrived. Above on a rock cliff, watching, a shore-bound audience held its breath.

Steamer *Whitehorse* running downstream on
Five Finger Rapids.
Credit: Yukon Archives, MacBride Museum Coll. Vol. 2,
Whitehorse.

Since they fought against the current, the boys decided to try the rock-free passage on the left, going upstream. Eddie carefully positioned the *Willie*. Finally, the *Willie* mounted the seething, milk white water, the boat vibrating with the engine's power, straining to make a foot or two and then sliding back. Inching forward a few more feet, the boiling steam pressure was so great the safety valve kept popping off. More and more the boat edged upstream, until the prow battled into the calmer waters above the rapid's edge. Spectators thought the crew had done it, and a half-cheer rose from their throats, but just as quickly the boat began drifting back, losing ground.

Ed called for full speed. Syd recounted, "I'd have the engineer screw the safety-valve down until it couldn't pop off, and heave pitch knots and slabs of fat bacon into the furnace until we got up enough steam to buck the rapids."[12]

Forward a few feet, drifting back—working the steamer over and over. The ship could not do it, the reason soon evident. As the boat reached the crest at the rapid's edge, the bow lowered, the paddlewheel lifting in the rear far enough out of the water to lose power; the *Willie* teetered at the brink.

Ed, realizing the left route useless, let the steamer drift back. He then tried the right, stony channel, urging the *Willie* at full speed, carefully threading between rocks. He wove to one side, then the other, gradually making ground. Finally the steamer drove ahead, forcing through "panting like some tired steed when its race is won."[13] Passengers and onlookers screamed with frenzy. The brothers came through, gaining a reputation for themselves. And a payoff.

The majority of the steamer runs, however, proved routine. The freighting trade showed such profit that Ed wrote a business friend in Seattle that the boat paid for itself in three trips.[14] Excitement rang in the letter Ed wrote home to Yorke: "We just arrived from Dawson after breaking the record up the River. The *Irving* is a fine little boat. We have got her all paid for!"[15]

Syd piloted the *Willie* also, for he spoke of the boat in Barrett Willoughby's book, *Gentlemen Unafraid*. He told of lining her propellers with steel. "When we'd hit shallow water and she couldn't go up bow on, I'd turn her stern upstream and set her engines going full speed. Say, you should have seen her wheel spin as she'd dig into that gravel!...But the little rascal could nearly always make a channel over a bar and get into deep water."[16]

Steamboats fired wood for fuel during gold rush days. A large steamer burned about ten cords a day[17] or more. At first companies running steamers hired Native crews to cut wood for each boat. Eventually so many steamers plowed along the river, captains had difficulty finding enough woodcutters.[18]

With everyone scrambling for gold, frantic to get to the goldfields, eventually few regular woodcutters or wood yards supplied the boats along the way. When woodcutters were scarce, the boat simply tied up at the bank, and everyone—including the passengers—helped with the "wooding up" for the day's run. All pitched in, either cutting or packing logs aboard. Sometimes passengers hesitated in taking on this labor. On Syd's steamboat he often told them, "Well, boys, we won't get to Whitehorse on time, unless you give us a hand."[19] That was all the motivation needed.

Through steamboating Ed did all right on his own account. "I have bought the *Clifford Sifton* boat for $21,000. I have 2 steamers and we will make all kinds of money. I think this first trip will cost us $5,500 in 3 days and it will get better later." Ever optimistic, Ed said total mining discoveries for all miners outside Dawson more than filled their expectations, "there will be about $12,000,000 cleaned up this spring," he wrote home, "but it will not go out on account of the [Spanish–American] war. Then maybe 2 or three million will go out."[20] A "hustler" everyone called Ed.

Before the gold rush with the town of Dawson mushrooming at the meeting of the Klondike and Yukon rivers, little had been there, only a sawmill and saloon.[21] It was a bleak, frozen wilderness in winter, a mosquito-infested swampland in the summer. "Moose pasture," miners called it. One missionary said the mosquitoes covered so thick that when a man wanted to tell the time of day he had to throw a stick into the air to be able to see the sun![22] In more explicit terms, Hill was fond of saying, "It was buggier than hell."[23]

Considering the thousands of stampeders converging on Dawson in 1898, the raw town springing up on a marshland, it was not surprising that disease followed. In early 1898, an epidemic of typhoid broke out. Just as the swarms of insects and body lice brought disease, the swarms of stampeders passed them on.

Hill Barrington caught the fever, but recovered. It was not long before the disease hit Ed Barrington, attacking him in August while running the *Willie Irving*. Only a month before, Ed had told his brother, Yorke, "There is a lot of scurvy cases here. The hospital is full and running over and there are many deaths. The boys are all well and happy. Tell Aunty that the boys are all feeling fine and I will look after them,"[24] an assurance he could not keep.

Becoming bedridden, a Mrs. Burrell ministered to Ed in Dawson, but in time, the disease prevailed. Surrounded by his brothers and relatives, Eddie Barrington, oldest of the boys, leader in the gold rush, family business head, died at thirty-two years of age on August 29, 1898.[25] It was an unexpected, shocking blow to the family. Ironically, Ed's boat, the *Aquila*, arrived in Dawson after its long trip up the Yukon from St. Michael the same day his body began its journey to Seattle.

A dismal family group headed south with the casket. Syd and Hill, along with uncle E.M. McCrohan, brother-in-law, Chris Fisher, and cousin, George Nunan, escorted the body aboard the *Willie Irving*. "It is particularly appropriate that the remains should be born *[sic]* up the Yukon by the *Willie Irving*," *The Klondike Nugget* stated, "the boat which pioneered the upper river and of which the Captain was so proud."[26] The sad party continued to Whitehorse Rapids, and eventually to Skagway. There the family put the body aboard the *City of Seattle* and accompanied it south,[27] telegraphing ahead from Victoria. They all dreaded the homecoming.

Heavy with grief, Washington relatives stood on the Seattle dock watching the ship come in, its flag at half-mast. With a crowd at the funeral, a reported seventy-five carriages rode behind the casket to the burial plot.[28] The family interred the body in the Lake View Cemetery in Seattle, next to his father.[29]

· · ·

1. William D. McBride, (Also spelled MacBride.) Compiler, "Saga of Famed Packets and Other Steamboats of Mighty Yukon River." *Cariboo and Northwest Digest*, Spring 1949–Winter 1948, pp. 97–114. AK Historical Library.

2. The *Wrangell Sentinel* of June 7, 1923, told of a unique scene passing Dawson during one ice breakup: three caribou calves were spotted standing on a slab of ice floating near the middle of the river. Few watchers expected the animals to survive in the grinding, tumbling ice floes. *The Dawson News* remarked: "The last seen of the caribou they still were standing calmly on the ice cake as it swept round the bend and past Moosehide and on toward Bering Sea, with old Death as pilot, and the sun smiling his gentlest on the silent victims of impending tragedy."

3. Edwin Tappan Adney, *The Klondike Stampede* of 1897–1898. Fairfield, WA: Ye Galleon Press, 1968, pp. 387–388. The first steamboat whistle blowing into town thrilled everyone. Even the dogs caught the excitement "as the deep whistle of the incoming boat was blown every Malamute dog lifted its voice in a

doleful wail. This wail began, we were told, at the first blast of the whistle, and the singular thing is that the leader struck the exact pitch, high or low of the steamboat. Then in waves the moan arose, breaking out in renewed and louder howls, each succeeding wave louder than the former, until...the volume...drowned the very whistle."

4. "Capt. Barrington of the Stikine Is Subject of Magazine Article." *Wrangell Sentinel*, February 10, 1933.

5. W.D. MacBride, "Saga of Famed Packets and Other Steamboats of Mighty Yukon River." *The Alaska Weekly*, August 25, 1944.

6. "Movements of the River Boats." *Yukon Midnight Sun*, June 11, 1898.

7. Letter from Ed Barrington to his mother, dated June 25, 1898. Courtesy of Peggy Darst Townsdin.

8. Ella Lung Martinsen, *Trail to North Star Gold*. Portland. OR: Metropolitan Press, 1969, p. 49.

9. "Finest Steamer on the River." *The Klondike Nugget*, Dawson, YT, June 28, 1898.

10. Jack L. Morison, "Steamboats on the Yukon." *Denver Westerners' Roundup*, Nov.–Dec. 1979, pp. 7–8.

11. Pierre Berton, *The Klondike Fever*. NY: Alfred A. Knopf, 1960, p. 284.

12. Barrett Willoughby, *Gentlemen Unafraid*. New York: G.P. Putnam's, 1928, p. 214.

13. Untitled newspaper item, undated, subheaded, "Through the Rapids." Probably a Seattle newspaper. Courtesy of Peggy Darst Townsdin of Coupeville.

14. "Capt. Edward Barrington's Funeral Largely Attended." *Seattle Post-Intelligencer*, Sept. 20, 1898.

15. Letter from Ed Barrington to Yorke, July 21, 1898. Courtesy of Peggy Darst Townsdin.

16. Ibid., Willoughby, *Gentlemen Unafraid*.

17. Melody Webb, "Steamboats on the Yukon River." *Alaska Journal*, Summer, 1985, p. 26.

18. Arthur E. Knutson, *Sternwheels on the Yukon*. Snohomish, WA: Snohomish Publishing Company, 1979, p. 184–185.

19. Barrett Willoughby, "Champion White Water Pilot of the North." *American Magazine*, Oct. 1928, p. 30.

20. Letter from Ed Barrington to his mother from the Steamer *Victoria*, June 25, 1898.

21. Ibid., Berton, *The Klondike Fever*, p. 75.

22. Ibid., Edwin Tappan Adney, p. 450.

23. Hill Sr. and Mildred Barrington tape, recorded by Eddie Barrington, II, 9/1/70, courtesy of relatives Marlene and Hill Barrington, III.

24. Letter from Ed Barrington to Yorke, July 4, 1898. Courtesy of Peggy Darst Townsdin.

25. "Capt. Barrington Dead." *Seattle Post-Intelligencer*, Sept. 17, 1898.

26. "Story of Steamboats." *Dawson Daily News*, May 19, 1900.

27. "The Rush from Dawson." *The Stikeen River Journal*, Sept. 24, 1898.

28. Ibid., "Capt. Edward Barrington's Funeral Largely Attended."

29. E-mail from Peggy Darst Townsdin, Oct. 22, 2003.

4: SOME YOU WIN, SOME YOU LOSE

After the summer of 1898 and burying his brother, Syd Barrington spent a short winter in the States. He had always looked up to his older brother, but Syd hid his grief and went on with life. Like Eddie, he did not believe in living in the past. Now, if Syd were to gain his fortune, he would have to go for it himself. Ed would want that too.

While in Seattle Syd heard the steamer *James Domville* was for lease. At the time, it wintered at Whitehorse. Syd understood what Eddie would have done, and he did it himself—lease the boat if possible. *Domville* owners in Seattle informed Syd a man was at that very hour making a trip to Dawson to take charge of the vessel. The owners could not, ethically, complete a deal with Barrington until they heard from the Dawson agent. Syd then knew it was a question of time. If he could overtake the man—his competition—and beat him to Dawson, he might yet succeed.[1]

To Skagway he traveled in February. Purchasing a dog team, Syd, along with companions, made tracks along the Yukon winter trail. Worried that his traveling party dawdled too much, Syd anxiously drove them on. After all, the whole next season's work depended on him leasing the *Domville*. He could almost feel the ghost of Ed behind him, pressing the race. When H.L. Miller overtook Syd's party, the two decided to charge the rest of the way by themselves.

Miller and Syd broke trail over most of the lakes, speeding past eighteen dog teams. Subzero cold, some days thirty below, tore at them and weakened the dogs. At Thirty-Mile, Miller fell through the ice and barely escaped drowning. From there the going went well.

Covering the 320 miles in near-record time, Barrington arrived in Dawson. He let out a sigh of relief to learn his competitor had not yet arrived. Syd quickly sold his interest in the *Willie Irving*, contacted the *Domville*'s representative there and leased the boat for $11,000 that season.[2] It proved a gratifying victory.

After another quick trip to Seattle[3] the end of March, Syd discovered the *Domville* owners had been offered $55,000 for lease of the boat during the 1899 summer season. Of course, Barrington had signed first, the contract held, and the company lost $44,000 on the deal.[4]

With that success, Syd headed north once more to await the ice breakup. He arrived in Skagway in May,[5] a day before a disastrous fire there consumed seven buildings downtown.[6] Barrington, accompanied by friends and relatives, then traveled to Whitehorse where the *Domville* wintered.

Built in 1898 in Vancouver, the owners had named the *James Domville* after a prominent Canadian banker and Member of Parliament.[7] Beside accommodations for cargo, Barrington fancied up the boat. He equipped the 125-foot boat with electricity and furnishings for 100 first-class passengers.[8] After all his trips south and hardships of the trail, Syd surely felt Eddie's excitement at sailing triumphantly through the 1899 summer—making a bundle. This was his own. Not only that, but he desperately wanted to be the first boat into Dawson that season,[9] for himself and for Ed. Would the gamble succeed?

By early June, the *Domville*, loaded with eight tons of supplies and 500 sheep,[10] ran down to Lake Lebarge with Barrington as pilot. Water in the Yukon flowed at an extremely low stage. No sooner had Syd begun the journey than the boat grounded on a bar at the head of the lake. Other boats experienced problems, too.

Syd, who was not a patient man, waited for a rise in water. Finally, the *Domville* edged off and drifted free. Down the vessel glided to the foot of Lake Lebarge. There Syd could have waited. Instead, the glory of being first into Dawson clouded his judgment. Leaving others behind, he decided to try the dangerous passage, the twisting switchbacks of the Thirty-Mile River. Surely he could do it.

Once in the current, the battle was on. Rocks appeared on every side as the boat wove through the channels. So careful was Syd, he navigated only six miles that day. The next morning he started off again, floating one mile…two…three, until the prow headed for a rocky bar on the left shore. Syd spun the wheel to compensate, but it would not respond, the fast current swinging the stern into deeper water. The *Domville* hovered for a minute, and then a cracking of the timbers snapped through the air. A split second later the boat broke in half.[11]

The *Domville*'s demise was simple, smooth and fast, nothing highly dramatic. All of Syd's rushing to Seattle and back, all his trials through the wilderness, all the timing and finally buying the ship, all Syd's hopes sank with the boat. Not only did Syd lose the profit for that season, but the ship that could have made him more. It was a disastrous blow. How quickly dreams of glory vanish!

While Syd stood on shore, the new *Bonanza King* came to the rescue. The *King* had already swept triumphantly into Dawson Wednesday night, the first steamer from the upper river that season. The boat, en route up river to Whitehorse Rapids, sidetracked to the site of the *Domville* wreck. Captain James Lee loaded on freight, sheep and passengers from the wreck. The defeat of the *Domville* proved more than uncomfortable for Syd Barrington. The accident proved a high price to pay for impatience.[12]

The *James Domville* had company along the rocks of the Yukon that spring—the *Australia*, the *Clifford Sifton*, the *Gleaner*, the *Humboldt* and the *Cottage City* all grounded from low water.[13] Many voyagers complained of the dangerous rocks.

"In fact, nearly every boat going through has suffered more or less," reported a Captain Richie in *The Daily Colonist* of Victoria, B.C. "It is not for me to say what the government should do in the matter, but the clearing of the channel would be a great benefit to navigation…"[14]

In the fall of 1899, public works officials from the Canadian government supervised the removal of several treacherous rocks from sections of the waterway. Work crews dynamited rocky areas at Thirty-Mile,[15] thus improving the safety factor. But it was too late for Syd.

With the death of their brother, and the destruction of Syd's boat, the Barringtons could have closed the book on their Yukon adventure. After all, they were able to make a livelihood piloting steamers in the Puget Sound area or along the Inside Passage of Southeast Alaska. But the routine, the ordinary, was not in the makeup of their genes.

The brothers, often with salty vocabularies, proved ideal for their

The *James Domville* lies wrecked on the
Thirty Mile River, June 7, 1899.
Credit: Yukon Archives, Gillis Coll., Whitehorse.

careers. Syd the promoter, the wild visionary, the most flamboyant, became the focal Barrington. He drew attention, and later became the subject of periodicals and books. Though it was Syd's photo in the national print, he always considered himself a partner and shared the limelight with Hill and Harry. The brothers were proud of each other.

Sydney did not mind being the center of attention either. He enjoyed an audience. In fact, he needed an audience, as he did not like being alone. For awhile, for instance, cousin Matt Nunan became Syd's "yes-man." When Syd told stories, he would turn to his cousin and say, "Ain't that right, Matt?" and Matt replied something like, "Right, Cap. You got it just like it happened."[16] For the most part, Syd's personality attracted people. Yet he had an explosive temper, which seldom lasted very long. He was not a patient man; he wanted to get things done—now.

Yet, "There is no bluster to the Skipper," one passenger stated. "Just a quiet self assurance that comes from knowing a job inside and out with presence of mind to use that knowledge in tight situations."[17] Syd put his forceful personality behind the wheel of his boat, as well as his business projects. Stuck on a sandbar? Ram through in reverse. No fuss, just do it.

Another determining trait defining Syd particularly was his craving to gamble. Proving a gambler to his very soul,[18] he bet on anything—which bird flew first, which floating branch passed the

STEAMBOAT SID

(To the Tune Casey Jones)
(By "SPLOTUS")

Come all you steamboat men and lis-
ten to me
I'll surely tell you something that
you seldom see.
Capt. Sid Barrington, you know him
well,
He's the gamest on the river, or I'll
go to—well.

Early this spring, about the middle
of May
He was told not to leave, so I heard
them say;
He jumped into the pilot house, the
wheel in his hand;
Then he gave three jingles to that
engineer man.

Chorus—
Steamboat Sid jumped into the pilot
house—
Steamboat Sid, he's the gamest of
them all;
Steamboat Sid jumped into the pilot
house;
He's surely got them bested in the
Spring and Fall.

He left Lake Labarge about the 10th
of May,
The water was low in the Thirtymile,
I heard them say;
When he left that lake it was half
past one,
But he got in Hootalinqua by the
setting of the sun.

The Delta and Evelyn were both
stuck tight,
But Capt. Sid never once turned his
searchlight;
Passengers shook his hand as they
gathered 'round;
In thirty-six hours they's in Dawson town.

Chorus—
Steamboat Sid on the mighty Yukon,
Steamboat Sid, he's the gamest of
them all;

Steamboat Sid on the mighty Yukon,
You have to hand it to him in the
Spring and Fall.

The first boat in Dawson with them
perishable goods;
Everyone in town, on the wharf they
stood,
To give three cheers for Steamboat
Sid,
'Cause they knew what a very good
job he did.

Then right up the Stewart with
a load of freight,
Stopped at every cabin and he put
off some weight,
Then way up the Procupine to Rampart House,
He was back in ten days looking
cute as a mouse.

Chorus—
Steamboat Sid, on the mighty Yukon,
Steamboat Sid, he's the gamest of
them all;
Steamboat Sid, on the mighty Yukon;
You'll have to hand it to him in the
Spring and Fall.

Late in the Fall, when the weather
was bad,
He's always feeling happy, and he
looks mighty glad;
All them other captains, why, they
don't think it's right,
Cause Capt. Sid never ties up at
night.

Up in the pilot house that wheel he
turns;
All them other captains, why a lesson could learn;
Give him a chance, he'll sure gain
fame,
As a steamboat captain, boys, he's
earned his name.

Steamboat Sid song by "Splotus"
(Location and date unknown).
Credit: Courtesy of Bill and Elna Barrington.

Hill Barrington, Puget Sound captain.
(Location and date unknown).
Credit: Bill and Elna Barrington Collection.

boat first, how many people met the boat, would boxer Vic Foley stay six rounds with Wild Cat Carter,[19] horse racing, anything. It made him reckless at times. It made him a loser as well as a winner. And everything was done on a grand scale. If he won at a wager, it proved a bonanza; if he lost, it was a fortune. The winning or losing never stopped Syd. It was the gamble that counted. As one prospector said of legendary money gamblers like Syd, "The bigger the odds or stake, the cooler and cannier they would get."[20]

In a very real sense, the search for gold also proved a gamble. Syd possessed a passion to make money, enjoyed it, and used its power. It was what riches could do that mattered. Money was to spend, be it on luxury hotel suites, gourmet food, high-end cars, travel and jewelry or on impressing people. The brothers would make a bundle, for instance, sail to San Francisco in the winter where cash streamed from their pockets like the always-flowing Yukon. There they lived in hotels and drank champagne from lady's boots. Or they liked nothing better than to tool around Seattle in a new Packard and live in the best hotels.[21] Then they often borrowed money to return north in the spring.

At times Syd shaved the sharp defining edge of honesty, for money could fix parking tickets, too, or possibly buy foreknowledge in an election. People understood that the actual gamble was the real goal, not the fortune in itself, for that never lasted very long. And easy-going Hill went along for the ride, enjoying every high and low.

Hill Barrington, the businessman, detail man and also the comedian, allowed his brother the spotlight. Hill might sit back on their boats, but he often instigated some outrageous goings on. While Syd promoted the business, Hill, who loved to dance, made a party of it. And then Harry, too, the solid, good common sense brother,[22] completed the set. They enjoyed one other and played off each other. Though Harry involved himself in mining and many of the boating and business operations throughout the years, he spent more time in Washington than the other brothers. His wives, first Kate who died, then Dora, were more rooted in Whidbey life. Hill and Sydney formed a dedicated partnership in all phases of the Barrington operations and, for the most part, their wives too enjoyed the ride.

Flamboyant the brothers were, and generous as well. No stranded miner cooled his heels along the riverbank for lack of a steamboat ticket. Syd simply glided the boat to shore, picked up the scraggly miner and allowed him to ride free. Later the Canadian government got wind of this frequent practice and, for a time, awarded Syd a yearly subsidy to help cover his expenses.

And the brothers sometimes went farther. When money jingled in their pockets, they often grubstaked other hopefuls, just as their father helped the less fortunate during his life. These selfless actions bonded friendships for the Barringtons, "buddies" who cheered them for a lifetime.

Participants in the gold rush realized quickly that the Klondike was a leveling ground, especially at the diggings; family position had little influence. People's actions defined them, not their money or social status. In the isolated wilderness then, a poor recluse with a loaf of bread held more status than a prince with no food. The Barringtons thus treated everyone on a fairly level playing field. They might make a fortune, use money, but they were not intimidated by it. Like their father, they generally treated all people fairly and remembered them.[23]

There may have been Barrington hangers-on, "the takers," those who enjoyed the flash and generosity of the boys, but their trip with the brothers did not last long. Did some people take advantage of the Barringtons? Sure, but the brothers simply shrugged their shoulders and eventually "left them on the river bank." The real friends and relatives stayed on, and their names reappear over and over through Barrington history. They all mutually enjoyed unique and exciting lives.

There is no reason to think their lifestyle in Dawson was any different. It is simple to imagine the Barringtons sauntering down busy Front Street, mixing with friends, to hear the blare of music in the air while passing one saloon after another. It is easy to see Hill and Syd enter a saloon and move to the card room, watch them intent on a faro game, drinks by their elbows, cigar smoke clouding the air, while the sounds of a vaudeville show drift in from the theater room beyond.

All in all, during the years as steamboat men, the Barringtons built a positive reputation. *The Klondike Nugget* newspaper commented on Syd. He was considered, "one of Dawson's best known and most popular young men...His sterling character and abilities easily carry him to the front..."[24]

No, the sinking of the *Domville* and Eddie's death did not end the Klondike adventure for the Barringtons. Actually, defeats only made the victories sweeter and more worthwhile. They were not leaving the Yukon, they were just getting started. They would navigate for the Canadian steamship companies and make money that way.

In the Yukon, the brothers Barrington and their relatives found their livelihood in years to come. Gold, whether coin from the river business, or from wilderness diggings, drew them north most summers. Thus, a seasonal rhythm emerged—operating in the north during warmer months and returning to Washington State for winter. The focal hub for the family was San de Fuca, a small town on Whidbey Island north of Seattle. At times, however, the brothers remained in the north during the dark months, working their claims. Or sometimes they obtained jobs in Dawson, like Hill, who weighed gold in the Northern Commercial store where they sluiced the floor mat for wayward gold flakes.[25] Other river men followed the same pattern.

Well liked or not, ambitious or not, the waters of the "Barrington River" found their rocky moments too.

• • •

1. Peggy Darst Townsdin, *History of a Whidbey Island Family*, p. 26. Clipping from undated, unknown source, "The Youngest Captain on the Yukon."
2. "Willie Irving Sold." *The Klondike Nugget,* March 25, 1899.
3. "Personal Mention." *The Klondike Nugget,* March 22, 1899.
4. Ibid., Peggy Darst Townsdin, p. 26, clipping.
5. "Preparing for Lake and River Trade." *Daily Alaskan,* May 4, 1899.
6. "Greatest Fire Ever in Skagway." *Daily Alaskan,* May 4, 1899.
7. William D. MacBride, Compiler, "Saga of Famed Packets of Mighty Yukon River." *Alaska Weekly,* August 11, 1944.
8. "Capt. Barrington in His New Boat." *The Klondike Nugget,* March 29, 1899.
9. Unknown title. *The Klondike Nugget,* Dawson, March 20, 1899.
10. Ibid., "Preparing for Lake and River Trade." *Daily Morning Alaskan.*

11. "Domville Rides to Her Doom." *The Klondike Nugget,* June 14, 1899.

12. "Doings on the Yukon." *The Klondike Nugget,* June 17, 1899.

13. "Yukon Boats Free at Last." *Seattle Daily Times,* June 17, 1899.

14. "Clearing the Yukon River." *The Daily Colonist,* Victoria, B.C., Oct. 27, 1899.

15. Ibid.

16. Conversation with Bill Barrington, Anchorage, April 11, 1998.

17. "Sid Barrington." Unknown author. Undated, unpublished typed article, possibly 1952.

18. Interview with Amos Burg who knew Syd Barrington. April 7, 1985.

19. Pat O'Cotter, "Thru Northern Glasses." *Alaska Weekly,* Jan. 20, 1928.

20. Ibid., "Sid Barrington." Unknown author.

21. Ibid., conversation with Bill Barrington.

22. Ibid.

23. Phone conversation with Edwin Callbreath, Seattle, with author, July 15, 1998.

24. Ibid., "Capt. Barrington in His New Boat."

25. Hill and Mildred Barrington tapes, recorded by Eddie Barrington, courtesy of relatives Marlene and Hill Barrington, III.

5: LEARNING THE WATERS

The Klondike years? Crazy times. No sooner had stampeding hordes reached Dawson, than rumors of gold in Nome drifted in. Many of the hopefuls arriving from Whitehorse swept right through Dawson, continuing west to the "beaches of gold."

Swiftwater Bill hustled his gear and left Dawson, along with stampeders Silent Sam Bonnifield and Arizona Charlie.[1] At Nome, people said, "The miners extracted gold from the beach sands with rockers and Tex Rickard extracted it from the miners with a faro layout."[2]

Because so many stampeders traveled west, roads from Valdez and Dawson opened up. Plans for other railways besides the White Pass company, in addition to a telegraph line, were the talk around the campfire. The more activity, the busier the Barrington boats.

In spite of Dawson's declining population and its constant flux, the town held its glitter. Tents, cabins and shacks littered the raw hillsides. Trails lead hither and yon, and logs stacked like matchsticks everywhere. Crowded boats ran up and down the Yukon. There was still plenty of activity. The Barringtons and other miners worked claims outside town and full services in town supported them.

"Full service" in Dawson meant just about everything. As author Pierre Berton said, "None of its citizens were ordinary." With their love of life, their gambling drive, you can be sure Syd and Hill enjoyed the open living in Dawson.

Anything could happen in the madness of the times, even wedding vows. No clear records exist, but there is some evidence that both men, Hill and Syd, decided to take the marital plunge.[3] In town at the time were sisters "Dirty Maude" Delisle (named for her habit of chewing fine cut tobacco and spitting over her shoulder as she danced), and her sister, Hazel, both song-and-dance performers from Ohio. Billed as the "Delisle Sisters," both performed at the 1898 Chicago World's Exposition before heading west and north to the Klondike.[4]

Whether well lubricated, whether on a bet or whether truly smitten, Syd married Maude in 1900. Hill followed suit, wedding a Washington prostitute, Babe Wallace, during the same time. Neither union lasted long, Babe dying of tuberculous[5] and Maude and Syd agreeing to a friendly divorce.[6] Considering the Barrington personalities and their youthful ages (barely into their twenties), the marriages have a ring of truth, though no actual certificates can be found. Accidental

Dirty Maude "Barrington" Delisle, c. 1900?
Credit: Courtesy of Bill Barrington

fires wiped out most records of these possible liaisons. Syd, nevertheless, kept an attachment to the Delisles, as later events proved.

Although the Barringtons focused operations on the Upper Yukon, they took piloting jobs in Alaska, too. Rivers, after all, knew no boundaries. And with officers on board carrying both Canadian and American licenses, travel between countries continued as a matter of course.

Hill remembered one experience coming out of St. Michael on the Lower Yukon. With a full load of cargo, returning upriver to Dawson, he came upon a steady stream of caribou crossing the Yukon at one site. The migrating herd headed north at the time. Rather than try cutting through the mass, Hill's boat tied up waiting for them to pass. The herd continued coming, moving, coming and crossing, crossing and moving, taking three days and two nights before the caribou completed the passage! Hill estimated 75,000 animals—and any number of caribou steaks—ambling past while he waited patiently.[7]

During these few years at the turn of the century, Barrington

Dirty Maude "Barrington" Delisle, c. 1900.
Credit: Courtesy of Bill Barrington.

Hazel Delisle Barrington, c. 1900.
Credit: Courtesy of Bill Barrington.

relatives stayed on in the Klondike area working their claims. Syd, however, grew restless. After losing the *James Domville,* Syd Barrington, himself, gambled on the Nome discovery in the fall of 1899.[8] With cash in his pockets, and prospects in his head, he joined the eager stampeders rushing west. He told Barrett Willoughby of his Nome trip, detailed in her book, *Gentlemen Unafraid.*[9]

Thinking to be a passenger for a change, Syd bought a steamboat ticket for St. Michael. No sooner had the vessel passed two bends, than the pilot grounded on a gravel bar. The captain, aware of Syd's ability, then asked him to take the boat the rest of the way to the coast. Arriving in St. Michael, Syd spotted a forlorn sternwheeler near the beach, searched out the owner and bought the ship and a barge for $15,000.

A storm, whipping into a gale, was blowing at the time. Syd bribed a tug skipper to take him, and to tow Syd's recently acquired barge and boat across the 100 miles of Norton Sound to Nome. Before leaving, Syd, a pushover for destitutes, gave in to a dozen begging, stranded men and promised them passage. The tug skipper, however, stubbornly refused to take the extra men. But since Syd could not disappoint the strays, he came up with a solution. Secretly, he hustled them to his own newly purchased boat towed behind the tug. The men scrambled aboard the empty boat and hid below. So the stowaways could not suddenly appear and be spotted by the captain taking them across, Syd shut the hatch and nailed the men in.

The ocean storm beat at the sea like some untamed monster. In truth, Syd never thought they would make it.[10] To his horror, the captain said he had to cut Syd's barge and boat adrift to save his own steamer. Barrington hollered at him, pleaded with him. "I managed," Syd related, "to keep him hanging on to that scow for twelve terrible hours—and believe me every hour was sixty minutes of hell. Then we reached Nome."[11]

What a sight—and stench—greeted Syd when he freed the men from the boat behind. All the stowaways had been sick, and they cursed him up one side and down the other, the tug captain adding his shrieks to the racket. Fury, nearly worse than the storm, heaped on Syd. But at least everyone came through. Then Syd remembered he was in Nome and his gambling blood started to simmer.

Upon arrival in the newly discovered gold town, Barrington heard the snap of cards and headed for Tex Rickard's northern saloon. Feeling favored by Lady Luck, Barrington sensed he owned the

Birds-eye view of Nome, Alaska in 1903.
Credit: Perry Palmer Album, UAF 2004-120-24.

world—a boat and scow in his ownership and $35,000 in his belt. He started playing at the faro table.

As Barrington stated the following day, "When I got up from that table at six the next morning I was clean. Money, steamer and scow were all gone."[12]

Shrugging off the experience, and temporarily broke, Barrington borrowed money and headed for Seattle to recoup and figure out how to purchase or lease another boat. After all, the Upper Yukon River still supplied a profitable livelihood, and he intended to go back.

But not all Barrington time was spent behind a boat wheel. Although Harry Barrington proved the constant miner in the family, Syd and Hill, too, spent periods on their claims during the off season. Christmas time brought nostalgia to Syd, as he told his mother the end of December from Dawson, "Well Mama [he wrote] there is another Christmas went bye without our Dear one. One Christmas but I can't say a happy one…God Bless the Boy we lost and Mama don't worry for we will all meet again where Eddie and Papa is."[13]

Also during the seasons, other projects kept Yukon boats busy. One job involved shuttling freight and workers for the American

Boundary Survey corps.[14] Once engineers mapped the boundary between Alaska and Canada, surveyors had to "run a line" and mark the border between the two countries. An important project, it continued for several years into the 1900s.[15]

Another key undertaking dealt with building a telegraph line, which residents commonly called the Marconi project. With the U.S. Army Signal Corps constructing lines in sections of Alaska, the Barringtons shuttled supplies from Fort Egbert at Eagle, Alaska, to Dawson, Yukon. Since Canadians already had a land line to British Columbia, the Eagle connection, when finished, tapped out the first direct telegraphic messages between Alaska and the contiguous United States.[16]

There was plenty of work to do.

After the Nome fiasco, the Barringtons did acquire another vessel in the spring of 1900. Believe it or not, with little money, they got to Whitehorse. There, Syd and Hill bought two bikes and rode to Dawson! To keep their money safe, they rolled it and shoved it up the hole in the handle bars. By the time they reached Dawson, the bikes were "shot to hell," But by salvaging enough, they pieced together one good bike and sold it for $20.[17] But they made it.

After winning a bet, Syd and Hill leased the boat, *Florence S.*, from Humboldt Gates and hatched a plan.

Built at St. Michael in 1898,[18] the *Florence S.* ran the Lower Yukon for summer. During the fall of 1898, the vessel steamed to the Upper Yukon, working stops between Dawson and Whitehorse. Since the *Florence S.* drew only thirteen inches of water, she could therefore thread upstream at low water stage if there was "even a trace of moisture."[19]

Anxious to pay off the boat and to drum up steamboat business, the Barringtons started a rumor. Hill admitted he and Syd began idle talk about gold up the Koyukuk River west of Fairbanks. Rumors of pay dirt there had already drifted in to Dawson. Why not give those whispers a stronger voice and make them full-blown facts? "Strike! Strike up the Koyukuk!" It was a dangerous plan, for gold strikers made it a practice to hang those who started a false stampede.[20] But by whispering such words to Scow Henderson, for instance, with a promise to say nothing, the rumor was soon all over town.[21] The daring Barringtons encouraged such rumors and added a few of their own.

As word flew from ear to ear, the air fairly tightened with tension. The next issue of the Dawson paper printed news of the strike. An advertisement stated, "First boat out of Dawson for the Koyukuk would be the Barrington Transportation Company's steamer and would take a limited number of passengers and a like amount of freight."[22]

But the gold strike rumor was nonetheless only a rumor, and the Barringtons had to make good. Their reputations hinged on that, and possibly their lives. Praying the strike to materialize, Syd, Hill and the *Florence S.* departed Dawson on May 22 with a full load of excited, expectant stampeders.

Day after day of the two-week journey passed, and the brothers grew more anxious. After all, it was the Barrington exaggerations that fired the men, and the brothers were trusted to deliver. Perhaps this was one trip they were not eager to hurry.

While plodding upriver, Syd spotted a stranded boy alone on the riverbank. The young boy's face was streaked with tears and dirt, and the men took pity. Stopping to check, the boy sadly reported all members of his family were dead from disease, and the Barringtons took him on board.

After questioning the boy, the youngster asked, "Where are you fellows going, up the Koyukuk to that gold strike? They know me up there."[23] Syd and Hill looked at each other, realizing they had called it right. Each heaved his own sigh of relief. This time their private wager paid off.

Soon, feedback told of Koyukuk diggings paying $100 a day to the man. People went crazy. More and more newcomers swarmed to the area, starting a new camp. Such was the frenzy that, on Syd's next trip, not only the passengers streamed ashore, but almost all the steamer hands abandoned ship. Syd had trouble snagging a skeleton crew to navigate the *Florence S.* back to Dawson.

Navigating through central Alaska at that section proved a challenge. As the silty Yukon flowed into the flats, over the years a saying evolved: "The river is too thin to plow, and too thick to drink."[24] Translated, that meant a skipper could see about an inch into the river. He took his reading from the surface of the water.

And sure enough, not far chugging back up the Yukon, Syd Barrington came upon the steamer *John C. Barr* and barge. Piloted by Captain John Healy, loaded with passengers, the *Barr* found itself well aground on a gravel bank up a side slough. Barrington wondered if he could net some money while helping out. Like his brother Eddie, Syd could add and multiply with the best of them; the *Barr's* 300 passengers represented a total fare of $28,000. Figuring he could do Healy a favor, and make a profit himself, Barrington offered to take the passengers to St. Michael for a cut rate of $12,000. Aghast at the price, Captain Healy's voice crossed the air with a few well-chosen adjectives, refusing the offer. Syd shrugged his shoulders and steamed away, leaving the captain to his own fate.[25]

About this time in Barrington history, an event occurred which nearly put a period to riverboating for young Sydney. The fervor of the times, the urgency to ferry people and supplies someplace quick, occasionally overshadowed safety. Perhaps, too, a bit of complacency in Syd Barrington, plus his willingness to play the odds, brought about a fatal accident. And it was he, as vessel owner and pilot, who had to assume responsibility.

No sooner back from the Koyukuk run in early summer, Syd Barrington took on another job. With low water on that return trip on the Thirty-Mile River, the *Florence* "stepped" carefully on the way out. Nevertheless, careless loading, or more likely overloading, nearly proved the downfall of Syd Barrington at this point in his career.

The accident occurred July 21, 1900, on a Saturday afternoon. Syd's steamer *Florence S.* chugged laboriously up the roiling Thirty-Mile River. It was headed for Hootalinqua River (now the Teslin),[26] heavily loaded with sixty tons of general merchandise and passengers. Syd, as pilot, held the wheel as they approached a sharp bend in the river. Ready for dinner with Hill, Syd turned the wheel over to Captain Ernest Jordan.

Only minutes later, as Captain Jordan swung the boat around the river bend, the cargo shifted to one side—too far. The *Florence S.* hung for a moment on her hull, and then almost leisurely, toppled over on her side. As the hull hit, the upper structure of the boat broke loose and landed with a splash. Instantly, most of the passengers flew into the water, where they struggled among the wreckage. Some grabbed parts of the boat, others fought for shore.

A Mrs. Stewart, caught in the eddying waters, flailed about helplessly. Her twelve-year-old daughter, clinging to the floating hull, spotted her and plunged forward to join her mother. Two men jumped into the water in an effort to save the two, and reached Mrs. Stewart, dragging her toward shore. However, probably thinking of her child, the woman fought free of their grasp, tried to find her girl, and went under with the current. No one spotted the young girl.

For a moment the tipped hull section floated. Then suddenly it eased over, bottom side up, losing the engine and boiler, and slowly sank.

Terrified, nineteen passengers clung to a floating section which took them along thirteen miles down river, until it lodged on an island opposite the mouth of the Hootalinqua. Syd, Hill and Jordan, in a stateroom at the time, had to chop their way out.[27] A small boat chugged around the bend at the time. Men from Victoria, B.C., landed their boat, threw off the cargo and rushed immediately to the rescue.[28] Fortunately, the steamer *Bailey* also swung by, and took on most survivors, transporting them to Dawson.

A few crew remained at Hootalinqua to salvage freight, and to retrieve, if possible, the three bodies of the drowned passengers. Two of the victims, Mrs. Stewart of Victoria and her daughter, having debarked from the ocean steamer *Amur*, were headed for Dawson.[29] The other fatality, seventeen-year-old steward Walter Monaster, had called Skagway his home for the previous two years.[30]

The Daily Colonist of Victoria, B.C., gave its own reason for the tragedy—overloading. "The river steamer…turned turtle in the Thirty-Mile canyon of the Lewes river…She was accounted very top heavy and rolled so dangerously that several of those who took passage from Dawson on her left the vessel at Five Fingers [Rapids] to await the arrival of another vessel."[31]

An investigation furnished several statements from survivors. Mrs. Annie Schmeer blamed the officers for the disaster. She stated the boat listed from overloaded freight and even took on water over the guards before the accident.

She believed the officers finally realized the danger and were trying to beach the vessel when the mishap occurred. Had the accident happened at night, she said, "Everyone would have been drowned in their berths like rats in a trap."[32]

Mechanic and engineer, R.E. Blake, stated that after the boat listed the last time, Barrington called for a "shut-off" bell, and then a "reverse bell," but it was too late. He believed the boat had not been overloaded and that the sharp turn at full speed caused the accident. Blake felt certain, in his opinion, that if Barrington had been at the wheel, the accident would never have happened.

The following day after Barrington arrived in Dawson, the unthinkable happened. Police arrested Syd for manslaughter. This "popular man" with "sterling character and abilities" was hauled off to jail. Officials released him when business partners Humboldt Gates and Tom Rockwell paid his $10,000 bond.[33] A warrant was also issued for Captain Ernest Jordan, the man actually at the wheel during the tragedy.

A subsequent court hearing a day later freed Syd Barrington of all blame in the wreck.

Witnesses repeated that if Syd had been at the wheel, the accident would not have occurred. Most also stated the cargo load was within acceptable limits. The turn around the river bend proved too sharp and dangerous, witnesses reported, thus the cause of the disaster. Only one survivor—Oliver Redpath, a well-known Canadian mining operator—continued to hold Barrington responsible for the loss of boat and lives.

Canadian police officer, Inspector C. Starnes said, "While there was plenty of evidence to show carelessness and neglect of duty on some one's part, he could find nothing in the evidence to sustain the charges against Barrington."[34] After all testimony, the court dismissed the case, and pursued it no further.[35]

News traveled south, of course, and Syd's brother, Yorke, came to his defense in a Seattle newspaper article, "Barrington Not Blamed." "I have all along known," he said, "that Sid [sic] could not have been to blame in the matter. He is much too careful a man for that."[36]

In August, Syd, free of legal blame and with no boat to pilot, decided to do something no one else had done before. Almost to prove their skill all over again, the Barringtons accepted a daring and reckless challenge, and a wager, from the Dominion Steamboat Company.[37]

• • •

1. Pierre Berton, *The Klondike Fever*. NY: Alfred A. Knopf, 1960, p. 412.
2. "Swiftest in Alaska." *Alaska Weekly,* August 6, 1954.
3. "1901 Census Records." *Filson's Pan for Gold Database*. Dawson City Museum, Canada.
4. Bill and Elna Barrington tapes, 2001–02, courtesy of relatives Marlene and Hill Barrington, III.
5. Lael Morgan, *Good Time Girls of the Alaska-Yukon Gold Rush*. Seattle: Epicenter Press, 1998, p. 66.
6. Ibid, pp. 63–66.
7. "Captain Born in 1877." *Oak Harbor News,* Dec. 29, 1966. Clipping in *History of a Whidbey Island Family* by Peggy Darst Townsdin.
8. "Story of Steamboats." *Dawson Daily News,* May 19, 1900.
9. Barrett Willoughby, *Gentlemen Unafraid*. NY: G.P. Putnam's Sons, 1928, p. 217–221.
10. R.M. Patterson, *Trail to the Interior*. NY: William Morrow and Co., 1966, p. 38–39.
11. Barrett Willoughby, "Champion White Water Pilot of the North." *American Magazine,* October 1928, p. 30, 148.
12. Ibid., Barrett Willoughby, *Gentlemen Unafraid*, p. 220.
13. Letter from Syd Barrington to his mother from Dawson City, Dec. 30, 1900. Courtesy of Peggy Darst Townsdin.
14. "Boat Crews Arrive." *The Weekly Star,* March 17, 1911.
15. Claus M. Naske and Herman E. Slotnick, *Alaska: A History of the 49th State*. Grand Rapids, Michigan: William B. Eerdmans Publishing Co., 1979, p. 79.
16. Stephen Haycox, *Alaska: An American Colony*. Seattle: University of Washington Press, 2002, pp. 213–214.
17. Hill Sr. and Mildred tape recorded by Eddie Barrington 9/1/1970, courtesy of relatives Marlene and Hill Barrington, III.

18. *"Florence* Turned Turtle." *The Daily Colonist,* Victoria, B.C., July 27, 1900.
19. Ibid., "Steamer for Koyukuk." *The Klondike Nugget,* April 22, 1900.
20. Ibid., Hill Sr. and Mildred Barrington tapes, 9/1/1970.
21. Ibid.
22. Frank Cotter, "Meet Sid!" No title on newspaper clipping, but probably the *Alaskan Weekly* (Seattle), Nov. 27, 1927.
23. "Captain Born in 1877." *Whidbey News-Times,* Dec. 29, 1966.
24. Barry C. Anderson, *Lifeline to the Yukon.* Seattle, WA: Superior Pub. Co., 1983, p. 11.
25. "Back From the Koyukuk." *Dawson Daily News,* June 23, 1900.
26. Norman R. Hacking and W. Kaye Lamb, *The Princess Story.* Vancouver: Mitchell Press, 1974, p. 161.
27. Ibid., Bill Sr. and Mildred Barrington tapes 9/1/1970.
28. *"Florence S.* Wrecked." *The Daily Klondike Nugget,* July 26, 1900.
29. "Mrs. Stewart and Her Daughter," *Dawson Daily News,* July 28, 1900.
30. "Skagwayan is the Victim in Wreck," *The Daily Alaskan,* July 30, 1900.
31. Ibid., *"Florence* Turned Turtle."
32. "Wrecked in Thirty Mile River." *Dawson Daily News,* July 23, 1900.
33. "Barrington Arrested." *Dawson Daily News,* July 24, 1900.
34. "Not Guilty." *The Daily Klondike Nugget,* July 26, 1900.
35. "Barrington Not to Blame." *Dawson Daily News,* July 25, 1900.
36. "Barrington Not Blamed," Unknown Seattle paper, July, 1900. Clipping courtesy of Peggy Darst Townsdin of Coupville. Sent to author Nov. 1998. [Maybe *Dawson Daily News.*]
37. "To Run Rapids." *Dawson Daily News,* July 28, 1900.

6: HIGHS AND LOWS OF THE BUSINESS

Through the late gold rush years, the riverboat *Clifford Sifton*, an elegantly appointed double-stacked sternwheeler, transported stampeders on Lake Bennett above Whitehorse. A Kansas syndicate of ladies contracted for the building of the *Sifton* at Lake Bennett in 1898.[1]

Sections of the White Pass and Yukon Route Railroad had already been completed from Skagway to Lake Bennett and from Cariboo Crossing to Whitehorse.[2] Along the south shore of Lake Bennett at that time, construction crews hacked and blasted out a railroad grade, hoping to connect Bennett with Cariboo Crossing. Eventually the White Pass railroad finished its entire route. Because of this, St. Michael, Alaska lost its trade. Skagway found itself the main port of entry to the Yukon.[3] Upper River travel continued to be strong.

With the railroad running from Skagway past the lake to Whitehorse in 1900,[4] the sternwheeler *Clifford Sifton* no longer found use at Bennett. The managers wanted to run her down the Yukon River from the lake, past the wild waters above Whitehorse.

Owners of the *Clifford Sifton* found Syd and Hill Barrington between jobs, ready to accept a risky undertaking and, of course, a wager. The brothers saw the trip as a welcome challenge, another adventurous gamble. They could hardly wait.

The job would not be an easy one. Two perilous obstacles on the water run blocked travel. The two barriers were Miles Canyon, which some stampeders called "a hell's caldron,"[5] and Whitehorse Rapids, both upriver of Whitehorse. On spotting the obstacles, stampeders took to land and portaged around these horrors. At different times,

First passenger train on the White Pass–Yukon Route
to the summit near Skagway. Feb. 20, 1899.
*Credit: Case & Draper: Alaska State Library/Alaska Railroad
Coll./PCA 275-12-64.*

The SS *Clifford Sifton* plowing through the
rapids of Miles Canyon.
*Credit: Yukon Archives, Canada, MacBride Museum
Coll., Whitehorse.*

more than 200 men thought they could master the waters and lost their lives taking the chance.[6]

In his book, *Klondike Fever*, Pierre Berton described these barriers. After rounding a turn in the river, a roaring din blasted the stampeders' ears. Before them "lay the gorge, a narrow cleft in a wall of black basalt with an unholy whirlpool at its center. Beyond this dark fissure lurked…White Horse Rapids, so called because the foam upon them resembled white steeds leaping and dancing in the sunlight."[7]

At Miles Canyon, water roared between rock walls 200 feet high, down a mile-long gorge eighty feet wide, squeezing through this narrow funnel at terrific speeds. Any number of nightmares could occur to an unlucky craft—the most likely being smashed against the side walls.

With the job in hand, the Barringtons followed one precaution— they fastened thick bales of hay around the entire steamer, bustles they were called, just in case it crashed against the rough canyon walls. "She looked like a woman going to a fancy dress party," Syd said later.[8]

The very air above, filled with the speed of the water, seemed to shriek in protest around them. Then with only one volunteer aboard, Syd in the pilothouse and Hill at the engine, they burst away.[9] A screaming blast from the whistle, and they rode the *Sifton* into that bucking foam. Above, a cheering Whitehorse population lined the cliffs.

The steamer swooped down the run, engine in reverse, taking the bends, barely dodging the walls. Syd read the water like a familiar book. After an intense couple minutes, the steamer blasted through the gorge, took on the rapids beyond and into the roiling crest of White Horse Rapids, its waters kicking ten, fifteen feet high and then, slowing, sliding with relief onto the quiet waters following. Everything happened so fast, but the Barringtons and the *Sifton* survived intact. The brothers might take risks, but they knew the job, too. Onlookers on the cliffs above went wild, though their voices drowned in the rapid's roar.

Once through, Hill summed up the adventure, "One ship, one mile, three men, three minutes, three thousand dollars."[10] The feat was written up in *Ripley's Believe It or Not*.[11] Captain G.G. Haley brought the steamer the rest of the way down river on its maiden voyage from Lake Bennett.[12]

The elation from the successful *Clifton* run did not last long. Within weeks, Syd Barrington received bad news. Though no criminal charge ever attached to him for the *Florence S.* disaster earlier in the season, the Washington Steamboat-Inspection Service reviewed the

Syd and Hazel Barrington taken in the early 1900s.
Credit: Courtesy of Bill and Elna Barrington.

tragedy over the summer. They decided punishment was due and withdrew Syd's pilot's license for two seasons. Not until January 1903 did inspectors reinstate his certificate.[13]

The license revocation was a shock to Syd. Even though not at the wheel during the accident, people died from his boat while he commanded. The positive reputation he built over the years as a skilled, even matchless, skipper was now marred by this tragedy. Syd was one to accept what happened and get on with his life, and that is what he did.

For the next two seasons, Syd stayed away from the wheelhouse. Few newspaper accounts mention the Barrington brothers or their whereabouts. All three are listed in Polk's Directory, the address book for Alaska/Yukon residents during those early years. Syd listed as pilot, Hill as bartender and Harry as miner. The restriction from riverboating afforded more time for mining their claims outside Dawson, and they literally dug in.[14] Quite possibly, they stampeded to other gold strikes in the area as well. *The Dawson Daily News* announced strikes at Fortymile, Flat, Clear Creek and five miles above Dawson, during the 1903 season alone.[15]

All three brothers visited relatives on Whidbey Island at various times as noted in local newspapers. Sometimes they worked. Hill, for example, was listed as freight clerk on the sternwheeler, *Fairhaven*, between Seattle and LaConner, making stops on Whidbey along the way. He also set up a "prosperous" cigar and tobacco business in the Hotel Stevens in Seattle.[16]

Though off river for this time, the years were punctuated with important events. Just as the Barringtons suffered river accidents, tragedy sought the brothers in a more personal form. During the early 1900s, the Barrington clan endured yet another family misfortune. Brother Yorke, who had gone to bat for Syd after the *Florence S.* disaster, often saw his brothers when they lived in Seattle. He operated a successful drugstore on Pike Street. At the age of twenty-nine,

Hazel Barrington lounging on the warm shore of Long Beach, California.
Credit: Courtesy of Peggy Darst Townsdin.

From a performing family, Hazel Delisle Barrington, poses for a serious moment in a clown costume.
Credit: Courtesy of Peggy Darst Townsdin.

totally energetic and healthy up to a week before his passing, he suddenly died of "tuberculosis of the lungs" at the Seattle General Hospital. Yorke's death on April 6, 1901[17] proved a shocking waste. Married in 1898, he left a young widow, Anna Phillips Barrington.[18]

After a somber summer, a happier event occurred that fall. Syd became a husband again. This time to his former wife's sister, twenty-four-year-old Hazel Delisle. Syd brought her south for the wedding, and the two married quietly at St. Mark's Church in Seattle Sept. 7, 1901, with Hill as a witness.[19]

Hazel proved a great match for Syd, sharing his philosophy: life was to enjoy, money to spend. She, too, owned a showy nature, a performer from a circus family and a Dawson song-and-dance girl.[20] Barrington relatives said, "She had a costume for every occasion."[21] Living it up was in her make up, for she encouraged Syd's wild living and concocted some of her own. While Syd gloried in an audience, Hazel provided the backdrop. She possessed a generous streak and loved to entertain.[22] Hazel adored Syd and felt somewhat possessive of

Yorke Barrington, the only brother who lived a landlubber's life, died unexpectedly before 30 years old, in 1901.

Credit: Courtesy of Peggy Darst Townsdin.

him. There were quiet, more thoughtful times, too. When not in the Yukon, the Syd Barringtons spent time in Seattle, on Whidbey Island, in California or traveling the United States.

Even though her sister, Maude, had been briefly married and then divorced from Syd, all three remained friends. On a few of Syd and Hazel's trips to Whidbey Island to visit Barrington relatives, Maude accompanied them.

Dawson was more a home to the newlywed Barringtons than Whidbey or Seattle. Due to his pilot's license cancellation, however, Syd was not riverboating when Felix Pedro struck gold in the Tanana Valley the summer of 1902.[23] Upon word reaching Dawson, 2,000 to 3,000 people—possibly Syd and Hill in the number—swept out of town as news of the Pedro strike spread.[24] This "floating" population scurried south and west down the Yukon into Alaska to the new diggings, at what would become Fairbanks. All this excitement spurred more construction. The Canadian government, for one, built a winter road between Dawson and Whitehorse during the summer of 1902.[25]

• • •

1. W.D. McBride, "Saga of Famed Packets of Mighty Yukon River." *Alaska Weekly,* July 28, 1944.
2. James Wickersham, *Old Yukon.* Wash. DC: Washington Law Book Co., 1938, p. 24.
3. "Battle for Control." *Klondike Gold Hypertext.* Hyperborean Productions, multimedia 1996.
4. *Facts About Alaska: The Alaska Almanac.* Anchorage: Alaska Northwest Publishing Company, 1980, p. 96.
5. Ella Lung Martinsen, *Trail to North Star Gold.* Portland, OR: Metropolitan Press, 1969, p. 44.
6. Barrett Willoughby, *Gentlemen Unafraid.* NY: G.P. Putnam's Sons, 1928, p. 223.
7. Pierre Berton, *Klondike Fever.* NY: Alfred A. Knopf, 1960, p. 279.
8. Helen Sefton, "Reporter Reveals Peculiarities Famed Stikine River Excursion." *Wrangell Sentinel,* October 3, 1941.
9. R.M. Patterson, *Trail to the Interior.* NY: William Morrow and Co., Inc., 1966, p. 39.
10. Bob Greenhagen, "Searching for Fortune On the Yukon Rivers." *Whidbey News Times,* April 13, 1972.
11. Trudy J. Sundberg, "Captains Sid and Hill Are Oldest Native Sons." *Whidbey Press Progress Edition,* June, 1961.
12. "Clifford Sifton Arrives." *Dawson Daily News,* August 3, 1900.
13. Steamboat-Inspection Service, Department of Commerce and Labor. *List of Masters, Mates, Pilots, and Engineers of Merchant Steam, Motor, and Sail Vessels.* Washington, DC: Government Printing Office, 1904, p. 16.

Telegram sent from Hill and Syd in Dawson after hearing the
news of Yorke's death in Seattle, April 1901.
Credit: Courtesy of Peggy Darst Townsdin.

14. "Dawson Couple Wed in Seattle." *Yukon World,* July 12, 1904.
15. "New Strike on Yukon." Dawson Daily News, Sept. 14, 1903.
16. Ibid., "Dawson Couple Wed in Seattle."
17. "Island News Paragraphs." *Island County Times,* April 12, 1901.
18. Bill and Elna Barrington tapes, 2001–02, courtesy of relatives Marlene and Hill Barrington, III.
19. Marriage Certificate #6061, State of Washington, King County, filed Oct. 1, 1901.
20. Lael Morgan, *Good Time Girls*. Seattle: Epicenter Press, 1998, pp. 64–66.
21. Ibid., Bill and Elna Barrington tapes.
22. Interview with Bill Barrington, Anchorage, April 11, 1998.
23. David Wharton, *The Alaska Gold Rush*. Bloomington, IN: Indiana University Press, 1971, p. 232.
24. John Scudder McLain, *Alaska and the Klondike*. NY: McClure, Phillips and Co., 1905, p. 44.
25. W.J. Roche, *The Yukon Territory*. Ottawa: Minister of the Interior, 1916, p. 194.

7: OVERCOMING SNAGS AND SWEEPERS

Once the Washington inspection service restored Syd's license in 1903, the brothers kept the sternwheels churning. During the same time, an ongoing shift of Yukon "players" occurred. Whereas miners originally dug with pick and shovel, now big business "plowed in" hauling heavy machinery. With the opening of the Yukon basin for gold, larger companies discovered and developed other resources such as copper, silver and coal.

The Barringtons kept busy. They shipped in and out of remote locations, often pushing heavily loaded barges before the boat. The more tonnage, the more barges, the more money. Some years so much freight waited to go downriver to Whitehorse, it could not be cleared out in one river season alone. Owners had to store it over the winter.[1]

Syd piloted for the river division of the White Pass (under the flag of the British Yukon Navigation Company).[2] The firm built their own steamers in Whitehorse,[3] as well as storing vessels over the winter. It was a sizeable operation. From the town's waterfront buildings, ramps sloped to the river. In the spring when the river ice broke, workers prepared stored vessels for launching. Using numerous heavy screw jacks, the "bull gang" levered the boats onto greased skids and slid them down the ways onto the Yukon. Once launched, the vessels moved upriver to freight docks where the railroad tracks ended. There, work crews loaded cargo onto the steamers.[4]

Spring charged the air with energy. Grocers filled bins with fresh produce. Storeowners stocked shelves. And when captains stepped off the train, newspapers announced steamboat officers' arrivals along

Panorama of Whitehorse looking southwest
from across the river, 1903.
Credit: Yukon Archives, H.C. Barley Coll., # 5538.

with river conditions at both Whitehorse and Dawson. Officers then—
Syd among them—took charge of their assigned vessels.

The Barringtons, when they could, preferred a Lake Lebarge
winter anchorage because it was closer to Dawson. Syd used his own
dog team while the ice held fast, dashing from Whitehorse to Lake
Lebarge.[5] The anticipation built; hearts pounded and adrenalin flowed
while waiting anxiously for Mother Nature to soften her grip on the
ice. When the Yukon did crack, skippers raced for Dawson to be first
and to win a substantial wager.

For years Syd and Hazel located at Whitehorse during the season,
becoming part of the community. Syd, for instance, captained the
Whitehorse baseball team.[6] It was their normal seasonal routine to
depart Seattle, sail up the Inside Passage and land in Skagway. When
laborers laid the last track for the railroad in 1900, it was a simple
matter to board the train and ride to Whitehorse. Tons of freight
traveled that way too. No more struggling over the mountains!

Syd, Baby Yorke, and Hazel; and father and son portrait.
Credit: Courtesy of Peggy Darst Townsdin.

Brother Hill, on the other hand, headquartered in Dawson each season. While Hill often rode the steamboats as purser, Harry, when in the north, focused on the gold claims at Bullion,[7] Sheep Creek[8] and Arch Creek[9] in the Kluane district.[10]

The minute the Washington Steamboat-Inspection Service restored Syd's pilot's license in 1903, he signed on with the White Pass for the run to Dawson. Finally he could get back into the business. Usually heading north in April or May, a special event delayed the journey. Syd remained in Seattle to witness the proud birth of his son, Yorke, who arrived May 31, 1903.[11]

With his pilot's license once more in hand, the White Pass assigned Syd to the steamer *Mary F. Graff*. Built in Seattle in 1898,[12] mariners called the *Graff* the battleship.[13] It provided more space for freight than any other steamer on the Dawson/Whitehorse run[14] and carried just about anything. The *Graff* hauled goods all summer. Barrington loads might have been a bit lighter to ease back into the job. By fall, Syd's careful wheelhouse attitude left the routine behind, and he was back in form.

Besides passengers, Barrington frequently carried live freight. Running from Whitehorse to Dawson late that summer, the *Graff* grounded near Minto on a new sandbar that was not on the chart, this one dubbed "Jackson's Discovery" after the captain who "found" it. The freight consisted of dynamite, hogs, gasoline, sheep, coal oil and 150 head of cattle.

While stuck on the bar for several days, crewmen lived in a hunter's paradise. They took time to stalk grouse, partridges and other game. Syd even shot a black bear that wandered too close to the boat.

When the *Selkirk* chugged by, it tried for five hours to pull the *Graff* off the bar, but the freight proved too heavy. With no luck there, crew finally pushed the cattle overboard to lighten the load. Forced off a gangplank, the cows hit water and drifted in all directions. A few struggled to nearby islands, a number floated to the mainland and the rest swept five miles downriver.

Once free of the sandbar, the scene took on a western flavor as crew set about corralling the cattle. Picture these northern "cowboys" shouting, howling, dodging, running, roping, calling and whistling to round up the anxious cows. Officers converted the upper deck into sheep pens to make room.

The job took eighteen hours, but the animals were finally reloaded. When the *Graff* tied up at Dawson, one reporter stated that the old ship "looked like...Noah's ark making her famous landing on Mt. Ararat."[15]

But as an ark of salvation, the *Mary F. Graff* was not to be. That fall it proved to be a jinxed vessel. Still, with extreme low water, every other steamer on the river "found" sandbars too. On an October 4, 1903 trip with Pilot Syd Barrington and Captain Jackman, the *Graff* ran upon rocks near the Little Salmon River and sprang a leak. Officers jettisoned the freight—again live cows—to browse for food on a nearby island. Trouble harassed the *Graff* that entire trip. Following is an excerpt from the actual log:

> At 1:20 p.m. we hit the sunk rock lying a quarter of a mile above the mouth of Little Salmon River...taking on water...ordered steamer beached...We landed her on a sand-bar beach...I found sixty-one timbers broken...I put on twelve soft patches, using blankets, bacon, sacked flour,

etc…On October 6th at 11:30 a.m. the steamer Columbian came alongside…she assisted us off bar and over to woodyard across the river.[16]

Six times the *Graff* grounded. Twice she had to be beached and patched to keep from sinking. Twice her steering gear broke. Other steamers helped pull her off sandbars, while she did the same for grounded cousins. A trip that normally took the *Graff* under two days to complete took ten! The "battleship" *Graff* had temporarily lost its battle. When towed back to Dawson, the boat remained there for repairs over the winter.

With the *Graff* out of commission, Syd and the crew transferred to the *La France*.[17] Since the ice was forming early, Syd finished one of the last runs to Whitehorse that year. As was the custom, pilots and captains often boarded the same large ocean steamer sailing down the Inside Passage at the end of the season. Thus completed the "winter of exodus south."[18]

Hill remained in the north two more months, a bright-eyed young lady the reason. Taking a later ship than normal from Skagway south to Washington that winter proved almost the last trip for Hill Barrington.[19]

Planning to arrive on Whidbey Island before Christmas, Hill boarded the 216-foot steel Canadian Pacific Navigation ocean steamship *Amur*. Fully loaded with passengers, the ship took off from Skagway. Halfway through the journey at the entrance to Port Simpson, Canada, the steamer hit a submerged boulder. Imagine the scare for sleeping passengers when a terrifying jolt at five o'clock in the morning nearly threw people from bed. In minutes the *Amur* piled upon the rocks. Crew and passengers nervously waited until high tide to float her off. Even at that, when full tide arrived and lifted the ship free, the current caught *Amur*'s stern and swung her around. Again she smashed against the reef, doing more damage. Finally a tug arrived from Port Simpson and towed the ship in.

Oh, how good to be on solid ground again. The relieved passengers waited until another steamer sailed them south to Washington.[20] Hill was assuredly pleased when he reached southern shores. There he shared his adventure with Whidbey relatives—no doubt with his own embellishments.

When the 1903 season ended, Syd made a change. He now carried a valid skipper's license, and he had once again proved himself with a successful piloting season. Deciding to give the job a rest for a period, he resigned from the White Pass. His wife, new son and family drew him south. Besides, he had noticed machinery practically replacing the pick and shovel miner.[21] Business had found rocky going. A number of large sternwheelers had been "laid on the shelf" or were out of commission due to lack of business.[22] It was time to rethink priorities.

Syd Barrington felt he needed to focus from a new perspective, to concentrate on mining. He had recovered from the disaster of the *Florence S.* and knew he was once again in good standing. He would be free to spend time south, or prospect up north. Therefore, he took the summer of 1904 and the next two seasons strictly for mining. His claims—#36 below on Bullion, among them—proved irrestible.[23] Harry and Hill spent several periods on Barrington claims, as well as more time south.[24]

Hill Barrington focused his heart not only on mining, but also on more tender affairs. As Dawson's *Yukon World* reported in 1904: "Hill Barrington, formerly purser of the steamer *Prospector,* and Miss Christine Anderson, a young woman very well known here, were married at the Lincoln apartments, Seattle, June 11. Both were in Dawson last year, but have lived in Seattle during the past spring and summer."[25]

Christine Anderson married Hill in June 1904. She died unexpectedly in Seattle in 1911. The photo was taken in Dawson. *Credit: Courtesy of Peggy Darst Townsdin.*

Once Syd moved back into steamboating in the spring of 1906, he relocated his family to a house in Dawson.[26] The location must have suited the Barringtons, as they headquartered there during the season for the next ten years. Syd's wife, Hazel, often invited relatives such as her mother, Mrs. Harry Crowhurst, to stay for the summer.[27]

Workwise, the White Pass assigned Syd as pilot on the *Victorian* for three seasons.[28] The 716-ton sternwheeler had been built in Victoria, B.C., in 1898 by J. Todd for the C.D. Company.[29] (This was not the same ship Syd's brother, Eddie, commanded in 1898, which was also called the *Victoria*.[30]) Little did Syd know, he and the *Victorian* would be saviors at the end of the summer.

Around this time "an uncommercial traveler, a man of color"[31] Mr. Hock Dennis—everyone called him "Splotus"—took a liking to the brothers and their manner of steamboating. He hooked up as crew for the next ten years. Every spring Splotus showed up in Whitehorse and hired on as cook and musician. A talented man, he played the banjo and sang songs aboard; many of the pieces he composed himself.[32]

The year of 1906, near the end of the river season, recorded the worst steamboat accident on the Yukon River. Although Syd was not involved in the tragedy itself, he and his steamer drew a hand as rescuers.

• • •

1. "Last Steamers From White Horse," *Dawson Record,* October 13, 1903.
2. Melody Webb, "Steamboats on the Yukon River," *Alaska Journal,* Summer, 1985, p. 25.
3. S.H. Graves. 1908, reprint 1970. *On the "White Pass" Pay-Roll.* NY: Paladin Press, p.142.
4. Helene Dobrowolsky & Rob Ingram. 1994. *Edge of the River; Heart of the City.* Whitehorse, YT: Lost Moose Publishing, p. 21.
5. "People Who Come and Go," *The Weekly Star,* April 14, 1911.
6. "Captain Now Miner," *Yukon World,* May 15, 1904.
7. "More Good News," *Daily Evening Star,* May 19, 1904.
8. "Syd's Brother," *Daily Evening Star,* July 17, 1904.
9. "Personal," *Daily Evening Star,* July 22, 1904.
10. "Kluane Activity," *The Weekly Star,* April 24, 1908.
11. "Happened at Home," *Island County Times,* June 19, 1903.
12. W.D. MacBride, "Saga of Famed Packets of Mighty Yukon River," *The Alaska Weekly,* August 25, 1944.
13. "Cattle in River," *Dawson Daily News,* Sept. 25, 1903.
14. "Big Loads the Rule," *Dawson Daily News,* July 2, 1903.
15. Ibid, "Cattle in River."
16. S.H. Graves. 1908, reprint 1970. *On the "White Pass" Pay-Roll.* NY: Paladin Press, pp. 161–162.
17. W.D. MacBride, *The Alaska Weekly,* August 16, 1944.
18. "Off for the South," *Dawson Daily News,* October 14, 1903.
19. "San de Fuca Notes," *Island County Times,* Jan. 1, 1904.
20. Untitled article, *The Mining Journal,* December 19, 1903, p. 1.
21. Howard Clifford. 1981. *Rails North.* Seattle, WA: Superior Publishing Co., p. 30.
22. "Fleet is Not Small," *Dawson Daily News,* June 3, 1905.
23. "Captain Now Miner," *Yukon World,* May 15, 1904.
24. "People Who Come and Go," *Daily Evening Star,* March 21, 1906.
25. "Syd's Brother," reported by the *Yukon World* (Dawson) in the *Daily Evening Star* (Whitehorse), July 19, 1904.
26. "People Who Come and Go," *Weekly Star,* June 29, 1906.
27. "Arrives From Up the River," *Dawson Daily News,* June 13, 1910.
28. "Seamen Bold," *Weekly Star,* June 8, 1906.
29. W.D. MacBride, *The Alaska Weekly,* Sept. 15, 1944.
30. Ibid.
31. "Building Boat for the Susitna," *The Cook Inlet Pioneer,* Anchorage, AK, May 23, 1916.
32. Barrett Willoughby, "Champion White Water Pilot of the North," *American Magazine,* October, 1928, p. 152.

8: GOING INDEPENDENT

On the clear fall evening of September 25, 1906, the *Columbian* steamed her way on the Yukon, downstream to Dawson. The boat, built in 1898 in Victoria,[1] cruised about twelve and one-half miles an hour. Captained by J.O. Williams,[2] she carried a crew of twenty-five, a stowaway, a number of cattle and three tons of blasting powder loaded in kegs on deck. Since the vessel carried explosives aboard, no passengers were allowed on the trip. That was law.

While rounding a bend, the steamboat surprised a flock of ducks. In a panic, the birds flapped to the air. Thinking to bag one, a crewman snatched up a rifle, swung to the birds, tripped and fell. The loaded rifle accidentally fired into the dynamite on deck. Instantly, a "dull roar" and a blinding explosion ripped off the front of the steamer and took six crew members. The blast demolished the engine controls, and only the skill of the captain—reversing the paddle against the current—managed to back the boat safely onto the gravel beach.[3]

Hurt, moaning, a number of crew suffered on shore waiting for rescue. Captain Williams sent several men ahead by land to contact a telegraph station and get help. When the *Victorian,* with Syd as pilot, received the news, he immediately beached the barge he was pushing and headed for the wreck. The steamer *Dawson* also heard the call, outfitted itself as a hospital ship and plowed toward the accident.

Shortly after 7:00 pm, Syd on the *Victorian* sighted the stricken crew and edged to shore. Deck hands helped the *Columbian* men and the injured aboard, and then hoisted the dead bodies on deck. Crew administered aid where possible. When the boat met the *Dawson* several hours later, deck hands again transferred the victims, put them under doctor's care and sped them toward Whitehorse. Eventually four other crewmen died of burns.[4] If the law about carrying passengers on boats transporting explosives had not been in effect, who knows how many lives would have been lost.

For the following three seasons, Syd concentrated on steamboating, navigating White Pass sternwheelers on the Yukon each summer. But to work for a salary, to sail on someone else's schedule, did not suit the Barrington nature. The brothers had long planned to build an independent steamer service. With that thought in mind, Syd had earlier contracted for a small sternwheel freight steamer, the *Hattie B.,* built in Seattle for service in 1906.[5] During this time, the other brothers worked the Barrington claims in the Yukon. Hill, Harry and Uncle J.P. McCrohan set up hydraulic operations on the Kluane northwest of Whitehorse and worked claims in the Sheep Creek district.[6] Life, however, was not to go on in any kind of settled routine for long. The brothers would see to that.

To further plans for an independent fleet, in the fall of 1908, Syd and his associates purchased the steamer, *La France,* a 201-ton boat built at Lower Lebarge in 1902.[7] The packet had been out of commission and overhauled in Dawson after running on a reef up the Pelly River two years previous.[8] In any case, the price was right. A powerful little vessel, the boat was a sister to the steamer *Thistle.*

Though no records exist, the Barringtons probably arrived late in the Yukon the following spring. Since the Alaska–Yukon–Pacific Exposition opened in Seattle in June 1909, it can well be imagined the Barringtons attending. In fact, it would be hard to think of them not using the opportunity to promote business or to trade Klondike tales with former stampeders and friends.

The year 1909 also proved a time of serious change for the brothers, for they made the break with the White Pass and became independent. Syd took the job as manager of the new firm. As their Dawson agent, the company hired A.W.H. Smith. Friends referred to Andy as "Alphabetical" Smith because of the string of letters before his name. Their new "Side Streams Navigation Company," (SSN Company) ran the "side streams" or tributaries of the Upper Yukon River—the Pelly, the Stewart, the Ross, the Porcupine, the White.[9] They went up farther on impossible rivers, often where no vessel had gone before.

The firm bought and piloted various boats in different seasons—

the *La France,* the *Pauline,* the *Vidette* and more. Hill Barrington, sometimes purser, and Captain Steve Martin, cousin by marriage,[10] as master often accompanied. Since Canadian rules required a Canadian captain in charge while in Yukon waters, Martin moved from Washington State and took up residence in Vancouver, B.C. Harry remained on land, working and watching over the gold diggings.

It was typical of the Barringtons to form such a company, finding a calling that supported miners and afforded a chance for real money. Left unsaid, perhaps, was the brothers' need for adventure. Independents could sail where they wanted. Navigating upstream where no steamer dared to go, forcing a sternwheeler against current, up and up, in narrow and often perilous waters, filled the brothers' craving for challenge. Everyday steamboat captains plied the Yukon, but who had the nerve to tackle the smaller, fickle side rivers far enough upstream where no paddlewheel had gone before—and still win? Moreover, conquering the side streams brought the gambling brothers themselves closer to the gold discoveries. There the real action took place.

During the summer of 1909 the Barringtons decided to test the *La France.* In Dawson at the time hundreds of stampeders with loads of supplies waited frantically to reach the Kluane diggings in Canada by way of the White River. With no railroad or road into the area, only loners poled against the terrific current as they attempted the trip. The Barringtons felt the need to battle up the river by steamer as far as possible. Few skippers even tried. A $5,000 wager added richness to the challenge.

The White River was named that for a reason. "In addition to the glacial silt with which the White River is charged," author Hudson Stuck reported, "it dissolved out of its banks great quantities of volcanic ash."[11]

The route flowed a heavy current, was lined with many channels spread over immense flats and entertained a multitude of snags everywhere. "So great is the speed of the current," said engineer Robert Lowe, "that the main channel runs on an average of eighteen inches higher than the water in the other channels and above the mud flats on either side."[12] Yet in some places, there was not enough water to "float a peanut shell."[13]

Author Barrett Willoughby described the White River valley more poetically through the eyes of a steamboat crew member. "Imagine a green valley seven miles wide and serpentining all over the bottom of it this river, swift and shallow as a creek, creamy-white and thick from the volcanic ash it churned up from its bottom, and actually split into fifteen or twenty channels by sand bars that shifted while you looked at them!…It's nearly impossible to read water that looks like a milk-shake in action but Captain Syd can do it."[14]

And Captain Syd did just that, collecting fourteen hull patches repaired with boards and wads of oakum along the way.[15] One passenger said, "The roar of our furnaces and the eternal pounding of water under our hull deafened us and tickled our eardrums; our teeth were nearly shaken loose from vibration as the boat bucked against that current; and how the old baby did eat up the wood."[16]

Yet for the first time, a vessel reached a site 100 miles above the mouth, hauling miners bound for the head of the river.[17] Because of Barrington boldness, the side streams of the Yukon were giving up some of their secrets.

Such news electrified prospectors intent on making the Kluane gold and the copper districts. Previously, stampeders poled up the White to its fork with the Donjek against a terrific current. Barrington's success cut the time from Dawson to five days; poling, besides being exhausting, would have taken about eighteen days. The run, according to Second Engineer Robert Lowe of the *La France* said the "trip was a marked success and one that must rank in the first place in the annals of steamboat explorations not only of the Yukon but of the world."[18] Such challenges, and victories, marked the Barringtons as unique in the business.

Syd knew the advantage for being at the immediate discovery site—that being payment, of course. No bouncing checks or credit cards then. For hauling supplies and equipment he was paid on the spot in gold dust.[19]

Even in the heat of gold discoveries and river traffic, the Barringtons understood change happened around them every day. Not only in methods, but in river travel itself. What helped the brothers to endure in business and prosper, in spite of difficulties, was their willingness to adjust and accept new ideas. Where many people resisted change, preferring to retain the "old fashioned way," the brothers studied change to see what it could do for them. When traditional tactics did not work, the Barringtons applied their ingenuity with unorthodox methods. They "bulled ahead," or tried something new, keeping their eyes open for ideas. Both Syd and Hill not only used innovations, but also devised them. It was this originality, and nerve, which brought success to the Barrington operations. Courage and confidence defined the men,[20] with a large dose of daring.

Newspapers tracked the *Pauline,* a boat built in 1907 at Whitehorse, and the *La France* the spring of 1910 as they touched at Hootalinqua, then Yukon Crossing, racing to be the first boats into Dawson following the ice. Triumphantly, the *Pauline* and *La France,* steamed into Dawson the evening of May 21, making a clean sweep. Lashed together, both pushed barges of freight for elated Dawson merchants. Several old timers traveled on the boats; possibly they smelled smoke on the air from a forest fire near Eagle. A few days later, the *La France* left for Mayo carrying supplies for miners and storekeepers.[21]

Wild fires plagued the area that season. Officers, and the *Pauline* itself, became "wood" rescuers the end of June, when fire raged at the mouth of Barker Creek. As the blaze consumed 200 cords of wood cut by wood dealer McNeil, the flames threatened another pile owned by a dealer, McLaughlin. Crew of the *Pauline,* on hand close by, used the power from the boat engine to throw a stream of water over the wood, thereby saving the day.[22]

As the air chilled in the fall, often a Barrington vessel ended the steamboat season, its decks crowded with last-minute passengers, every inch occupied. [23] Other than an occasional stray rider picked up along the way, the boat pointed toward Whitehorse in a mad push to beat the creeping ice. Once upriver, the Barringtons routinely wintered the vessels at Lake Laberge. As mentioned, by leaving the boats at the foot of the lake, the steamers would be ready to load freight and fly down the river following the ice breakup in the spring.

Caught by the challenge and wildness of Alaska, Syd and his brothers continued to divide their time between the adventurous north, and the more urban, sophisticated Seattle living. Whenever the Barringtons headed south for 'the winter—sometimes stopping at Tenekee Hot Springs in Alaska before finishing the trip[24]—if their wallets bulged, they traveled and lived high. They also made it a point, every season, to visit relatives in Washington State.

The Puget Sound area had drastically changed in the time since father Edward Barrington pioneered on Whidbey Island in the 1850s. By 1910, ocean ships from Alaska shifted focus from Port Townsend

Steamer *La France* plying the Yukon River.
Credit: University of Alaska: Carla Rust, 67-110-361.

to the Seattle/Tacoma area, which then supported a population of nearly 250,000.[25] The urban region was, as well, the terminus for four transcontinental railroads.[26] Steamer travel throughout Puget Sound had evolved from canoe to sailing ship to sternwheeler and steamer.[27]

The family matriarch, Christina, into her sixties by 1910, lived in San de Fuca, Whidbey Island with her second husband, school director and sheriff, Joseph Power. Memories recall Christina as a well-loved woman, describing her as a "tough old gentle lady."[28] Daughter Sibella Barrington Fisher and her own family lived close by. Harry bought a house nearby also, while Hill settled in his winter home in Oak Harbor only a few miles away. Syd purchased property in San de Fuca also, but lived in Seattle. The half-sister, Olivia Monroe, made her home more distantly in Spokane and Seattle,[29] but visited often.[30]

When in San de Fuca, the family often gathered for Sunday dinner with everyone bringing a dish.

Hazel Barrington, Syd and Christina Barrington
Power. Photo possibly taken in the early 1900s.
Credit: Courtesy of Peggy Darst Townsdin.

For the most part, there were amiable feelings among family members. They never talked about religion, but politics proved a loud and quarrelsome topic. It made no difference whether it was a local bond issue or the presidential election, everyone had a definite and noisy opinion. At times debates grew quite ferocious. Then a discussion might end with, "Well, that's what I told you in the first place, damn it!" In any case, before separating for their own homes, everyone kissed as if nothing had happened. Quite a kissing family, the Barringtons. They fully enjoyed each other.

• • •

1. W.D. MacBride, "Saga of Famed Packets of Mighty Yukon River." *The Alaska Weekly,* July 28, 1944.
2. "Seamen Bold," *Weekly Star,* June 8, 1906.
3. Melody Webb, "Steamboats on the Yukon River." *Alaska Journal,* Summer, 1985, p. 26.
4. "Columbian," *Fort Wrangell News,* August 10, 1898. Lloyd Bayers card, MS 1, Juneau Alaska Historical Library.
5. Gordon Newell, *The H.W. McCurdy Marine History of the Pacific Northwest.* Seattle: Superior Publ. Co., 1966, p. 118. The original pamphlet by W.D. MacBride [also spelled McBride] entitled "Saga of Famed Packets and Other Steamboats of Mighty Yukon River," housed in the Alaska Historical Library states the *Hattie B.* was a tug from San Francisco, arriving in Dawson July 10, 1898. That information was not in the printed *Alaska Weekly* series of "Saga" articles in 1944. Some discrepancy here.
6. "Captain Syd Is Pleased." *Daily Evening Star.* April 27, 1906.
7. Ibid., W.D. MacBride, "Saga of Famed Packets of Mighty Yukon River." August 16, 1944.
8. "On Side Streams." *Weekly Star,* April 23, 1909.
9. R.M. Patterson, *Trail to the Interior.* NY: William Morrow and Co., 1966, p. 38. There is some disagreement as to who began the Side Streams Navigation Co. In Barry C. Anderson's book, *Lifeline to the Yukon* (page 59), he states the White Pass expanded and formed the SSN Company in 1909. The Whitehorse paper (4/23/1909), however, states that the *La France* was sold to Syd. The *Vidette* followed, as did the *Pauline.*
10. "Pioneer Lady Laid to Rest in Family Burial Plot May 20." *Island County Times,* May 25, 1939.
11. Hudson Stuck, *Voyages on the Yukon and Its Tributaries.* NY: Charles Scribner's Sons, 1917, p. 40.
12. "Kluane in Touch." *Dawson Daily News,* July 21, 1909.
13. Barrett Willoughby, *Gentlemen Unafraid.* NY: G.P. Putnam's Sons, 1928, p. 226.
14. Ibid., pp. 226–27.
15. Ibid., p. 229.
16. Barrett Willoughby, "Champion White Water Pilot of the North." *American Magazine,* October, 1928, p. 150.
17. "From White River." *Weekly Star,* July 30, 1909.
18. "Kluane in Touch." *Dawson Daily News,* July 21, 1909.
19. Kent Sturgis, *Four Generations on the Yukon.* Fairbanks: Epicenter Press, 1988, p. 22.
20. Ibid., R.M. Patterson, p. 40.
21. "*La France* Departs for Mayo." *Dawson Daily News,* May 26, 1910.
22. "Wild Fire Rages on Stewart." *Dawson Daily News,* June 27, 1910.
23. "Last Dawson Boat." *Weekly Star,* October 28, 1910.
24. Untitled article. *Daily Alaskan,* Oct. 8, 1914.
25. Norman H. Clark, *Washington.* NY: W.W. Norton and Co., 1976, p. 75.
26. "Seattle Timeline." Seattle Public Library flyer, 1995.
27. Gordon Newell, *Ships of the Inland Sea.* Portland, OR: Binfords and Mort, Publishers, 1960, pp. 2–3.
28. Copy of letter from Bill Barrington to Peggy Darst Townsdin, Dec. 6, 1998.
29. Flora Pearson Engle, "Recollections of Early Days." *Whidbey Island Times,* Feb. 1, 1929.
30. "San de Fuca Notes," *Island County Times,* Nov. 17, 1938.

9: WHERE NO STEAMER GOES

Anxious to get a jump start on spring, the Barringtons and other captains arrived in the Yukon in March of 1911. Jack Frost, however, shattered those hopes with a snap of his icy fingers. Though warming toward spring during the month, temperatures plunged to well below zero by mid-April. "Readers!" declared the *Whitehorse Weekly Star,* "April Is Backward."[1] Snow drifts piled over twelve feet on sections of the White Pass railroad track between Skagway and Whitehorse.[2] The train had difficulty plowing through and frequently arrived late, even with a rotary snow plow clearing the rails.

The continuing gold strikes—shouted from isolated wilderness areas—were just the places the Barringtons wanted to be. But with the various shipments from the Stewart, the Pelly and other tributaries, they never seemed to have enough boats or barges. The brothers would have to remedy that.

When river operations finally opened at the foot of Lake Lebarge the spring of 1911, Syd and Hill were in the thick of it. They brought along a crew of ship carpenters from Seattle. Other owners, too, hired men to construct scows for carrying the heavy volume of cargo. Tons of freight-supplies for the boundary parties, the Northern Commercial Company and towns along the route sat piled on the ice at the foot of the lake, waiting to be loaded and transported down river.[3] The *Whitehorse Star* estimated 100 men would be building barges there by mid-March.[4] The ring of hammers and the hum of saws blew across the windy lake.

In addition to running the *La France* and the *Pauline,* the Barringtons

Steamer *Vidette*, formerly the *May West*, pushing
up the White River about 1914.
Credit: University of Alaska, W.F. Erskine Coll. 70-28-706.

decided to build a new and larger steamboat called the *Yorke Barrington*
named after Syd's son.[5] At the same time, several barges would be
constructed; the Barringtons then having eight scows in their fleet.

Syd Barrington had purchased the old police riverboat, *Vidette,*
the previous fall.[6] Its timbers held years of history. Originally named
the *May West,*[7] ship workers built the 134-ton vessel in 1897 at St.
Michael. From the start, the *May West* acquired a noted tag: not only
was it hailed as first steamer arriving in Dawson June 8, 1898 (beating
out Eddie Barrington), it then carried on board sixteen barrels of
whiskey, which sold for $1 per drink (about $26 today).[8]

The *May West* soon changed her name and her character when the
North West Mounted Police purchased the boat from the first owner,
renaming it the *Vidette*. After a colorful ten-year career, in an effort to
reduce the police force in the territory, the constables sold it to the

Perhaps Syd liked the *Vidette* best, as it did anything he wanted—
broke through ice, pushed itself to Mayo, hit Dawson first and last
many seasons. The Barringtons bought the boat the fall of 1910.
Credit: Courtesy of Peggy Darst Townsdin.

Barrington brothers.[9] At completion of the sale, a disappointed
reporter said, "[Now] there will be no flagship to the police fleet of
cruisers and torpedo boat chasers, and the water transportation will be
limited to a covey of mosquito canoes propelled by the strong arms of
the constables."[10]

That spring on Barrington's order, carpenters cut the *Vidette* in half,
adding forty feet to her middle, along with new engines.[11] This larger
vessel was then to be named the *Yorke Barrington,* but the title never
stuck. The brothers themselves, along with everyone else, continued
calling the boat the *Vidette.* The vessel would become Syd's favorite.

While construction continued, 200 people, Dawson bound,
gathered anxiously at the foot of Lebarge for the river ice to break.
The *Pauline, La France, Vidette* and *Evelyn* steamers paused there
along with the mountain of freight. At the Dawson end—its

With Syd at the wheel, the *La France* pushed up the White River in 1909, going "where no steamer had gone before." It burned to the waterline in 1911.
Credit: Courtesy of Peggy Darst Townsdin.

population then at 1,000[12]—May weather reports claimed an approaching ice breakup any moment. Both destinations waited with mounting eagerness.

In mid-May, with a creaking and groaning for miles, the river ice broke, and the race to Dawson was on. The Barringtons, fighting low water and high rocks, could not get the speed they needed. The *Vidette* streamed into Dawson a few days later, second only to the *White Seal,* with four hours separating their times.[13] That first run from Lebarge to Dawson hit ill luck along the way, for the *Vidette* as well as other boats.

But a more serious snag soon caused further delay for the Barringtons. Worse news arrived as Syd stepped on the Dawson shore; his other boat, the *La France,* burned to the waterline in the Thirty-Mile River after striking a rock. Captain Steve Martin[14] quickly offloaded passengers and freight, and watched from shore as most of the *La France* settled underwater. Efforts to bring her up failed, and two days later the boiler room—still above water—caught fire and took the rest of the vessel. One of the accompanying barges with freight also wrecked while floating a few miles down river.

These setbacks seriously worried the Barringtons, with the massive freight loads they had contracted to carry. They would have to work harder, longer hours, push heavier loads, but it could be done. The brothers, however, had long ago learned a financial lesson; insurance, thank heavens, covered the *La France*.[15]

Work continued. Piloting the *Vidette,* Syd navigated in and out of Alaska that spring on the Porcupine, the longest tributary of the Yukon River. Besides carrying horses, dogs and freight, the boat shuttled the Canadian Boundary party to Rampart House on the border. The American Boundary contingent had already landed there. "With the two big survey parties occupying the front," Hill remarked, "Rampart House had one of the liveliest tented cities seen in the Yukon basin in many years."[16]

Another important project drew the Barringtons attention during that summer—dispersing Canadian census workers to their area of enumeration.[17] Census employees gathered statistics relating to furs, fishing, mining and deaths, as well as counting residents.

Not everyone was happy with the census results. The published headcount, for instance, did not sit well with established Dawsonites. The flood of newcomers who built the town more than ten years before, had now settled to a much lower population mark. The British Columbia *Vancouver Province* newspaper, all too smugly, reminded residents of this fact. "'Dawson But a Shell of Its Former Self,'" the headlines stated. "Corporations have taken over the mining, and little ground was being worked by the private individual."[18]

Government officials saved face for Dawsonites. As population figures amassed, the Census Commissioner said, "Few mining countries have stood the exodus that has taken place from the Yukon to new gold diggings in Alaska and other places and sustained the family and mining population as well as this territory."[19]

The lower population trend was not lost on the Barringtons. They absorbed the data along with other changes in the transportation industry—roads being built, tracks being laid. But, the shout of "Gold!" still rang from northern hills. There were men to be shifted, supplies to be transported, money still to be made.

In mid-June 1911, business took a back seat to personal matters. Hill received a telegram with shocking news delivered to him on the *Vidette*. Before sailing north that season, Hill said goodbye to his wife Christine on Whidbey Island, knowing she was scheduled for a routine appendicitis operation. Somehow the operation turned sour. Christine suddenly died[20] in Seattle's Providence Hospital June 15, at the young age of thirty-one years.[21] That she was pregnant at the time of her death was further tragedy.[22]

Christine's untimely death dealt a numbing blow to Hill. He sailed on the *Selkirk* immediately from Dawson to Whitehorse, catching the *Princess Royal* to Seattle.[23] The family buried Christine Anderson Barrington in the Lake View Cemetery, attended by her sisters, Mrs. F.F. Welch of Fairbanks, and Mrs. Harold Malstrom of Dawson.[24] A saddened Hill returned north on the *Humboldt* in July.[25] He might have wondered about his luck: possibly two marriages under his belt, twice a widower and only in his mid-thirties.

River work flowed on nonetheless, the side streams of the Yukon the focus. Piloting the *Vidette,* Syd navigated the first boat up the Pelly River that summer, turning in a record run—on a bet for sure. He completed the round trip to and from the town of Ross River in six days, a total of 460 miles in thirty-four hours coming down.[26] That translated to about fourteen miles an hour, several miles faster than a normal run. Dawsonites soon learned the reason for all the speed.

In July, tall, gaunt Bob Henderson sailed into Dawson with news of his strike somewhere near the mouth of the Macmillan River. When Henderson first arrived, he shied from answering questions about his claim, stating he did not want to start a stampede.[27] "What's this?" people questioned, their eyebrows shooting up. As a discoverer of the original Klondike fortune in 1896,[28] Henderson's secretive actions only aroused more curiosity. Rumors flew through town and excitement climbed, setting off a flurry of high hopes.

Finally induced to talk about the Pelly and Macmillan Rivers, Bob Henderson ran on like a mining scientist, speaking of schist and quartz formations, granite, coal, crystallized lime and sulfur and red ochre. Ending, he spoke more generally about the area: "I would say that both rivers afford an excellent opportunity to both the quartz and placer prospector, and anticipate seeing the country yet have the reputation of being a good producer."[29]

Even modest optimism from a Klondike discoverer was enough.

The Barringtons were more than eager to go. Men snatched their packs, bought supplies and scrambled aboard the *Vidette* for the quick run up the Pelly.

Bob Henderson—perhaps his Scotch origins taking over—bought passage on a White Pass boat to Selkirk and poled up the Pelly, starting several days before Syd's boat. The *Vidette* overtook Henderson on the river and picked him up, carrying him as near as they could to the new creek.

The strike proved almost a total bust. Once on scene, stampeders found the site not at all likely for claims—boulders in evidence, not enough gravel, creek too short. All fifty-six hopefuls except two returned on the *Vidette* to Dawson. No one blamed Henderson for the false strike. Hadn't he, after all, tried to keep men from stampeding in the first place?

On the heels of the Henderson gold rush up the Pelly, word filtered down in August of "$30 a day" panned from quartz up the Stewart River in the Mayo district—this from a ledge nine feet wide. The *Dawson Daily News* quickly responded.[30] "Great Excitement over Mayo Quartz," one headline called.

Syd Barrington, about 1910 in the Yukon area.
Credit: Barrett Willoughby from Gentlemen Unafraid, Putnams, 1928.

Another side stream and the brothers eagerly loaded on the wood.

The Stewart River, about fifty miles south of Dawson, had long been called the "Grubstake River" because prospectors could always mine enough gold along its banks for another season of supplies.[31] A rich silver specimen had been uncovered on the trail in 1903. Prospectors poked along the rivers in the district, and in 1911 an important gold find on Dublin Gulch caused stampede hysteria.

This discovery sounded like it had more substance to it. When Hill and other eager miners arrived in Dawson on the *Vidette,* they spoke of nothing else. "Strike, strike, up the Stewart!"

*York*e *Barrington* steamer (the *Vidette*), summer of 1911,
last trip to the Stewart River, Yukon Territory.
Credit: Bill and Elna Barrington Collection.

And which boat, you might ask, turned around and made a quick
return to Mayo? Why the *Vidette,* of course. Only three weeks later, the
Vidette brought down gold pokes running $3,000 per man from the Mayo
diggings[32] (roughly $128,000 in today's gold market[33]). The rush proved
productive enough for the Barringtons to set up a scheduled run over the
250 miles from Dawson to Mayo once a week during the summer.

The Yukon side streams produced work for the Barringtons. But
perhaps more importantly, down deep, they offered a battle of skills,
and the ever-present wager. Often a river looked impossible to
navigate due to shallow water and sandbars, but this only whet Syd's
determination and heightened the odds. Yet the trip often cost in time.
With groundings, careful and slow steering, a boat took three days to
work over a stretch of ten miles, a Dawson paper reported of one trip.[34]
Eager prospectors there expected the Mayo diggings to explode to
15,000 miners before two years passed.[35] Activity at the camp kept the
Vidette busy for the next few seasons.

With several companies navigating boats on the Yukon,
competition proved brisk, but not without its humor. Near the close of
the 1911 season, a rate war developed between Barrington's Side
Streams Navigation Company and the White Pass. To attract a crowd
for a last seasonal run from Dawson to Whitehorse, prices on the

Vidette dropped dramatically. The *Dawson Daily News*—tongue in cheek—reported that spielers on the street kept disappearing. As they touted low prices either for the White Pass or the SSN, they kept getting "kidnapped" or "bought out" by the opposition. They seemed to vanish as soon as they appeared.[36]

The passenger list on the *Vidette,* however, filled up fast. Syd made the year-end run for Whitehorse on October 18. As it drew away from the wharf, the boat gave a long brazen whistle blast, good-naturedly thumbing its nose, so to speak, at the White Pass.[37]

The grateful passengers of that final trip, richer because of the lower passage prices, decided to share the savings. Once safely in Skagway, the travelers awarded Syd a Howard watch in the parlor of the Golden North Hotel. The presenter said, in part, "Take it, and wear it, and may it ever be as faithful a time keeper as your ship has been in making time...It will be a remembrance...caused in no small degree by the affable manners and good fellowship of the Barrington boys..."[38]

Thus, another season ended, the *Vidette* secured at the foot of Lake Lebarge, ready for the coming year. The Barringtons headed south to spend the winter.

Each spring, that same sense of excitement still continued at Lake Lebarge waiting for the river ice to break above and below the frozen lake.[39] Tons of freight and mail clustered on the lake shore; carpenters repaired boats and constructed barges. Since the swift Yukon River broke up first, steamboat captains poised on the open river at the foot of Lebarge. Impatiently they waited for the sight of sleds or horses racing toward them over the frozen lake. Then the wild steamboat race to Dawson could start. Syd and the other gambling captains knew thousands of dollars waited there for the winner each spring. As in other seasons, the April of 1912 proved no different. Except Syd made it different.

That spring, Hill Barrington took charge of 300 passengers from Whitehorse,[40] transporting them safely down twenty-five miles of open river to frozen Lake Lebarge. At the end of the lake miles away, Syd and the *Vidette* paused on the open river, ready for the straight shot to Dawson.

Hill had arranged for dogs to sled the passengers across the frozen lake to the *Vidette*. His group eventually took off on sleds, racing down the "thirty miles of sinking [lake] ice" to meet Syd on the river beyond.

Anxious eyes watched the rotten ice soften and settle fast,

showing black spots, becoming dangerous. Every minute, every foot, the journey grew more desperate.

Around them other riders dashed on sleds drawn by horses or by dogs. Loud cries shouted through the air urging their animals forward. But as the ice grew softer in spots, some travelers raced past on solid ice, others bogged down in the slush, while still others actually slipped through the rotten ice into the water. The pace proved frantic.

Hill did not give up. On and on he charged with his passengers and loads, dashing ten miles, on and on, twenty, twenty-one, twenty-two…Finally down lake, a bare four miles from open river and the *Vidette,* the weakened ice proved too spotty. Hill knew he had to deliver his passengers to shore or they would all surely hit a soft area and sink.

Just before he signaled change of direction to nearby land, Hill heard a blast over the noise around them. Looking ahead, not a quarter mile, a steamboat charged, bucking toward them on the frozen lake, ice "splintering high into the air." It was Pilot Syd Barrington. He and the *Vidette* had rammed through three miles of ice to connect with Hill's passengers sledding down the lake! Time was eating at Syd. He had to save the passengers and then fly to Dawson. A heavy packet weighed in the balance.

Finally meeting, crew loaded the dripping, relieved people on board. The steamer turned, followed its path back to the open river and sped ahead. The *Vidette* sailed into Dawson beating the other steamers that spring,[41] making a "clean sweep." The triumphant boat arrived at the Dawson wharf May 15, 1912, with a huge audience cheering them on. The brothers had gambled, and won, you can be sure, a sizeable wager.

· · ·

1. "April Is Backward." *Weekly Star* (Whitehorse), April 14, 1911.
2. David B. Wharton, *The Alaska Gold Rush.* Bloomington, IN: Indiana University Press, 1972, p. 40.
3. "More Lake Freight." *Weekly Star,* March 31, 1911.
4. Ibid.
5. "Boat Crews Arrive." *Weekly Star,* March 17, 1911.
6. "Steamboat Crews Arrive in Yukon." *Dawson Daily News,* March 30, 1911.
7. This *May West* was the same boat which made it first into Dawson in June, 1898, beating Ed Barrington on the *Victoria* from Circle City. "Movements of River Boats," *Yukon Midnight Sun,* June 11, 1898.
8. W.D. MacBride, "Saga of Famed Packets of Mighty Yukon River." *The Alaska Weekly,* August 25, 1944.
9. Linda E.T. MacDonald and Lynette R. Bleiler. *Gold and Galena.* Mayo, YT: Mayo Historical Society, 1990, p. 179.
10. "To Be Sold." *Weekly Star,* August 24, 1906.
11. "In From Up the Yukon." *Dawson Daily News,* May 23, 1911.

12. "Dawson Knocked in a Vancouver Paper." *Dawson Daily News* (information taken from the *Vancouver Province*), May 18, 1911.
13. Ibid., "In From Up the Yukon."
14. "*La France* Burned to Waters Edge." *Dawson Daily News,* May 23, 1911.
15. "River Disasters Very Numerous." *Weekly Star,* May 26, 1911.
16. "*Vidette* In From Long Run." *Dawson Daily News,* June 13, 1911.
17. "Workers Are Busy." *Dawson Daily News,* June 6, 1911.
18. Ibid.
19. "Progress With the Census Workers." *Dawson Daily News,* June 17, 1911.
20. "Daily Statistics – Deaths." *Seattle Daily Times,* June 17, 1911.
21. "Mrs. Barrington Called to Rest." *Dawson Daily News,* June 16, 1911.
22. Hill Sr. and Mildred tape, recorded by Eddie Barrington 9/1/70, courtesy of relatives Marlene and Hill Barrington, III.
23. "Called South by Wife's Death." *The Daily Alaskan,* June 24, 1911.
24. "Hill Barrington Back to Dawson." *Dawson Daily News,* July 17, 1911.
25. "Town Talk." *The Daily Alaskan,* July 12, 1911.
26. "Makes a Good Run." *Dawson Daily News,* July 4, 1911.
27. "*Vidette* Is Back in Port." *Dawson Daily News,* July 22, 1911.
28. "Bob Henderson on M'Millan." *The Daily Alaskan,* August 4, 1911.
29. "To Navigate the Pelly." *The Morning Sun,* June 4, 1902.
30. "Great Excitement over Mayo Quartz." *Dawson Daily News,* August 16, 1911.
31. *Gold and Galena.* Mayo, Yukon: Mayo Historical Society, 1990, p. 28.
32. "Gold Arrives From the Mayo District." *Dawson Daily News,* Sept. 11, 1911.
33. John J. McCusker, "Comparing the Purchasing Power of Money in the U. S. (Or Colonies) from 1665 to Any Other Year Including the Present." www.eh.net/hmit/ppowerusd/
34. "Great Excitement over Mayo Quartz." *Dawson Daily News,* August 16, 1911.
35. "*Vidette* Is Back After a Trying Trip Up Stewart." *Dawson Daily News,* Oct. 2, 1911.
36. "Rate War Is on Between *Vidette* and White Pass." *Dawson Daily News,* Oct. 11, 1911.
37. "*Vidette* Sails on Her Final Trip of the Year." *Dawson Daily News,* Oct. 18, 1911.
38. "River Skipper Given Watch." *The Daily Alaskan,* October 25, 1911.
39. Pierre Berton, *Klondike Fever.* NY: Alfred A. Knopf, 1960, p. 276. When trucks eventually freighted goods down the frozen lake, workers discovered, by accident, that an oil drip from one truck changed the solid ice to slush. From then on, a company truck sprayed a 40-foot-wide path of Lamp Black on the lake ice a month before breakup each spring. (Ripley, "Believe It or Not." *Seattle Post-Intelligencer,* Feb. 24, 1939. From Knutson's book *Sternwheels on the Yukon.* Snohomish, WA: Snohomish Publishing Co., 1979, p. 48.
40. "Barringtons Here." *Weekly Star,* April 19, 1912.
41. Barrett Willoughby. *Gentlemen Unafraid.* NY: Putnam's, Sons, 1929, pp. 234–40.

10: A NEW PARTNER CLIMBS ON BOARD

The Barringtons had long made Dawson their home. On occasion, Yorke and Hazel rode along on one of the boats heading up the side streams.[1] While in town, the brothers became part of the community. For instance, Hill and Syd—like they had on Whidbey and in Whitehorse—played on a baseball team.

A 1912 issue of the *Dawson Daily News* reported one baseball game when the *Vidette* crew went up against the Cascades, the town's laundry workers, and lost. In good humor, the paper bantered: "Hill Barrington was a polar marvel. His greatest feat was in being hit on the bone where he used to part his hair. Hill soon swelled to mountain proportions, but he showed the stuff of which he is made and pluckily remained in the game…The *Vidette* crowd…could not understand how the soap and starch aggregation managed to put the steamboat gang through the mangle."[2]

Later in the summer Syd made a run to Rampart House on the *Pauline*. Once again the Alaska and Canadian boundary parties hired the Barringtons to move supplies. One survey man said the boundary between the two countries had been set through to the Arctic; only the monumenting and finished work remained.[3] No small task faced the boundary surveyors with that job. Besides clearing a twenty-foot-wide swath through the wilderness 1,200 miles[4] along the 141st meridian, they had to set up forty monuments in concrete bases weighing one ton each.[5] Imagine the materials and manpower that project took.

Those boundary supply trips up and down the Porcupine River that summer were no easy task for pilots, either. Forcing the boat through low water, and return, proved a real skill. No matter how difficult, however, Syd carried the boundary parties as far upstream as humanly possible. Stated one traveler, "Navigators of the *Pauline* literally made the craft walk over sandbars for miles, and at other places snaked her over the dew. Some places the anchor and a cable were used, with aid of the capstan, to dig out a channel."[6]

While the *Pauline* was busy, the *Vidette* continued scheduled journeys through to the Mayo region too, but the going had its own problems. The camp had not mushroomed to the 15,000 predicted in the original heat of discovery the year before. Instead, population settled to 100, and the gold showing proved decent. The Stewart River rose and dropped with the weather, and running a vessel through to Mayo, again, took a well-experienced—and fearless—pilot. Often, boats off-loaded freight in order to work through shallow water. Dr. William Catto, investor in the district, expressed the gratitude of the passengers for the Barringtons. "They are the only people who have made a success of navigating the Stewart river regularly. Other companies left goods scattered all along the river."[7]

Near the end of the 1912 season, Syd Barrington took sick with pleurisy, and did not pilot the journey to Whitehorse, leaving the job to a fellow captain. Eventually, his health restored, Syd managed the final trip, which left Dawson in November. In fact, the *Dawson Daily News* reported, a large steamer had never before departed Dawson for Whitehorse later than October.[8]

Leave it to Syd to break the records—or at least try. Because of ice already thrown down into the Yukon from the Stewart and White tributaries, plus the lateness of the trip, Syd decided to haul little freight to avoid making landings, which could be dangerous that time of year.[9] Anxious last-minute passengers squeezed onto deck space and into staterooms. Knowing Syd Barrington, they would take a chance, in spite of the perilous departure. Even Syd might have refrained from wagering on this journey. The odds were too heavy against. For his own protection, he had passengers sign an agreement to ride at their own risk. In her book, *Gentlemen Unafraid,*[10] author Willoughby told of this trip. Only Barrington's knowledge of the river averted a tragedy.

Dawson travelers hopeful of making stateside through Whitehorse and Skagway, persuaded Syd to try for that one last trip upriver before the ice closed in. With the gambling devil prodding him and 128 people egging him on, Syd began the trip from Dawson later in the fall than ever before.

It did not take long to know the risk was a mistake. Thirty miles out of Dawson—as far as Indian—Syd knew. Temperatures kept dropping and dropping. With the ice thickening too fast, Syd realized he could not go on. He turned the wheel and steered the *Vidette* near shore.

There he remained, ice getting worse both up and down stream, threatening to crush the boat. Besides, the passengers, thinking they would eventually end their journey in Seattle, were hardly dressed for ten-below weather. Reading the river movement, Syd also sensed an ice jam blocked the lower bend by then. "If I went back through that thick-running ice my steamer would be carried on to that jam and smashed to smithereens," he told Willoughby. Retracing his course to Dawson was simply too dangerous. Barrington would not risk the passengers' lives or his boat.

The travelers insisted Syd take them back to Dawson. Barrington explained and said no. The passengers persisted; after all, the river still flowed, didn't it?—anybody could see that. Still Syd resisted. Instead he sent ahead by land for blankets and dog sleds to transport the passengers back overland to Dawson. The travelers then became nasty and threatened to hang him. Still Barrington stood firm.

While everyone waited for transportation, Barrington hiked down river, and sure enough, an ice jam clogged a narrow channel and was still building. If he had backtracked, trying to make Dawson, everyone would have been lost.

The dog sleds from Dawson finally arrived at the boat. Passengers saw the ice jam from shore on their return to town. All the travelers landed at the Klondike city safely, if not well ashamed of their actions against the good captain.

In spite of the passenger mutiny during the voyage, Syd had not followed through to Whitehorse. There might be times when he shaved the edges of honesty a bit, but he was always more than fair with his passengers. Since he had not completed his part of the bargain, he refunded all the money.

In the end, the grateful passengers presented Syd with a heavy gold watch fob, lined with nuggets, a diamond, emeralds and a ruby. On a gold disk attached, an engraver had etched a likeness of the *Vidette*.

The presenter in Dawson's Regina Hotel dining room said that while it was customary to give a token to the captain of the last boat up river each year, this trip proved more of an ordeal than usual. Syd needed especially to be remembered.[11]

On receiving the fob, Barrington responded that, "He saw no reason why a man should be given a prize for landing the outfit in a slough instead of at Whitehorse. He just did his best," adding, "but for the other officers and crew, and the passengers, things might have ended much worse than they did."[12]

Barrington skill for sure. About that skill, one passenger said, "Mostly it is lightning judgment and the experience of a skipper who knows his rivers as a scholar knows his books."[13] Thus finished another season.

Hill Barrington traveled north from Washington State earlier than usual the following spring of 1913, arriving May 2. He spent time in Skagway and Whitehorse, the reason soon becoming apparent. He planned to marry Mildred Clare Ward of Skagway.[14]

Born in Washington, Mildred was the daughter of Frederick C. and Margaret (Condon) Ward.[15] She

Syd and Hazel's boy, Yorke, on the Yukon with his dog, July 1911.
Credit: Courtesy of Peggy Darst Townsdin.

moved north at age seven when her father obtained a job working on the railroad.[16] Between school years in Seattle and her mother sick with the flu in Skagway (she spent nine months in the hospital), Mildred never knew her too well.[17] Employed as a clerk at Case and Draper in Skagway, Mildred met Hill on one of the Barrington boats.[18] She had been on her way to visit her father who owned a roadhouse on the Stewart River. A romance blossomed.

Syd soon followed his brother north, sailing into Dawson on the *Vidette,* with a full load of passengers—the first boat of the season again. The *Vidette* was almost always crowded with passengers because, according to the *Whitehorse Weekly Star,* "Those who have traveled on the *Vidette* say her tables are not excelled by those of any steamer on the river."[19]

The Side Streams Navigation Company ran several vessels on the Yukon that season.[20] Syd piloted the speedy steamer, *Norcom* (a

Syd Barrington hunting swans on Lake Lebarge in the
Yukon, summer of 1910.
Credit: Courtesy of Peggy Darst Townsdin.

reconstructed *Evelyn*) a time or two,[21] while also using the *Vidette* for
certain trips. Hill was often his purser. In addition, the American
steamer *Tanana* ran under the SSN operation, this time traveling
between Dawson and Eagle on the Lower Yukon.

While in Dawson, Hill obtained a marriage license on June 30.[22]
Hill was fond of saying, "She chased me around Skagway until she
caught me."[23] Mildred and Hill took the matrimonial plunge a week
later on July 7, 1913. The vows were spoken at four o'clock in the
morning—not the bride deciding the time, but a boat schedule.

The bride-to-be, Mildred, had traveled by train from Skagway to
Whitehorse accompanied by her mother, Margaret. Even though Hill's
boat arrived at three-thirty Saturday morning, Mildred refused to marry
without her brother, William, who could not reach Whitehorse for
another day. Mildred and her mother whiled away the time at a friend's
house. After William's train arrived at three-thirty a light Monday
morning, Mildred and Hill tied the knot. Of course some token

Sunday.

Dear Mrs. Barrington—
                Will you and
your 'good' husband have dinner
with us at 6 o'clock, this evening,
very informally, of course.
I may meet you at church, but
will not run any danger of
missing you.
                Very Sincerely Yours
                Martha Munger Black.

To the Hll Barringtons, members of the Dawson social scene. Invitiation
from Mrs. Commissioner George Black (Martha Munger Black).
Credit: Bill and Elna Barrington Collection.

remuneration was required for the clergy. But since the couple was
married by two bishops and a priest, Hill did not pay each. Instead, he
tore a $100 bill into three pieces and let the clergy sort it out.[24] Within an
hour after the ceremony, the happy pair left on the *Vidette* for Dawson.[25]

Twenty-three-year-old Mildred felt somewhat in awe of these older
people—Hill was thirty-six at this time, Harry forty-three and Syd going
on thirty-eight. With a conservative outlook, Mildred brought a
steadying, more traditional influence to Hill; she would not let him
gamble for one thing, which slowed his flamboyant lifestyle. She could
not cook,[26] but playing the piano was one of her joys, and she was
musically talented in other ways.

Mildred fit into Dawson life like a custom dress. In spite of the
population downturn from the gold rush, the capital of the Yukon
Territory still held its glamour, with a governor's mansion and social
layers of society. The "upper crust" bought their gowns and suits in San
Francisco in the winter and wore them in Dawson during the summer

Steamer *Vidette*, Clear Creek on the Stewart River, June 22, 1914. Mildred and Hill are on the bridge to the left, and Mrs. Commissioner George Black is to the right. *Credit: Bill and Elna Barrington Collection.*

season. It was all quite refined. Mildred found herself in a quandary when, one spring, her trunk of new dresses fell off the cart during the race through rotten ice for the boat to Dawson. She lost all her finery—it was quite a disaster.[27]

Not only was Mildred active in the social life of Dawson, but she felt strongly about Canadian involvement in World War I in Europe. There was an encampment of the St. John's Ambulance Corps on the banks of the Klondike River, and Mildred volunteered. Among other activities for practice, she hiked into the brush to give first aid to the "wounded." Eventually, the Corps headed for Europe and Mildred wanted to go. It was always a disappointment to her that Hill would not let her.[28]

The male Barringtons had little time for social events, for soon news of another gold strike rang through the air—this time in Alaska. Later that summer miners from Valdez, Cordova, McCarthy and Chitina stampeded to the Shushanan River country in central/eastern Alaska. The Dawson paper reported it to be the richest since the famous Klondike, with its discoverer taking out $100 to the shovel per day; $30,000 out to date.[29]

In a fever to access the Shushanan strike more easily, Syd and Captain Steve Martin aboard the *Vidette* made headlines by plowing even farther up the White River. The vessel fought up the tributary, mere miles from the Alaska border. There Syd took on the Donjek River, fed from Kluane Lake.[30] The Barringtons had battled the White before, but never so far upstream. Another victory for the SSN.

As Syd expected, the river caused problems all along the way. "The White," he reported, "is very swift, contains many snags, has many sweepers and has a very hard marl-like bottom...While there are shoals on the river, the steamer can get through, but a heavy rain up the White would raise the river four or five feet in a very short time, and thus greatly aid navigation."[31]

What a break for stampeders rushing into the Shushanan district. Men poled their small boats, launches and steamers as they struggled up and down shuttling stampeders. Because the Canadian government thought the strike valuable enough, it assigned ten Royal North West Mounted Police along the run.[32]

It was an emergency on the river in late August, however, that brought the Barringtons together with an innovative man who would become an important influence in their lives. The original accident happened like this.

The *Vidette* chugged along, pushing a barge up the White. Constable Michael Fitzgerald of the Royal North West Mounted Police, sent to the new diggings to establish a post, stood on the barge. He and a companion worked a sweep (a long, paddle-shaped pole) nudging the barge back from the shoals. Suddenly the current swished the sweep in such a way, it knocked Fitzgerald off into the water. Instantly the deck crew launched several small boats to rescue him.

The nearby fifty-foot gasoline launch belonging to Max Nelson that was heading downstream also sped to help. On board was Charles M. Binkley who designed the vessel. Binkley said of Fitzgerald, once retrieved and on shore, "The boys put the body over a log and worked with it over the bank..."[33] Finally, crew hauled the constable aboard the *Vidette*.

In a letter written by a *Vidette* passenger, the man said, "Fitzgerald shows just a little improvement. Sid [sic] Barrington and Hill Barrington and crew are working like heroes to save his life. Gasoline launch men also showing every consideration."[34]

The efforts, however, proved fruitless. Police officials later buried thirty-seven-year-old Fitzgerald at Dawson with full military honors. It was a sorrowful accident in a busy year.

The Fitzgerald death later exposed a bizarre incident. The *Whitehorse Weekly Star* reported: "A strange coincidence in connection with the death by drowning of Constable Fitzgerald is that ten or eleven years ago he was stationed at a post far up the Stickine *[sic]* river, there being four men on the detachment. The other three started for Wrangel, Alaska, in a small boat for their mail, leaving Fitzgerald alone at the post. The boat was wrecked and all three of the men were drowned. As it was supposed all four had gone in the boat, Fitzgerald knew nothing of the fate of his fellows until he saw an account of the drowning in a paper, his own name appearing as one of the lost."[35] An odd twist to a sad ending.

Apparently no written record exists of the first Barrington/Binkley meeting. It could have occurred at any period during the Klondike, since all were there at the same time.[36] Though the Barringtons and Binkley spoke during the Fitzgerald tragedy, another encounter soon after intrigued the brothers, and they pursued a friendship and business arrangement with Binkley.

A week later while Syd struggled up the White, he again saw the gasoline launch owned by Max Nelson and partners powering as far as the Donjek River—no problem. On board, again, rode Charles Binkley.

As skillfully as the *Vidette* performed at bulling up the White hauling prospectors and supplies, the boat often could only struggle so far. At this time, the *Vidette* grounded due to low water at the mouth of Katrina Creek, White River. One day, two, three days, the boat just sat there. While settled, waiting for higher water, Syd watched the Nelson gasoline launch approach and pass him, continuing on toward the Donjek.[37]

Pass the *Vidette*! What a thought-stopping sight. Another pilot might be angry, or jealous—and even those feelings might have zipped through Syd's mind. But Syd was more intrigued, impressed. And since he felt challenged to deliver passengers and freight as far as navigation allowed, he decided to catch the launch on the way back and check out the competition, maybe negotiate. And that's what he did.

A *Vidette* passenger wrote up his experience. "We were the least disappointed in not getting up the White by steamer further than Katrina, but are fully satisfied that Barrington did all possible to get us up as far as he could…The *Vidette* laid up for three days in the hope that weather would turn milder and the water rise…While marooned at Katrina, Mrs. Hill Barrington kept up the spirits of those on board by her sweet singing and guitar playing and a goodly supply of angelic candy…Sid finally decided to pull out for Dawson. Before doing so, however, he showed his every consideration for the welfare of the passengers by purchasing the Nelson gasoline launch and arranging for the transfer to the Donjek of all goods left at Katrina by the *Vidette*."[38] Here the more contemporary saying might apply: if you can't lick 'em, join 'em.

After purchasing the Nelson launch, *Olof Splegatus,* Barrington put Steve Martin in charge. The newspaper stated: "Binkley, the clever designer and builder of the *Splegatus* is with the craft as engineer…Binkley ran similar boats of much larger capacity on the North Thompson river with great success."[39]

The new launch designed by Binkley proved invaluable. Steve Martin transferred supplies from the *Vidette* and the *Pauline,* and the *Splegatus* managed to run an additional thirty-two miles to the Donjek River where larger riverboats could not go.[40] What a coup. It followed that the Barringtons took note of Binkley and his special skills for designing boats. Innovation had always been a Barrington priority, and hooking up with Binkley seemed inevitable. The men built a lifelong friendship.

Born in Indiana, Charles Binkley proved a fine inventor and artisan, fascinated in designing boats. This craftsman played a major role in custom designing riverboats used by the Barringtons to navigate more difficult streams that larger boats failed to negotiate. Binkley also spent time in Seattle during the winter. He built and raced boats on Seattle lakes with his half brother, Emerson "Emmy" Reid.[41]

With access now farther upriver, excitement continued high throughout the fall of 1913. Stampeders rushed up the White and Donjek, trying to get through to the Copper River strike, while activity continued up the Stewart to Mayo. And when the *Vidette* arrived in Dawson from the Mayo District with $20,000 in gold from the placer streams, the news spread and fired up the residents. Syd told the newspaper that every trip down from Mayo was like that.[42] Mining there continued through the teen years, with another big silver strike in the early 1920s,[43] keeping Canadian boats and railroads busy.

Such was the eagerness accompanying new gold discoveries that the Barrington brothers decided to buy another light draft steamer for the White run. The SSN company sent Harry Barrington to the coast to complete the plans.[44]

That fall the *Vidette* tied up at Hootalinqua for the winter, ready to "get into the game" early next season.

• • •

1. "*Vidette* Is off for Trip up the Pelly." *Dawson Daily News,* June 25, 1912.
2. "Great Game of Ball on the Minto Grounds." *Dawson Daily News,* July 6, 1912.
3. "Pauline Is Back from the Porcupine." *Dawson Daily News,* July 31, 1912.
4. Thomas Riggs, Jr., "Marking the Alaskan Boundary." *National Geographic Magazine,* July, 1909, p. 596.
5. "Prosecuting Boundary Survey." *Alaska-Yukon Magazine,* April, 1911, p. 50.
6. Ibid., "Pauline Is Back from the Porcupine."
7. "Mayo District Is a Place With Future." *Dawson Daily News,* Sept. 17, 1912.
8. "Pauline and Falcon Are on the Way." *Dawson Daily News,* Oct. 31, 1912.
9. "Many Plan to Leave Here on the *Vidette*." *Dawson Daily News,* Oct. 29, 1912.
10. Barrett Willoughby, *Gentlemen Unafraid,* (N.Y.: Putnam's Sons, 1929), pp. 241–45.
11. "Captain of *Vidette* Honored with Gift." *Dawson Daily News*. Dec. 19, 1912.
12. Ibid.
13. "Capt. Barrington of the Stikine Is Subject of Magazine Article." *Wrangell Sentinel,* Feb. 10, 1933.
14. "People Who Come and Go." *Weekly Star,* June 6, 1913.
15. Lloyd Spencer and Lancaster Pollard, *A History of the State of Washington,* 1937. (Northwest Collection, University of Washington. 38-11577). pp. 66–67.
16. Peggy Darst Townsdin, *History of a Whidbey Island Family,* p. 25. From an Oak Harbor clipping dated Dec. 29, 1966 entitled "Captain Born Here in 1877."
17. Hill Sr. and Mildred Barrington interviews 9/1/1970 by Eddie Barrington, courtesy of relatives Marlene and Hill Barrington, III.
18. Conversation with Elna Barrington, Anchorage, August 29, 1998.
19. "Doing Big Business." *Weekly Star,* June 27, 1913.
20. "Norcom Has Speed." *Weekly Star,* June 13, 1913.
21. Ibid.
22. Marriage license # 906 taken out at Dawson, June 30, 1913.
23. Hill Sr. and Mildred Barrington tapes recorded by Eddie Barrington 9/1/1970, courtesy of relatives Marlene and Hill Barrington, III.
24. Ibid.
25. "Happily Married." *Weekly Star,* July 11, 1913.
26. Ibid., Hill Sr. and Mildred Barrington tape 9/1/1970.
27. Ibid.
28. Ibid.
29. "Writes of the Strike on the Chisana Side." *Dawson Daily News,* August 28, 1913.
30. Canada map. Washington, DC: National Geographic Society, 1995.
31. "Successful Trip Up White River." *The Alaska Times Cordova,* August 24, 1913.
32. "Police to Go on the White River Patrol." *Dawson Daily News,* August 13, 1913.
33. "Life is Lost at Mouth of White River." *Dawson Daily News,* August 28, 1913.
34. Ibid.
35. "Victim of White." *Weekly Star,* Sept. 5, 1913.
36. Kent Sturgis, *Four Generations on the Yukon.* Fairbanks: Epicenter Press, 1988, p. 6.
37. "New Strike Is Reported Up River." *Dawson Daily News,* Sept. 6, 1913.
38. "Writes of the Conditions on White River." *Dawson Daily News,* Sept. 23, 1913.
39. "*Vidette* Gets In From Trip Up the White." *Dawson Daily News,* Sept. 8, 1913.
40. "Good Work Is Done on White by the Olaf S." *Dawson Daily News,* Oct. 1, 1913.
41. Ibid., Sturgis, p. 28.
42. "Gold In From Mayo Camp on *Vidette*." *Dawson Daily News,* Oct. 1, 1913. One young passenger traveling to Mayo harbored a concern that had nothing to do with gold. The boy and his family were crammed on the *Pauline*. The bunk/cot above the young boy was occupied by an enormously fat woman. Every time he got into bed, and she onto the top bunk, the boy reported, the upper cot "sagged down and touched the tip of my nose." *Gold and Galena,* 1990, p. 319.
43. "Mayo Strike Is Rich." *Seattle Daily Times,* October 22, 1922.
44. "Will Go In for a Steady Run on the White." *Dawson Daily News*. August 13, 1913.

11: DECISIVE YEARS FOR THE BARRINGTONS

After buying out the Northern Navigation Company, which controlled most of the Lower River business in 1912, the White Pass Company on the Upper River enjoyed a near monopoly of the entire Yukon waterway.[1] Yet a few independent firms like the Barrington's Side Streams Navigation Company survived. They operated where the action and money were—up the side river tributaries. The SSN still kept a decent business going, though the brothers knew of the declining trends.

While the Barringtons sailed the side streams in their battle with the rivers, more serious problems accelerated in Europe. With Great Britain threatened during World War I and its tie to Canada, young Yukon citizens of military age soon joined the service. Such headlines as "Attack Is Made on Port Said by Two Aeroplanes,"[2] and "Kaiser's Best Could Not Stem Anzac's Flood,"[3] cried from Dawson's front pages.[4] The Barringtons felt the loss of their bookkeeper, A.W.H. Smith who enlisted in the Canadian Railroad Troups No. 10 and fought overseas.[5] As mentioned, Mildred Barrington got caught up in wartime activity and wanted to join the ambulance corps in Europe, but Hill would not let her.[6]

In spite of the distant war, Barrington life coursed on as usual. Cruising through Alaska's Inside Passage the spring of 1914, Hill's wife, Mildred, stayed on in Skagway to visit her mother, Margaret, while Hill continued to Whitehorse. They had spent the last part of the winter in southern California and were ready for the river season up north.[7] Syd, too, completed several trips to California that winter and was primed for work in the spring.

As ice melted on Lebarge again, boats poised for the race down river. While at the Dawson end, everyone waited for the ice breakup as they had for years, ready to make their fortune on the exact moment. A reporter said the ice breakup stage was set: the whistle was lubricated and the 600 feet of rope well anchored to the ice with a downstream pull. A flag floated above the anchor.

Gamblers—which included just about everyone in town for this event—once again placed bets well ahead of time. Some based their wagers on dreams, superstitions, scientific calculations and pure guesswork. Dawsonite George McLachlan reported: "Sid Barrington busy figuring out a scientific deduction at Lebarge, taking into account, the winter snowfall, the Japan current, the influence of the sun, the tarif and the conditions in Ireland and Mexico."[8] And true to form, the *Vidette* swept into Dawson first that spring, flag flying proudly.

Though Syd operated the *Vidette* during the 1914 season, he arranged to have a new gas boat built at Lake Lebarge, one that could maneuver in very shallow water. No doubt Syd's confidence in boat builder Charles Binkley made such a design possible. It's not hard to picture the Barringtons and Binkley, sprawled in chairs, discussing the pros and cons of boat design over a drink in the galley. Always looking forward, Syd and Hill tried new methods, and they understood power-driven gas boats taking the lead in river use over wood-driven steamboats.

Linking an association with Charles Binkley proved beneficial to all three men. Using Binkley's ideas and installing the first gas engine in a Barrington boat, Syd contracted for a *Hazel B.* launch to be constructed. Built knocked-down in Seattle, it was later assembled on the Yukon River.[9]

In mid-summer, the new gas launch made her fame up the Porcupine, more than likely on wagers. She ran the fastest round trip to Rampart House—Syd as pilot and Binkley as engineer. With two daredevils and gamblers plowing ahead, the operative word was "fast." One can almost feel the thrill of speed roaring under the hull. This new shallow draft vessel, named for Syd's wife, Hazel Barrington,[10] proved the first of many *Hazel* boats custom styled for river use. On one of the first runs up the Forty-Mile, Chief Binkley handled the engines and said, "The spoonshull climbed the waters like a hydroplane."[11]

In spite of the new gasoline boat venture and a rather slow 1914 season, Syd Barrington extolled the prospects for the Mayo and Stewart River country. He said to a Whitehorse newsman, perhaps over-optimistically in light of his later plans, that businessmen

Side Streams Navigation Co.'s first *Hazel* boat, a gas launch, built in 1914 with design by Charles Binkley.
Credit: Courtesy of Peggy Darst Townsdin.

displayed more confidence in the future than he observed at any time during his ten years experience on the Stewart River.[12]

Weather pulled a surprise the spring of 1915. After a mild winter, river ice "done went" April 6, a good twelve days earlier than previous years, breaking all records in Yukon history.[13] Syd might have been relaxing in Seattle with his family, but he hustled to sail north and take advantage of the extended season. In tow, he brought a crew of about ten men to ready the *Vidette* at the foot of Lake Lebarge. Syd and the crew arrived in Whitehorse April 21, and drove an auto truck shipped ahead from the States.[14] The Barringtons were becoming further mechanized.

Off raced the *Vidette* from the lake on May 5, again very early. When Syd steamed into Dawson, the vessel had cracked two records—first on May 11 with a "clean sweep," and second as earliest arrival in the city's history.[15] No record of how much cash changed hands for this victory.

Friends enjoyed playing jokes on Syd, and he took it with good-nature. On tying up in Dawson, newsmen deluged Syd. It seems a rumor had circulated up north—and someone played a joke—that Syd had lost a leg in an auto accident in "the wicked village" of Seattle. A reporter stated, "On his [Syd's] arrival here today, he found stacks of letters awaiting him, and on opening them found they all were from supply houses wanting to sell him wooden feet, wooden legs, cork legs and

Alaska Railroad construction in south-central Alaska, about 1915. Two pile drivers work toward each other in construction of a bridge.

Credit: Regina Knill Cope Coll. UAF 1991-156-5.

glass arms. Sid is right side up on even keel, and can navigate without the use of wooden, glass or cork attachments or money rudders, and is prepared for a season of hard work."[16]

Barrington's first trip for the season from Dawson ran to Mayo and Stewart River destinations, returning on May 16.[17] Mayo remained a vibrant camp, working out silver-lead ore, which owners shipped to a San Francisco smelter.[18] The work helped to keep the Barringtons busy.

No sign of Hill Barrington early that season, as he remained on Whidbey Island until his wife gave birth to a baby boy, May 25,[19] Hill leaving a week later for the Yukon. As an honor to his brother, Hill and Mildred named the baby Sydney Ward. Soon after, Mildred Barrington took the new baby to Providence Hospital in Seattle for a checkup, returning to San de Fuca several days later.

Once Hill landed in Dawson, Syd left the business in his brother's hands and departed for Whitehorse, planning a jump to the west coast of Alaska, then to Whidbey Island. "As Captain Sid usually starts something wherever he is," the Whitehorse *Weekly Star* reported, "results are likely to follow his visit to the westward."[20] This item proved the first public hint that the Barringtons might be mulling business changes in their minds, which indeed turned out to be true. Construction of an Alaska railroad was the reason.

With permission of Congress, in 1914 U.S. President Woodrow

Wilson authorized building a federal railroad in Alaska Territory. The sprouting railroad construction camp called Ship Creek Landing,[21] on the shores of Cook Inlet, would soon become the growing city of Anchorage. The Barringtons took on the job of shipping supplies for this project, Syd in charge.

Hill remained in the Dawson area, worry about his son at the front of his mind. But it seems parenthood was not in the cards for Hill at this time. Readers can be sure his heart dropped when he was handed a telegram in mid-July. Telegrams meant bad news. He opened the wire to find his infant son died on July 14th of meningitis, only seven weeks after his birth. How many of these disasters could he stand? The devastated Whidbey family buried the baby in the Barrington plot in Seattle, the Lake View Cemetery.[22] The news slipped Hill into grief. Soon after, a disheartened Mildred Barrington sailed north to join her husband in Dawson.[23] Syd followed later.

At the close of the 1915 season, the *Weekly Star* of Whitehorse reported Hill, Mildred and Syd passing through on their way to Skagway and Seattle. A newsman said, "They report a good season with their steam and will be back by the time the pussy willows are in bloom."[24]

The Barringtons soon settled back into their easier winter living. The gaiety plus the warmer weather drew the families to San Francisco. There they took in the Panama–Pacific Exposition, viewing Alaska relics and partying with Klondiker[25] friends also attending. Certainly Mildred and Hill needed diversion from their summer of sadness.

The brothers had considered business changes before 1916, but it proved the pivotal year for the family. Harry Crowhurst (Hazel's stepfather[26]) and George Waltenbaugh opened the Side Streams Navigation office that spring, coming over the ice to Dawson where the *Vidette* spent the winter. Hill and his wife planned a later arrival on one of the vessels from Lebarge.

By then, Syd's railroad job west of Dawson was made public knowledge. "Sid Barrington, the manager," Crowhurst told the paper, "may not be here until after the river opens from Whitehorse. He is superintending the construction of two large modern gasoline boats for the American government for use on the coast rivers in connection with the new American government railway system in Alaska."[27] It was expected that Harry Barrington would run one of the new government boats. Crowhurst further stated the Barringtons had figured on a gas boat for the Stikine, but since business dropped, they canceled construction.

Life went on, Hill Barrington knew, in spite of his own misfortune. He learned that from the past. Piloting the *Vidette*, he kept the Side Stream operations going in the Yukon.

Since the beginning of their boating careers, it was a given that the Barringtons enjoyed mixing with boat passengers, weaving yarns, placing bets and showing them a good time. After all, they had been at it for more than fifteen years and earned the respect of those they dealt with. Running the SSN vessels performed a genuine service by freighting miners and supplies to wilderness camps and hauling out minerals. The Barringtons also made it an enjoyable experience.

One trip up the Stewart River to Fraser Falls during the 1916 season exemplified the tone of a river voyage. As was the rule over the exception, a trip was often "fun" for passengers. No other word described it. No other word conveyed the playfulness or spontaneity of a Barrington run, especially if Hill rode on board. He allowed just about anything.

On this journey, the skipper and crew hosted a honeymoon trip and dinner for passengers Dr. and Mrs. Norman Culbertson. Steward Harry Crowhurst, who had been a "star fun maker of the Barnum circus, and sawdust king later with the Ringling shows," decorated the dining hall and had a special menu planned for a wedding dinner. "I never had a more pleasant trip in my life," stated the newly married doctor. "My only regret is that we could not stay longer."[28]

By this time, most of the serious gold strikes in the north were ending. Big business had taken over, and river traffic supplied their limited needs.[29] Regardless of continued riverboat traffic on the Canadian tributaries, times had adjusted to other methods. Transportation had taken a faster travel pace.

It was impossible to look around and miss the travel changes in the northwest. Not only did the Barringtons plan on using gas engines themselves, but they contracted jobs to help supply a competitive mode of transportation—the railroad. Still, another technology was beginning to lift off in Alaska, one that would eventually affect the Barrington business.

In her book, *Flying North,* Jean Potter told of the first Alaska plane flight during the Fourth of July in Fairbanks only two years previous. Aviator James Martin traveled north to perform an "Aerial Circus" for the celebration. True, the several brief stints in the air were short, but they were flights nevertheless. Flying seemed a natural to cover the vast distances in Alaska and Canada.[30]

Then too, because of highways and railways, the steamboat

business slowed. The fiery excitement that once blazed every newcomer's hopes during Klondike days had burned down. Steamers that once had "every foot on board crammed with people," now carried only a "good list of passengers." Runs to discoveries had become routine rather than frenzied. For the Barringtons, it was as though their inner engines, like the Yukon steamers, had cooled. The brothers needed a fire to rev things up. A discontent stirred, and they looked farther afield for business.

After closing the Side Streams Navigation Company in Dawson, and putting the boats to rest for the 1916 season, Hill expected to remain in the Yukon. In fact, he and Mildred planned to spend the winter at the new Rude Creek gold placer camp there.[31] But in the next two weeks a restlessness, or something more concrete, changed their minds. Most likely it was the brothers' decision to sell the SSN Co. to the White Pass, which they did. Instead of remaining north, Hill and Mildred sailed to Seattle for the winter.[32]

Meanwhile during the same 1916 season, Syd traveled between Seattle and the growing Cook Inlet area, its "Anchorage" population at the time topping 2,000.[33] He and colleague Charles Binkley developed and designed special ship adaptations, and engineers commissioned them to build several boats for interior travel.

The vessels themselves were constructed by the Canal Manufacturing Company in Seattle. The plant, between Lake Union and Salmon Bay, then knocked down the completed boats and shipped them to Anchorage. Working together, Syd and Charles Binkley designed the eighty-seven-foot boats especially for river movement. "The twin screws of each vessel operate in tunnels running through the bottom from stem to stern," the *Seattle Times* reported. "In this way they are protected from snags and other obstructions to river navigation."[34] It was a genius solution to a knotty problem.

The first Barrington and Binkley boat—the *B & B No. 1* (Barrington & Binkley)[35]—which tested a new hull up the Ross and Forty-Mile Rivers in Alaska and the Yukon, was sold to the Alaska Engineering Commission to help with railroad work.[36] Hazel Barrington did the christening honors to the *B & B No. 2* at the Canal boatyard in Seattle, when she broke a bottle of champagne over its hull. No.'s 3, 4, 5 vessels also ran on rivers backing Cook Inlet.[37]

While in Anchorage, Syd decided to build a boat for himself—the shallow draft freight and passenger *Hazel B. No. 2*,[38] again, named for his

The *B & B No. 2* (Barrington and Binkley) transports Alaska Railroad officals and supplies in the Southcentral Alaska area, circa 1915.
Credit: Anchorage Museum of History and Art.

wife. Ninety feet long with a twenty-foot beam, two ninety-five-horsepower gas engines powered the vessel.[39] Syd planned to take advantage of all the jobs near the Susitna River, operating it there. Built in Seattle, the hull was then knocked down and sent to Anchorage where workers constructed the superstructure.[40] Tide dictated the launching at 3:05 in the early morning of June 14, 1916. An asset of the new boat, the captain stated, was the continued presence of cook "Splotus" Dennis, who had been with the Barringtons for ten years while on the Yukon. One of the first commissions for the vessel was transporting passengers to Talkeetna for railroad work.[41]

Of course the Barringtons and Binkley could not know the exact effect the Alaska Railroad would have on Yukon River travel. But having worked in the north for more than twenty years, they understood the signs. A map of Alaska was like a blueprint of what could happen.

When workers completed the railroad in 1923, changes were immediately evident. For one, Yukon River traffic decreased and St.

Wrangell, summer of 1929.
Credit: Courtesy of the Wrangell Museum, 91.10.05.02.

Michael became a steamboat "has been." The railroad not only supplied interior Alaska faster by distance and time, but it could be used twelve months a year. The rails patterned their own artery directly into the heart of Alaska. The Barrington brothers could envision this outcome.

Because of the changing travel modes, the Barringtons kept an eye out for a location where river operations had a longer "run."[42] They could of course stay in Puget Sound and navigate the inland sea; with years of piloting experiences, obtaining jobs or running their own boats there would be no problem.

But no ordinary, predictable waterway would do. The brothers required a river of challenge—and one with gold prospects not too distant. Syd even considered a trip to South America during the winter of 1916, to investigate the navigational possibilities there.[43] The Barringtons eventually took a second look and decided the Stikine River out of Wrangell, Alaska, held the future for them.

The Stikine area afforded obvious advantages the Yukon did not.

For one, commuting time would be shorter from Washington. Second, working on one river instead of many as in the Yukon, would allow for a more rooted family life. Third, river competition was practically nil. And last, the gold-bearing Cassiar proved comparatively close.

A reader might think the Barringtons managed two separate careers—one on the Yukon, one on the Stikine. They did. But the prospecting lines were not that distinct. The brothers worked in a traveling business, and stampeders traveled. Many dedicated miners/gamblers rushed to the Yukon earlier and moved on to the Cassiar later, just like Syd, Hill and Harry. They just approached the general gold fields from a different direction. Studying a map, one can see that the White River, the Kluane in the Yukon district and the Cassiar River in British Columbia touch—gold streaking through all.

Prospecting proved such an uncertain provider, and in the end, everyone had to eat. The rivers afforded a livelihood. Business on the Yukon had slowed, and the Stikine was waiting for daring captains to defeat the waters.

Working new goldfields no doubt proved a strong lure for the brothers. However, another reason, under the surface, helped decide the Barringtons on a southern location.

The Stikine River had a challenging reputation, plus a stunning backdrop. Author C.L. Andrews called the Stikine, "The most picturesque of all the waterways of the Northwest, the most thrilling stream of the swift water routes of the land..."[44]

Once decided, the Barringtons made arrangements to sell their Dawson operation to the White Pass and Yukon Company,[45] which they completed in 1916.[46]

Syd brought Hazel and Yorke—now a teenager—and barged[47] the *Hazel B. No. 2* to Wrangell that summer. He navigated several trips around the area, perhaps to get a feel for the town and the job. Neither Syd nor Hill wavered in this decision for a new location. In fact, quite the opposite, they looked forward to the change.

The winter back in Washington proved a quiet, happy one for the most part. Young Yorke was sure to enjoy the wider spaces in the new, beautiful home Syd had built on Queen Anne Hill.[48] And what a great life the boy lived with his family, not only spending time with friends going to school during the winter in Washington, but also heading in the summer to the wilderness and steamboating adventures in Alaska. Gold mining, ever-changing locations, spellbinding people, space, animals—what a life for a boy. Sometimes Yorke took a friend to share the summer vacation.

In Seattle, the Barringtons hosted a belated party in January celebrating their fifteenth wedding anniversary.[49] Syd's mother, Christina, sister Sibby and the Hill Barringtons helped celebrate. The sixteenth year, in a new river location, would have unique challenges.

As spring approached, flickers of the old excitement ran through the families as they anticipated the coming move to Wrangell. There would be new people, an unknown yet challenging river and, certainly not least, the chance to find the elusive gold close by in the Cassiar. So many daring gambles along the route—a journey the Barringtons were eager to make. Perhaps they did not consider there might be misfortunes as well.

• • •

1. Melody Webb, "Steamboats on the Yukon River" *Alaska Journal,* Summer 1985, pp. 27–28.
2. "Attack Is Made on Port Said by Two Aeroplanes." *Dawson Daily News,* May 10, 1916.
3. "Kaiser's Best Could Not Stem Anzac's Flood." *Dawson Daily News,* Sept. 13, 1916.
4. "Boys of the Yukon Are Entertained." *Dawson Daily News,* May 22, 1916.
5. "War Medal Awarded to A.W.H. Smith." *Wrangell Sentinel,* July 29, 1938.
6. Hill Sr. and Mildred Barrington tape, recorded by Eddie Barrington 9/1/1970, courtesy of relatives Marlene and Hill Barrington, III.
7. "*Vidette* Crew Arrives." *Weekly Star,* April 17, 1914.
8. "Whistle Oiled and Ready." *Dawson Daily News,* May 18, 1914.
9. Gordon Newell (Ed), *The H.W. McCurdy Marine History of the Pacific Northwest.* Seattle: Superior Publishing Co., 1966.
10. "Captain Barrington Arrives," *Weekly Star,* May 1, 1914.
11. "Fast Trip Is Made on the Fortymile Run." *Dawson Daily News,* June 11, 1914.
12. "Coming to Front." *Weekly Star,* Oct. 9, 1914.
13. "River Is Now Open." *Weekly Star,* April 9, 1915.
14. "Due Next Tuesday." *Weekly Star,* April 16, 1915.
15. "Earliest In History." *Weekly Star,* May 7, 1915.
16. "First Boats of Season Make Port." *Dawson Daily News,* May 11, 1915.
17. "*Vidette* Is Back from Mayo Camp." *Dawson Daily News,* May 26, 1915.
18. Ibid.
19. "San de Fuca Notes." *Island County Times,* June 4, 1915.
20. Untitled article. *Weekly Star,* June 25, 1915.
21. Stephen Haycox, *Alaska: An American Colony.* Seattle: University of Washington, 2002, p. 231.
22. "San de Fuca Notes." *Island County Times,* July 16, 1915.
23. Untitled article. *Weekly Star,* July 30, 1915.
24. Untitled article. *Weekly Star,* Oct. 15, 1915.
25. "Glad to Be Back to the Halcyon Land." *Dawson Daily News,* May 23, 1916.
26. "Alaska Pioneer Drops Dead at Wrangell." *Anchorage Daily Times,* Aug. 4, 1925
27. "Getting Busy on Vidette for Season." *Dawson Daily News,* April 14, 1916.
28. "*Vidette* Back from Fraser Falls Trip." *Dawson Daily News,* July 24, 1916.
29. Ibid., Stephen Haycox, p. 210.
30. Jean Potter, *The Flying North.* NY: The Macmillan Company, 1965, pp. 26-27.
31. "Local Notes." *Weekly Star,* Oct. 6, 1916.
32. Ibid, Oct. 20, 1916.
33. Kent Sturgis. *Four Generations on the Yukon.* Fairbanks: Epicenter Press, 1988, p. 25.
34. Ibid., "Glad to be Back to the Halcyon Land."

35. "New River Boat Breaks All Records." *Wrangell Sentinel,* August 2, 1917.
36. Ibid., "Glad to be Back to the Halcyon Land."
37. Ibid.
38. Gordon Newell (Ed.), *The H.W. McCurdy Marine History of the Pacific Northwest.* Seattle: Superior Publishing Co., 1966, p. 268.
39. "Building Boat for the Susitina." *Cook Inlet Pioneer,* May 23, 1916.
40. "Barringtons Close 19th Season on Stikine Riv." *Wrangell Sentinel,* Oct. 26, 1934.
41. R.N. DeArmond (compiler), "Down Through the Years." *The Alaska Journal,* Winter 1979, p. 43.
42. R.M. Patterson, *Trail to the Interior.* NY: William Morrow and Co., Inc., 1966, p. 38.
43. "Capt. Barrington Is Going to South America." *Wrangell Sentinel,* Sept. 9, 1916.
44. Clarence L. Andrews, *Wrangell and the Gold of the Cassiar.* Seattle: Luke Tinker, Commercial Printer, 1937, p. 57.
45. Ibid., R.M. Patterson, p. 40.
46. Bob Greenhagen, "Searching for Fortune on the Yukon Rivers." *Whidbey News,* April 13, 1972.
47. *The Stikine River.* Anchorage: Alaska Geographic Society, 1979, p. 55.
48. *Polk's Seattle City Directory 1941.* Seattle: R.L. Polk and Co., 1941. (Address: 1426 11th Avenue West)
49. "San de Fuca Notes." *Island County Times,* January 5, 1917.

12: CHALLENGE OF THE STIKINE

A great deal of thought went into the location change for the Barrington boat venture. "What I heard of the Stikine made me think it would be interesting and profitable," Syd stated to author Barrett Willoughby. The captain later admitted, "Beside her [the Stikine], the Yukon is a sluggish stream."[1]

Soon to follow the Barringtons to Wrangell was bookkeeper and "bookmaker" A.W.H. "Andy" Smith returned from war duty in Europe. Twice wounded, Smith readily looked toward civilian life again. Another transplant to Wrangell proved to be Barrington business associate and friend, Charles Binkley. Hock "Splotus" Dennis never made the shift.

Once settled in, Wrangellites cast a skeptical eye at Syd's plans for making scheduled trips to Telegraph Creek. Nudging each other, residents might have said, "Oh, he'd probably start out all right, but a weekly run? Well, we'll see."

On his initial voyage, Syd could not even hire a local pilot to show him the route, to point out where the mountain river emptied into tidewater. No one helped him. Syd explored the flats area himself, finally chancing upon the yellow streak that flowed down from the Stikine and joined the bay.[2] As a river man, he knew what that meant.

Local opinions turned shortly, however. For it did not take people long to admire the Barringtons and their friendly style. Syd soon thought of a more tangible way to win over Wrangell residents. He offered a pleasure excursion trip to Petersburg over the Memorial Day

Telegraph Creek about 1926.
Credit: Barrett Willoughby, from Gentlemen Unafraid.
Putnams, 1928.

weekend in 1917 on the *Hazel B. No. 2.* The weather turned ideal, and both towns enjoyed the visit.[3]

This trip was the first of many. With Syd telling yarns and Hill playing tricks, the Barringtons became famous over the years for their "excursion" trips around Wrangell or to nearby communities. They filled the boat with residents, found an island where passengers could picnic, swim, fish, bathe, dance and experience a grand time. On one outing, a *Wrangell Sentinel* reporter exaggerated a bit on the great fishing. "A fresh water stream was nearly so full of fish that the fishermen say they had to hide behind trees while baiting their hooks to keep the fish from jumping from the stream and taking the bait from their fingers."[4]

At that period in 1916 and 1917, about 800 people resided in Wrangell, a southeastern Alaska coastal town kept alive by fishing and logging.[5] As an aside, not all of Wrangell's past was that obvious or harmless. There was even the hint that Wrangell proved the location for an opium business outside town at a saltery. At one time, opium was supposedly brought from Victoria, B.C. to the saltery, where workers stuffed it into salted salmon bellies and packed it in barrels. From there the drug was shipped to all parts of the United States, according to Clarence Andrews in his book *Wrangell and the Gold of the Cassiar*. Historians gave Wrangell significance by noting it the only town in Alaska that had been ruled by four nations: Tlingit, Russia, Britain and the United States.[6] The local *Wrangell Sentinel* in 1916 printed items and features about World War I in Europe. But other than a few enlistees and others who helped with Red Cross projects, the war did not seriously touch the community.[7]

Tlingit Indians lived in this southeast area for centuries. They used the river as a highway, poling their canoes through the changeable waters, struggled upstream to trade with the Tahltan Indians of the Interior.[9]

As early as 1840, the Hudson Bay Company, interested in furs,[10] built trading posts along the Stikine. Boats poled from Fort Wrangel[11] upriver several times a year.[12] Although early day Indians canoed up the Stikine, Captain William Moore, in 1862, was the first swiftwater captain who fought to the head of navigation by steamboat[13] in his *Flying Dutchman*.[14] Gold discoveries brought stampeders into the Cassiar during the mid to late 1800s, and soon after the Stikine River became one of the routes to the Klondike. At that time, thirty sternwheelers pushed up the torrent—fifteen operated by the Canadian Pacific Railway.[15]

The relocation from Dawson to Wrangell proved a satisfying move, for the Stikine turned out to be Barrington's river. First the green and white[8] *Hazel* boats—numbering them and renumbering new ones—*Hazel B. No. 1, Hazel B. No. 2, Hazel B. No. 3,* and *Hazel B. No. 4,* ran the river. Then Al Richie's *Judith Ann.* For years the brothers made their livelihoods during the warmer months hauling freight and passengers up and down the waterway. Energized by periodic gold and mineral strikes in Canada's Cassiar region, big game hunting interests, fur trapping and a growing tourist industry, the vessels did a brisk business. The brothers had made the right move.

In the earlier years of the 1900s, "Deaf Dan" McCullough[16] operated before Barrington. So did Captain C.A. Gardner, running the *Port Simpson* for the Hudson's Bay Company.[17] Normally the *Port Simpson* worked the Skeena River out of Prince Rupert, Canada. Every summer she plied north and completed several trips up the

Iceberg along the Stikine River.
Credit: Nancy Warren Ferrell.

Avoiding a sweeper on the Stikine River.
Credit: Courtesy of Edith Carter.

Stikine to service Telegraph Creek residents.[18] However, the Barringtons established a constant passenger/freight schedule people could depend on.

The Stikine, a 400-mile[19] water artery running through steep glaciated mountains, was said to be the swiftest navigable river in Alaska—called "The Child of the Glaciers."[20] Fed by countless tributaries, the river rushed downward into the silty delta several miles from Wrangell itself. There the Stikine braided through ever-changing mud flats and sandy islands nearly impossible to navigate. There were stretches so shallow, a boat seemed to glide on the sand.[21] In winter when the river froze, dog sleds traversed the iceway, carrying people and freight.[22]

No placid river the Stikine. From its head of navigation above Telegraph Creek, the river plunged about 600 feet in 160 miles. Those figures proved more impressive when compared to the Mississippi River which dropped nearly the same amount, but over a 1500-mile run.[23] A captain sailing upstream then, to Telegraph Creek, found the route almost a constant climb. At one stretch—Buck's Riffle—the river steepens seven feet in a 150-foot expanse![24]

In addition, the sandy Stikine river bottom always moved—building up in sections, washing out in others. The shifting river eroded the shoreline, exposing tree roots, felling trees and sending them sweeping down the river.[25] For many years during the Barrington era, there were "snagging" cabins along the route. Workers moved up and down the river from one cabin to another, clearing snags off the water.[26] A captain had to "read" the river changes and react to danger instantly.

Riding a *Hazel* boat from Wrangell upstream, Captain Barrington steered through a variety of landscape. From its mouth at sea level, the Stikine wound through tidal flats, gradually narrowed and climbed through hemlock and spruce hugging the waterway. Thick berry bushes, ferns and devil's club choked the underbrush. Forests and mountains bordered the lower section—a wilderness for bear, goat, moose and sheep.

At times, with the shifting bottom, no channel ahead seemed available. Then Syd called out to the deckhand who lolled on the scow being pushed ahead by the boat, "Willie, get the sounder working. I'm going to take her through that hole in the woods."[27]

Syd then called for "the mark."[28] Into the water until it hit bottom plunged a red and white pole about fifteen feet long, painted in one-foot sections. As the crewman shouted out the depth, the skipper flipped the number of fingers on his hand, as a visual signal—three, four, five feet. All the time, bells rang furiously, giving orders to the engine room,[29] accompanied by Syd's salty language. "Four and a quarter. Four and a half. Five. Quarter less three!" the captain shouted.[30] Crew and captain worked together until they discovered the best channel. As a reporter said, the boat "...wriggles and squirms up through the shallow, swift water like a salmon headed for the spawning grounds."[31]

Occasionally, the vessel hit bottom. One traveler reported, "The boat struck bottom with a terrific jar. The passengers looked at Captain Syd apprehensively and he, without batting an eye, observed, 'Must have hit a steelhead salmon.'"[32]

Before long, gleaming glaciers striped the landscape—more than 100 lined the route.[33] If there was time to stop, Barrington might have the cook prepare ice cream; a simple task of mixing a pail of condensed milk, eggs, corn starch, vanilla essence and sugar. Cook then placed the pail in a hole in the glacier, covered it with ice from the same glacier and left it to freeze.[34] In contrast to the icy glacier, a short walk into the heavy brush nearby brought a traveler to Chief Shakes Hot Springs. There, hot water spilled out beneath granite rock,[35] steamy heat swirling the air.

The mountains grew steeper as the river pushed past the International Boundary between the U.S. and Canada, for these were the Coast Mountains that define the border. Watching the landscape as they floated by, travelers spotted terns and sandpipers swooping low, visiting sand bars or lighting on the river bank.[36]

About nine o'clock each evening, the *Hazel* tied up to a tree for the night. Time for leisure then, or playing cards with the crew.[37] On a fall evening, the Northern Lights might put on a display. Engine sounds often woke passengers at 4:00 in the morning for a long day.

Just across the border into Canada flowed the Stikine's largest tributary, the Iskut. Used heavily by Tlingits and Tahltans in earlier days, the area supported an abundance of goats, moose, wolves and salmon.[38]

Still battling upstream, the *Hazel* ascended through a valley, blue-gray limestones visible on both banks. Side streams flooded into the Stikine, the scenery dotted by occasional cabins occupied by prospectors or trappers. In the distance rose 10,000-foot Kate's Needle.

When the waters rushed stronger than the riverboat engine going upstream, the boat needed to be lined or winched—much the same technique as on the Yukon River. Lining meant that two of the crew launched a small skiff on which they hauled a cable. They fastened the cable around a tree or stanchion a quarter mile upstream. On the crew's return, the cable was fastened to the bow of the boat. From then on, deck hands literally cranked the vessel upstream,[39] a small boat pushing the *Hazel* from behind.[40]

As Syd steered the vessel farther upstream, the river narrowed. Ahead ran Klootchman's Canyon, a mile-long gorge. Conquering the canyon proved particularly difficult and claimed all of Barrington's attention. As a *Wrangell Sentinel* writer reported, "the canyon was a churning, seething mass of water with a power of resistance that was nearly too much even for the *Hazel B. No. 3.* The engine worked faithfully but there were minutes when no progress was made…Everyone watched the struggle with bated breath and the women of the party sat in silent dread of what might happen—but the *Hazel B. 3* won, and the canyon was left behind."[41]

In an *Alaska Sportsman* article, passenger Anton Money wrote his own account of Barrington's skill negotiating this canyon. "He would let the writhing current catch the bow so that the boat skittled sideways over the surface like a water beetle racing across a pond. Then just as we seemed about to strike the granite wall, he would give the wheel a twitch, the stern would swing in and the bow out, and we would gain another few feet upstream. Logs raced past us, bobbing up and down like porpoises passing a ship in the ocean, and water foamed around the bow and sprayed the passengers who had gathered to watch our progress."[42] Ever so slowly the climb continued until the *Hazel* reached the head of the canyon.

Because of the narrowness and ferocity of the canyon, flag men were stationed at the lower end. If the flag were down, it signaled a boat was coming from the upper end, and the lower boat had to wait. If the flag stood up, it was safe to go through. Logically, the boat coming down always had priority because of the swiftness of the current, and the fact that the course was too narrow for two boats at the same time.[43]

Above the canyon another world opened to view. The land was

Nine-Mile Canyon of the Stikine, one of the very swift sections.
Credit: Barrett Willoughby book, Gentlemen Unafraid, Putnams, 1928.

dryer, receiving about thirteen inches of rain a year, whereas at Boundary, eighty-six inches was the norm.[44] Volcanic action had rounded the practically bare mountains. Sparse, evenly spaced poplars and pines edged the riverbank. So even and neat were the trees, one passenger remarked that they looked like they had been trimmed.

"Why, hell," Captain Barrington responded. "That's the rabbits. When the snow's deep they eat the tops off the trees, leaving 'em all the same height."[45]

A few miles up was Jackson's Landing, named after a man who discovered anthracite in the area and sold his claim to a German firm. He left for Outside, married, couldn't stand being away and returned several years later.[46] Along this mile the Chutine River enters the Stikine from the west.

And then Barrington brought the boat past the town of Glenora, a stop on the route to the Klondike in 1898. Once busy during several gold rushes, the dilapidated town then sat deserted.

Almost across the river was the landing for George Ball's ranch. Visitors hiked or took a cart on a wagon path about four miles to the ranch, a guest resort and site for big game hunters.[47] Another guide, J. Frank Callbreath,[48] also led hunting parties into the Cassiar to get their "bags" of game.

Still plowing toward Telegraph Creek, the *Hazel* approached the Three Sisters—three gigantic rocks jutting from the river's center, one of which resembled the head of a lion. Indian legend had it the rocks signified three Indian women who did not obey their husbands. As a result, the wives were turned to stone.[49] After that, legend said Indian canoe travelers threw tobacco to the sisters to assure a safe journey.[50]

Only a few short miles took the *Hazel* to her goal—Telegraph Creek in Canada. The town itself received its name when the government proposed a telegraph line to cross British Columbia and

Three Sisters Rocks. Iron rings are fastened into the rocks to hold boats on the river there. Ships had to make their way around the rocks.
Credit: Kay Jabusch, Wrangell.

connect with Europe in the 1860s[51]; officials eventually abandoned the project.[52]

About 160 miles upstream from Wrangell,[53] with a population of about twenty Caucasian and 200 Natives in 1923,[54] the Telegraph settlement was a jumping off spot for miners, travelers into the interior and big game hunters. Beside headquarters for a chain of Indian fur trading posts, Telegraph Creek supplied big game hunters for their hunt into the wilderness; more than 100 horses grazed there, kept on hand for outfitters. World record specimens have been "bagged" from the area—especially sheep and caribou.[55]

Above the town several miles, the Indian village of Tahltan and volcanic lava beds drew interested tourists. Riverboats did not travel that far.

During the Barrington era, a riverboat pushed up the Stikine course in three days, but floated back down in twelve hours and normally used one-fifth of the gas fuel on the downstream run.[56] One passenger said, "Coming downstream was the most extolling and thrilling; we literally zipped along…we dodged and twisted our way through snags so close together they seemed to form an impassible barrier to navigation. It is in places like these that Captain Sid shows his genius as a river pilot."[57] Syd demonstrated his years of experience with easy confidence.

The hectic seasons were just beginning.

• • •

1. "Capt. Syd Barrington of the Stikine." *Pacific Motor Boat Magazine,* Jan. 1933, p. 12.
2. Barrett Willoughby. "Champion White Water Pilot of the North." *American Magazine,* October 1928, p. 156.
3. *Hazel B. II* Makes Voyage to Petersburg." *Wrangell Sentinel,* May 31, 1917.
4. "Big Time at Big Bay." *Wrangell Sentinel,* August 7, 1919.
5. "Community Profiles." Alaska on the Internet.
6. "Welcome to Wrangell." *Wrangell Guide 1998,* p. 4.
7. Claus-M. Naske and Herman E. Slotnick, *Alaska: A History of the 49th State.* Grand Rapids, Mich: William B. Eerdmans Publishing Co., 1979, p. 92.
8. "Navigation on Stikine Opens This Week." *Wrangell Sentinel,* May 12, 1927.
9. *The Stikine River.* Anchorage: Alaska Geographic Society, 1979, p. 9.
10. Bess Winn, "The Stikine." *Alaska Sportsman,* Sept. 1947, p. 12.
11. Fort Wrangel was changed to Wrangell in 1902. Donald J. Orth, *Dictionary of Alaska Place Names.* Wash. DC: U.S. Government Printing Office, 1967, p. 1061.
12. Ibid, Bess Winn, p. 13.
13. Ibid., *The Stikine River,* p. 52.
14. Norman R. Hacking and W. Kaye Lamb, *The Princess Story.* Vancouver: Mitchell Press Limited, 1974, p. 71.
15. Leslie Deane, "The Stikine-River of Beauty." *Alaska Sportsman,* August 1937, p. 19. The waterway was so narrow in places, with all that travel, boats could not pass each other. Signal men as lookouts were stationed at points to direct traffic.
16. "Stikine Is Open To Navigation." *Wrangell Sentinel,* May 11, 1916.
17. "Port Simpson Is On First Trip Up River." *Wrangell Sentinel,* July 15, 1916.
18. "Excursion to the Great Glacier." *Alaska Sportsman,* April, 1963, p. 26.
19. Bob Henning, et al (Eds.) *The Stikine River.* Anchorage: Alaska Geographic Society, 1979, p. 6.
20. "Much Activity In the Cassiar." *Wrangell Sentinel,* May 15, 1924.
21. Author's trip up the Stikine to Boundary by jet boat. Summer 1998.
22. Ibid., Leslie Deane.
23. "Swiftest in Alaska." *Alaska Weekly,* August 6, 1954.
24. Ibid., Bess Winn, p. 12.
25. Ibid., p. 14.
26. Phone conversation with Verna Kaer in Wrangell, Sept. 19, 1998.
27. "Sid Barrington." Unknown author. Undated, possibly about 1952. Supplied by Bob DeArmond, June, 1998.
28. Anton Money, "A Voyage Up the Stikine." *Alaska Sportsman,* August, 1964, p. 46.
29. "Reporter Reveals Peculiarities Famed Stikine River Excursion." *Wrangell Sentinel,* Oct. 3, 1941.
30. Ibid.
31. Ibid.
32. Ibid., "Sid Barrington," Unknown author.
33. Ibid., Bess Winn, p. 13.
34. "Hooper Tells of Trip Up Stikine." *Wrangell Sentinel,* June 19, 1924.
35. Ibid., Bess Winn, p. 45.
36. Ibid., Leslie Deane, p. 18.
37. "The Passing of an Era..." *Alaska Life,* April, 1948, p. 23.
38. Ibid., *The Stikine River,* p. 77.
39. Richard A. Rammer, "They Rule the Stikine." *Alaska Life,* Feb. 1942, p. 16.

40. Conversation with Amos Burg, April 7, 1985.
41. "Excursionists Report Delightful Trip to Telegraph Creek." *Wrangell Sentinel,* June 20, 1918.
42. Ibid., Anton Money, September, 1964, p. 19.
43. Phone conversation with Verna Kaer in Wrangell, Sept. 19, 1998.
44. R.M. Patterson, *Trail to the Interior.* NY: William Morrow & Co., Inc., 1966, p. 25.
45. Ibid., Anton Money, p. 19.
46. Ibid., Bess Winn, p. 47.
47. Phone conversation with Verna Kaer of Wrangell, Sept. 28, 1998.
48. "Our Trip Up the Stikine." *Wrangell Sentinel,* Sept. 13, 1917.
49. Ibid., Bess Winn, p. 48.
50. Ibid., Leslie Deane, p. 16.
51. Ibid., *The Stikine River,* p. 53.
52. "107 Years of Stikine Riverboating." *The Stikine River.* Anchorage: Alaska Geographic, 1979, p. 53.
53. "Much Activity In the Cassiar." *Wrangell Sentinel,* May 15, 1924.
54. Ibid., Anton Money, August 1964, p. 59.
55. Ibid., Leslie Deane, p. 18.
56. Untitled article. *Alaska Sportsman,* July 1954, p. 13.
57. Helen Sefton, "Reporter Reveals Peculiarities Famed Stikine River Excursion." *Wrangell Sentinel,* Oct. 3, 1941.

13: BREAKING ALL RECORDS

To Syd, the challenge of the river proved his greatest satisfaction. Nothing could stop him from getting through. People said he was so excellent at his job, he could take his boat "over the dew on the grass,"[1] and get it there. If the vessel, by its design, could not do the job, the Barringtons, with boat designer Charles Binkley,[2] fashioned devices that solved the problem.

Binkley, an idea man as well as a true craftsman, fit in with Syd's plans perfectly. For his first Wrangell job, he designed and built the new *Hazel B. No. 3*. Though smaller, it carried more power than the *Hazel B. No. 2*.

The sixty-two-foot boat was small and light, with such a shallow draft, it could run in nine inches of water. Because of this, skimming over shallow sandbars would be easier. While native cedar and spruce made up the housing above, the underneath planking was constructed of fir, reinforced by strong bracing boards. The lightness of the hull gave a springiness to the boat, which permitted it to "bend" with the stream movement. This bending also allowed a flexibility in the upper housing, keeping it from becoming rickety.[3]

The Barrington brothers and Binkley also customized upper tunnels on the back of their boats. This modification worked from the boat's pilothouse. When hitting shallow areas or avoiding submerged branches,[4] the captain could flip a lever in the wheelhouse, which lifted the propeller into a tunnel, clear of the water.[5] A six-cylinder Wisconsin 95-horsepower engine propelled the *Hazel B. No. 3*.

The vessel plan allowed for passenger comfort, too. Barrington

Wrangell shipyard.
Credit: Wrangell Museum, P80.12.17.04.

and Binkley furnished the boat with electric lights and first-class staterooms. An upper deck permitted unobstructed viewing of the spectacular scenery. Since the river proved too silty for a drinking water supply, room was allotted on board for large cans of water.[6] Though the *Hazel 3* sprouted no really fancy fixings, both tourists and miners delighted in the vessel. Designers thought of just about everything.

Not that she and other Stikine boats had no problems, for the fickle waterway took its toll on the vessels. Photographer Amos Burg recalled a later voyage. "The trip I was on, the propeller on the boat bent 16 times on the way to Telegraph Creek. Captain Barrington changed propellers that many times. When we got back down to Wrangell, the captain had the propellers bent back and repaired for another trip. There was no trouble on the way down the river, because the boat drifted."[7]

The Hudson Bay Company ran their lumbering 137-foot sternwheeler, *Port Simpson,* up the Stikine to Telegraph Creek in 1916, offering both "berth and bath" to thirty-six passengers. A round

Colleague and friend, Charles Binkley, the
innovative boat designer.
Credit: Wrangell Museum, P82.06.13.06.

trip cost $25.[8] The boat certainly was a convenience, but it worked no regular schedule. During warmer months, she generally made two to five round trips to Telegraph Creek per season.[9] Smaller and swifter, the *Hazel B. No. 2* proved no real competition to the larger *Simpson*.

When Barrington launched the *Hazel B. No. 3* in 1917, Syd's gambling blood fired up. In Syd's eyes, one might compare the new *Hazel* to a thoroughbred horse. No sooner did the new gas boat hit water than Syd began taking bets; the *Hazel 3,* he claimed, could well outstrip the plodding *Port Simpson*.

One day soon after, with the *Port Simpson* already on her way to Telegraph Creek, Syd wagered he could not only beat the *Simpson* to Telegraph Creek, but the new *Hazel* could run up, collect the mail and return to Wrangell before the Hudson Bay vessel even *reached* Telegraph Creek. Odds placed heavily against *that* happening.

And so the contest was on. Syd pulled out all stops, forced the *Hazel* through calm and rapids and climbed the 555-foot up-slant of water all 160 miles.[10] At Telegraph Creek, he unloaded freight and passengers, grabbed the mail and floated back down. Syd must have waved triumphantly as the *Hazel* swept past the laboring *Port Simpson* still struggling toward Telegraph Creek. Syd Barrington broke all records for the route, completing the total run in twenty-six hours.[11, 12] Soon after, the Hudson Bay Company ceased running the *Port Simpson,* and the Barringtons filled the gap. After all, who could compete with the *Hazels*. Syd became known as "Dean of the white water skippers."[13]

Brother Hill remained in the Dawson area as manager of the Side Streams Navigation Company through the 1917 season,[14] no doubt tying up loose ends from the business. He then joined Syd in the Wrangell operation, naming the new business the Barrington Transportation Company.

Harry Barrington arrived in Wrangell later, as he spent more time in Washington—running the Steamer *Tourist* during 1918 between Seattle and Bremerton—as well as other locations.[15] By then, Washington ferries touched port at Whidbey communities, carrying travelers to the mainland where they drove to Seattle by car.[16]

Syd's mastery of the Stikine meant everything to Telegraph Creek residents, who practically revered him. Frequent trips, every forty-eight hours, added to the Barringtons' popular standing. In turn, people at the headwaters showed hospitality to passengers by performing what they called the "Telegraph Shuffle"[17]—meeting the boat and making visitors welcome.

The brothers were often on the receiving end of Telegraph's gratitude. The Rev. Will Thorman of the town presented Hill with a monstrous head of cabbage one time. "Thirty-five pounds," at least, said the reporter.

Since Hill frowned on exaggeration [!], he answered, "Don't lie about it. It weighs twenty-five pounds." Actual weight was only fifteen pounds.

"But," the reporter persisted, "A fifteen-lb. head of cabbage is really some size and the discussion proves that sometimes one head is better than two."[18]

However accommodating Syd felt to people in the area, the challenge and speed of the boats may have appealed to Barrington more than its convenience to residents. What trips had taken days before by other skippers, Barrington completed in hours. Soon after breaking the speed record, Syd further reduced it, running upstream in twenty-four hours and fifty-six minutes, while returning in half that time.[19] Anyone knowing the Barringtons felt sure heavy wagers backed the outcomes.

The challenge itself proved important, too. Suggest to Syd that a boat could *not* do something, or could *not* go somewhere, and Syd proved otherwise. Such was the case with the Iskut River, a tributary in Canada emptying into the Stikine over the U.S. boundary.

The Iskut flowed so rapidly, it made navigation nearly hopeless. "The river's impossible," everyone said. For years, Indians avoided the upper country to the Iskut headwaters having heard tales of a *Kustika-a,* or bad spirit, who lived there and ate all invaders.[20]

As the tale originated, about 1910 a German count, hearing glowing rumors of gold in the area, offered Indian Chief Shakes enormous amounts of money to mine the area. Shakes refused the proposal. Rumors persisted over the years, peaking the interest of miners. Finally, the Canadian government granted holdings in the Iskut district. But how to get there conveniently with supplies?

Needless to say, the Barringtons answered the call. With the new, light *Hazel B. 3,* Syd covered the distance with no difficulty in August of 1917, offering the boat and himself for further use. Without even lining, Barrington ran up thirty-five miles to a mining camp in only eight hours, coming down in two. Thus he opened up a new district for mineral exploration.[21]

A number of buildings still stand at Telegraph Creek. Here is the Old Pioneer Outfitters owned by Callbreath. It was a restaurant, store at one time. It may have been built between 1850 and 1875. Now a family lives in the house.
Credit: Kay Jabusch, Wrangell.

Syd and Hill learned to love the Stikine. "She has a different mood for every foot of her channel," Syd said, "and she's three times faster than she looks...I don't dare take my eyes off her a minute. She's always got some new trick to spring on me...I watch her—every minute."[22]

Certainly the Stikine's challenge decided the Barringtons on a Wrangell location, but another factor proved just as important: the proximity to the busy Canadian gold-bearing Cassiar district. The gamble of uncovering a bonanza lode held a permanent craving in their souls.

In those years and later, periodic reports of new finds drifted to Wrangell, and another surge of interest brought prospectors. The brothers kept busy during the years transporting miners and equipment into and out of one area or another. No problem keeping track of the latest gold discovery, for the Barringtons offered the only transportation company heading up the Stikine, and they caught every clue. Syd, himself, always focused on gold strike news, just as he had for Cook Inlet, the Klondike and Nome.

The scheduled runs to Telegraph Creek offered Hill and Syd opportunities to dig around themselves. They followed up leads on different tributaries, hand-panned hopeful locations, investigated property. The "big one"—they were always looking for the big one. Ever hopeful, the incurable gamblers never gave up.

The 1918 season closed in October that year, with the *Hazel B. No. 3* making its last trip October 17. The World War, far away in Europe, had little direct impact on Wrangell, though the *Sentinel* stated a slow down of activities in the Cassiar district.[23]

Wintering the *Hazel* boats in Wrangell with Dan McCullough as caretaker,[24] the Barringtons headed south in October. Out of sight of Wrangell, however, was not out of mind. Syd the promoter talked up the area wherever he went, drumming up business. "To my mind," he told the stateside periodical *Railway and Marine News,* "the Stikine River district and the Cassiar country of Northern British Columbia are the most wonderful hunting grounds on the entire continent."[25]

As in Yukon years, wives Hazel and Mildred accompanied their husbands to Wrangell from Seattle. Yorke came too, of course. The sister-in-laws were friendly to each other, though both had different personalities: Hazel showy, direct and outspoken; Mildred quiet, more traditional. It was a family secret that Mildred always felt a bit miffed that none of the Barrington boats carried her name.[26]

Since Mildred's mother, Margaret Hayward, resided in Skagway, Mildred often visited her while in the Yukon or Alaska. The Hill Barringtons had lost their infant, Sydney, several years before, but Mildred became pregnant again in 1918. Because of this mother/daughter visit, Mildred nearly lost her next baby, as well as her own life.

While Hill finished the Wrangell season and cruised south to Washington, Mildred visited in Skagway. Three months pregnant, she booked passage that fall from Skagway to Washington on the steel 245-foot *Princess Sophia.*[27] Since October signaled the end of the steamer season north in the Yukon, eighty-eight river men as well boarded the *Sophia* south for the winter.[28] Thus pilots, captains and possibly their families, many of whom Mildred knew, settled aboard. She expected a pleasant voyage, with plenty of good company.

During the time, influenza raged throughout the northwest as well as the rest of the world, and at the last minute, Mildred became ill. She canceled her ticket and remained in Skagway for a later ship. Out of Skagway the ill-fated *Sophia* struck Vanderbilt Reef, thirty miles north of Juneau, Alaska, and all 398 passengers and crew drowned.[29, 30]

What Mildred's reaction to this near-death experience was, can only be guessed. Horror certainly, some relief, too. Little mention of the *Sophia* tragedy found its way to print in the Skagway paper, for global news releases squeezed out many of the local articles. Instead, the front pages cried such headlines as "Kaiser Quits," announcing the end of World War I, which occurred in early November.[31]

The Yukon River lost many of its captains in the *Sophia* disaster, and Mildred lost many of her friends. She did, however, give birth at San de Fuca—in fact, in the old captain's house[32]—to a healthy boy on April 10, 1919. This time Hill and Mildred named the baby William Hill after his father.

The first several years in Wrangell convinced the Barringtons the business could use another vessel. Word of gold discoveries and trophy game specimens coming from the Cassiar passed south from one ear to another, and more interest turned toward the Stikine. The war was finally over, too. Following a regular time schedule to Telegraph Creek along with the enjoyment of the trip encouraged increased boat use. Builders finished the new sixty-five-foot *Hazel B. No. 4* the summer of 1919. It, like her predecessors, was designed for lightness, with specific elements to blend boat with river.[33]

Syd, however, did not forget about his first love—prospecting. In the summer of 1919, he hit pay dirt 100 miles northeast of Telegraph Creek.[34] Close-mouthed at the time, it was later revealed that, by hand panning alone, he took away $150,000 (roughly, over $6 million in today's gold market).[35] What a bonanza! The Barrington gamble was paying off.

But of course the amount was not substantial enough, certainly not "the big one." Would anything be big enough? Such a find, however, spurred Syd's exploration in an expansive way. Never thinking small, he bought claims in the Cassiar, brought in six men and equipment to work the ground, and left them in the goldfields during the winter.[36] In the years following, Barrington added to his properties. And no old-fashioned methods for Syd. Miners said he owned the biggest hydraulic proposition on the continent.[37]

In addition to gold, outside businesses from Vancouver took

Hill and Mildred Barrington with Billy, taken in the mid-1920s.
Credit: Courtesy of Bill and Elna Barrington.

interest in locating cattle in Klappan Valley. A petroleum company sent men to the same area to drill for oil.[38] All these activities decided Syd to run a boat on Dease River so movement into and out of the interior would be cut to days rather than months.[39]

You can be sure the Barringtons lived high during the winters of those years, akin to jet-setters in this day.

However, with the birth of little Bill Barrington, Mr. and Mrs. Hill took on a more staid life on Whidbey Island.[40] Because of the flu epidemic not only in Alaska but in Washington as well, Mildred did not want to "move around" with a baby, and Hill agreed. In fact, Mildred refused to move to Wrangell at that time.[41] First the family rented, and then with money sent from Mildred's father, they purchased a house (in her name) in Oak Harbor.[42] Hill bought a drugstore and pharmacy[43] on Barrington Avenue, now Pioneer Way, and there they remained for the next five years or so.[44] During that time, citizens elected Hill mayor of Oak Harbor,[45] where he filled two terms between 1920 and 1924.[46]

Mayor Hill Barrington might not have been the perfect role-model in public office, but he reflected a general view toward Prohibition at the time. Hill always managed to have a few liquor bottles under his pharmacy counter. One day an Oak Harbor preacher came in. Reaching under the counter, Hill opened the wrong bottle, and a pressure-powered cork zipped past the preacher's nose. After a minute of silence, the two left words unsaid.[47]

Living a more rooted life in Oak Harbor for a time did not mean that Hill cut himself off from mining activity entirely. An item in the July 14, 1922 issue of the *Farm Bureau News* of Oak Harbor mentioned that Hill, his wife and son, visited "the new mine at Hope, B.C., Monday last, and were well pleased with the prospects. The mill will commence crushing ore this week." Because of their mobile lifestyle, the Barringtons thought nothing of traveling. Hill probably made many trips during this stay in Oak Harbor.

Before 1925, the Hill Barringtons resumed the Alaskan commute to Wrangell, and Hill took up captaining on the Stikine.

While in Seattle, during the winter, the Syd Barringtons enjoyed their grand, new home constructed on Queen Anne Hill. Spacious rooms gazed out on a lovely view. The family welcomed relatives and visitors.

Hazel designed the house and, leaning toward the theatrical, the house decor also tended that way. She decorated with a Chinese motif, though she was fond of changing styles. Philippine mahogany patterned the floors, and it was always a wonder to the family why Hazel covered them with black and gold carpets.[48] Red silk embroidered drapes brightened the windows. A six-foot long fireplace adorned the dining room wall.[49] In some of the rooms, painters gilded portions of the windows.[50]

Syd entertained lavishly in his home, using it to backdrop the deals—and gambles—he promoted. He invited important people to visit, impressed them and sometimes swayed them to "the Barrington view."[51]

Besides the joy of having a beautiful new home in Seattle, over the years the Barringtons nurtured a large orchard in the backyard. Apricot, peach and plum trees grew in abundance. So much so, that Hazel had to prop eight poles under one especially heavy crop. "All we have to do," said Syd, "is to carry pitchers of cream into the backyard, pick the peaches, and dream we are in the heart of Georgia."[52]

And that was the high point of many Barrington dinner parties: after a sumptuous meal, guests picked fruit from the trees and created their own dessert.[53]

• • •

1. "Sourdough Memories." *Alaska Weekly,* July 8, 1955.
2. "Personal Item." *Wrangell Sentinel,* April 18, 1918.
3. "New River Boat Breaks All Records." *Wrangell Sentinel,* August 2, 1917.
4. Richard A. Rammer, "They Rule the Stikine." *Alaska Life,* Feb. 1942, p. 16.
5. Bess Winn, "The Stikine." *Alaska Sportsman,* September 1947, p. 14.
6. Untitled article. *Alaska Sportsman,* July 1954, p. 12.
7. Conversation with Amos Burg, April 7, 1985.
8. Bob Greenhagen, "Searching for Fortune On the Yukon Rivers." *The Whidbey News Times,* April 13, 1972.

9. R.N. De Armond, "Riverboating on the Stikine." *Alaska Journal,* Autumn 1979, p. 77.

10. R.M. Patterson, *Trail to the Interior.* NY: William Morrow & Co., Inc. 1966, p. 51.

11. Ibid., Bob Greenhagen.

12. Norman R. Hacking and W. Kaye Lamb, *The Princess Story.* Vancouver: Mitchell Press Limited, 1974, 168–69. In 1898, the Canadian Pacific Railroad built the *Ogilvie* steamer to ply the Stikine. Early in the summer, under the command of W.D. Moore, son of the well known William Moore, the steamer made a record run from Wrangell to Glenora in thirty-five hours, while a month later, she made a forty-four-hour round trip, breaking the down run time to nine hours and twenty-five minutes.

13. "Sid Barrington No 'Desert Rat'." *Alaska Weekly,* April 12, 1935.

14. *Polk's Alaska-Yukon Gazetteer and Directory,* 1917–18. Seattle: Alaska Directory Co., 1917–18, p. 728.

15. "San de Fuca Notes." *Island County Times,* August 23, 1918.

16. "Bert Nunan Tells Whidbey History, Water Travel Days." *Island County Times,* Nov. 14, 1946.

17. Conversation with Edith Carter, Juneau, April 1, 1998.

18. Ken Neville, "Stikine and Cassiar Hotshots," *Wrangell Sentinel,* Sept. 30, 1938.

19. "Our Trip Up the Stikine." *Wrangell Sentinel,* Sept. 13, 1917.

20. "Iskut River Navigable." *Wrangell Sentinel,* Aug. 30, 1917.

21. Ibid.

22. Barrett Willoughby, "Champion White Water Pilot of the North." *American Magazine,* Oct. 1928, p. 154.

23. "*Hazel B. III* Makes Last Trip of the Season." *Wrangell Sentinel,* Oct. 17, 1918.

24. "Barrington Boats Make Last Trip." *Wrangell Sentinel,* Oct. 20, 1934.

25. "The Most Wonderful Hunting Grounds on Entire Continent." *Wrangell Sentinel,* January 8, 1920.

26. Conversation with Bill Barrington, Anchorage, April 11, 1998.

27. Ibid., Norman R. Hacking and W. Kaye Lamb, p. 243.

28. Jack L. Morison, "Steamboats on the Yukon." *Denver Westerners' Roundup,* Nov.–Dec. 1979, p. 22.

29. "Disasters." *The World Almanac and Book of Facts—1995.* Mahwah, New Jersey: World Almanac, 1994, p. 565.

30. Conversation with Bill Barrington, Anchorage, Alaska, April 11, 1998.

31. "Kaiser Quits." *The Alaskan,* Nov. 11, 1918.

32. Conversation with Bill Barrington, Anchorage, Alaska, April 11, 1998.

33. "*Hazel B. No. 4* Makes Initial Voyage Up River." *Wrangell Sentinel,* July 3, 1919.

34. "Good Reports from Barrington Property." *Wrangell Sentinel,* Oct. 23, 1919.

35. Ibid., Bob Greenhagen.

36. "Sid Barrington Takes Up Mining as Side Line." *Wrangell Sentinel,* Sept. 11, 1919.

37. "Activity in the Cassiar Region Begins Early." *Wrangell Sentinel,* February 10, 1921.

38. "Callbreath Says Cassiar Will Boom Next Season." *Wrangell Sentinel,* Oct. 23, 1919.

39. Ibid.

40. Conversation with Elna Barrington, Anchorage, August 29, 1998.

41. Bill and Elna tapes, recorded in 2001–02, courtesy of relatives Marlene and Hill Barrington, III.

42. Ibid., Bill and Elna interviews, 2001–02.

43. "Capt. Hill Barrington, son of pioneer, celebrates 82nd birthday Saturday." *Oak Harbor News,* August 25, 1959.

44. Conversation with Elna Barrington, Anchorage, August 29, 1998.

45. "A New Mayor and Council." *Farm Bureau News,* Dec. 8, 1922.

46. Trudy J. Sundberg, "Captains Sid and Hill Are Oldest Native Sons." *Whidbey Press Progress Edition,* June, 1961, p. 4.

47. Hill Sr. and Mildred Barrington tapes, recorded by Eddie Barrington 9/1/1970, courtesy of relatives Marlene and Hill Barrington, III.

48. Conversation with Elna Barrington, Anchorage, August 29, 1998.

49. Ibid., Hill Sr. and Mildred Barrington tape.

50. Conversation with Bill Barrington, Anchorage, April 11, 1998.

51. Phone conversation with Jim Binkley in Fairbanks, with author, August 9, 1999.

52. "Barrington Once Again on Yukon." *Island County Times,* August 17, 1944.

53. "Guests Pick Their Own At Barrington's." *Alaska Weekly,* Sept. 1, 1944.

14: TIMES OF GRIEF AND GLORY

A once-in-a-lifetime historical event spotlighted the 1920 riverboat season in Wrangell. All eyes searched the sky expecting the first U.S. continental airline flight to touch down—Wrangell the first stop in Alaska. Led by Captain St. Clair Streett, the U.S. Army Air Service's Black Wolf Squadron's flight from New York to Nome landed in Southeast.[1] Never before had Alaskans witnessed such a continental milestone.

The first airplanes arriving east out of Canada were due at Wrangell on August 14, 1920. The mayor received word the four army De Havillands were scheduled to land on Sergeif Island, twelve miles north of Wrangell. When residents caught wind of the stopover, a festive spirit prevailed; flags flew from buildings and the mayor announced a holiday. About noon on the 14th, bells rang and the mill whistle blew, calling the town to the distant landing field. Syd Barrington hitched a scow to the *Hazel B. No. 3,* and loaded passengers to the limit. With other small boats on the way, the town of Wrangell emptied.

Glances kept to the sky as vessels made their way to Sergeif Island, no one wanting to miss the important event. Once offloaded, the crowd waited and waited on Sergeif that Saturday, and waited some more, but nothing happened. The afternoon grew longer. Finally a few sightseers decided the squadron was not arriving that day. Just as one family prepared to leave in their own boat, someone shouted, "There they come!" And there they were, flying over Wrangell.

Hundreds of eyes followed the open-cockpit aircrafts as they

A *Hazel* boat and scow load up with Wrangell people going to see the Nome-bound planes from New York in 1920. Ed Arola is the little boy in front with his mother.
Credit: Courtesy of Wrangell Museum P80.12.155

Planes making the New York-Nome flight on Sergief Island outside Wrangell.
Credit: Courtesy of Wrangell Museum, P80.12.448.04.

approached, awed by a sight most had never seen before. Swooping low, the squadron prepared to land. The grassy field, however, proved wet, and a danger to flipping the planes. While the pilots steadied the light aircraft gliding in, the back rider in every plane climbed out of the rear cockpit!

The crowd gasped in horror and held its breath.

Finding a grip where they could, each airman shimmed back and straddled the rear of his plane. There he rode to earth on the tail like a cowboy calming a skittish bronco.[2] What a sight! After safe landings and collective sighs, wild shouting ranged through the air.

Such excitement residents had seldom experienced. Once in town, Wrangellites hailed and feted the visitors. After several days of festivities, the flights continued north. Eventually the squadron landed in Nome, August 23, 1920, completing the transcontinental flight.[3] Editor of *The Nome Nugget* envisioned air paths as "highways of the future,"[4] as must any land traveler or riverboat captain. Journeys that previously took weeks or months could now be completed in hours.

Syd and Hill, of course, foresaw the inroads air transportation was pioneering as railroads had up north. The knowledge neither slowed the brothers' work nor their ambitions. They might not like it, but they knew it was destined to be. Rather than buck air competition, they used it themselves.

Into the early 1920s, the Barringtons experienced joys tempered with tragedies. Death seemed to come in numbers to the family. Mother Christina's second husband, Joseph Power, died in San de Fuca Oct. 20, 1922, at the age of seventy-six. After Joseph's death,[5] the brothers financed a California trip for Christina during several months each winter. She either stayed in a hotel or visited relatives in Long Beach.

Christina, an independent woman, went on with her life. Grandson Bill Barrington remembered one story about the grand old lady. Christina Barrington Power violently opposed drinking alcohol in any form. However, when Hill settled in Oak Harbor with the pharmacy store during the first five years of Billy's life, he acted as doctor to his mother. He supplied her with a large bottle marked with Rx, filled with "medicine." In reality, the bottle contained port wine. Christina downed several tablespoons each evening before retiring. Every month or so, she called her son, saying she was almost out of her medicine, and Hill refilled her bottle.[6]

Getting together with friends. Mildred is left in
the back row and Hazel is right in the back row.
Circa 1930s.
Credit: Courtesy of the Wrangell Museum, P89.31.02.

The year 1923 unfolded as a tragically unhappy one for the Barringtons. By this time, Charles Binkley had married and fathered a son. His wife, Peggy,[7] grew unhappy with the union and separated from him, traveling to California. Depressed over his personal life, Binkley died in January in a Seattle hotel of pneumonia, his obituary stated. A broken heart might be more the cause. The Wrangell newspaper said, "Friends in Seattle who learned of Mr. Binkley's illness and who saw him on the two days preceding his death, say that he was indifferent as to whether he recovered or not. They reported that he was so heart sick that he felt that he would just as soon be dead as alive."[8] The Barringtons grieved their best friend and colleague.

As the months passed up north, national news stirred Wrangell residents. The President of the United States, Warren G. Harding, was planning an Alaska trip, and Wrangell was to be one of his stops. Officials began arranging an appropriate welcome.

Life looked brighter for the Barringtons in June when twenty-

Wrangell Alaska = June 18th

Dear Grandma

Just a line to let you know how everything is up in the wilds. This is a picture of my first Goat. The goat is the one underneath — Hope you are feeling well and having a good time. I am getting a lot of good pictures for my album. Love Yorke.

Yorke Barrington, newly graduated from high school, poses for a postcard picture with his first wild goat. The card was sent to his grandmother, Christina Barrington Power, on Whidbey Island during the summer of 1923.
Credit: Courtesy of Peggy Darst Townsdin.

year-old Yorke graduated from Seattle's Broadway High School.[9] The family once again took up summer living in Wrangell, bringing Yorke's young friend, Dennis James, along to share the adventures.

Of course the loyal Republican Barringtons would never miss the Harding celebration. Before the dignitaries arrived, however, there was time to take a goat hunting trip up the Stikine. In high spirits, the Barrington party chugged up the river a few days later to do their own big game hunting. Yorke bagged his first wild goat, recording his picture next to the goat on a photo. A proud Yorke pasted the photo on a post card and sent it to his grandmother, Christina, in San de Fuca. The card said: "Dear Grandma. Just a line to let you know everything is fine up in the wilds. This is a picture of my first goat. The goat is the one underneath. I am getting a lot of good pictures for my album. Love Yorke."[10]

Then, five days after July Fourth, the steamer *Henderson*, convoyed by two torpedo boats, glided into Wrangell harbor under

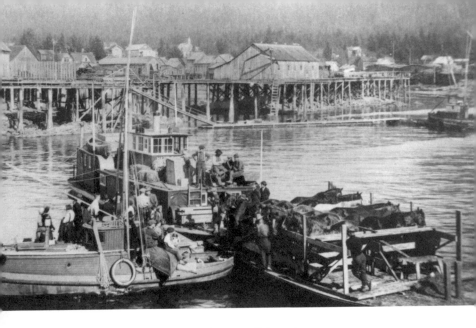

One of the *Hazel* boats transporting horses to Telegraph
Creek for the hunting season.
Credit: Courtesy of the Wrangell Museum, P 80.12.460.16.

ideal weather. From the visiting marine band, brass notes blared and
drum rolls pounded the air with patriotic fervor as the Presidential
party rode a launch to shore. Those aboard included Mr. and Mrs.
Harding, Governor Scott Bone, Herbert Hoover, Henry Wallace and
other dignitaries. The executive party finally stepped into a crowd of
flag-waving, camera toting onlookers, no doubt the Barringtons among
them. After speeches and handshaking the Presidential party again
boarded the *Henderson* and continued the journey.[11] After leaving
Alaska, the President became ill and died in San Francisco August 2,
1923.[14]

The freedom and happiness experienced through the summer
months proved a sharp contrast to events that fall. High spirits soon
plummeted to devastating anguish for the Barringtons.

With Hazel in Seattle taking care of her mother that September, the
men planned a Sunday duck hunt on the wetlands outside Wrangell.
Ironically, Dennis James did not want to go on the trip, but his hosts
talked him into it.[12]

The hunting party consisted of Yorke, Dennis, Syd Barrington and several other hunting friends. Early in the morning they all stepped aboard the *Hazel B. No. 4* and cruised to the Stikine River flats.[13] The weather matched the event that would follow—a cold wind blew across the wetlands, and rain pelted down. Once on the duck grounds, the group spread out over a five mile area, Dennis and Yorke on their own.

Spying ducks on the flats, the boys stealthily crept forward. Quietly, guns cocked and ready, the two slogged through deep mud, Yorke three feet away in the lead. Suddenly, Dennis stumbled. His readied gun exploded, and the discharge blasted Yorke in the side, killing him instantly.

Dennis began screaming and screaming and screaming, bringing Syd from a half mile away. Imagine Syd's shock, his agony. He carried his son's body to a canoe and later placed it on the *Hazel,* where one of the party remained.

A painful waiting period followed, for the party could not immediately leave. The tide would not be high enough until midafternoon, and the other men hunted over a wide area. Syd had to remain there, sitting on the boat, grieving his son. He lowered the ship's flag to half mast, but it claimed no attention from the distant hunters, as United States flags were already at half mast because of President Warren Harding's death.

Shots fired from the *Hazel* over several hours eventually brought in the remaining hunters. Then again it was more waiting for the tide. Once on the move, the vessel tied up in Wrangell at six o'clock that evening. In spite of Syd's grief, he treated young Dennis James with the kindest tenderness, realizing how close the two boys were.[15]

A Stateside ship not reaching Wrangell until Thursday, Syd took the body of his son to Ketchikan on a small boat, hoping to catch the earliest steamer south.[16] Relatives buried Yorke in Seattle, and the family grieved quietly.

Understandably, the loss of their only son proved an unrecoverable blow. Both Hazel and Syd continued with their lives, but several people remembered Hazel, at times, becoming quieter, losing some of the flamboyant gaiety of earlier years. Perhaps by way of partial compensation, both Hazel and Syd developed a deep love for dogs—two Boston Bulls to be exact—and they traveled everywhere with them.

The following year, another death took place in San de Fuca when sister Sibella's husband, sixty-six-year old Christian Fisher, died suddenly May 7, 1924.[17] In the living room of their home, he had assured Sibella he was feeling fine, gave a goodnight and went to bed. Ten minutes later, Sibella heard a knock on the wall, hurried to check and found him dead.[18] Much of the family were there, on the island, to support her.

Harry Barrington felt his own loss eight months later when his sixteen-year old adopted son, George Morice, died suddenly of septicemia in San de Fuca.[19] Apparently healthy about a week earlier, he developed an infection and eight days later died on January 12, 1925. The only Barrington name surviving at that time from Edward Sr.'s direct line was young Billy, Hill's son.

During the early 1920s, half-sister Olivia Monroe moved closer to the family on Whidbey Island. Olivia, offspring of Edward Sr. and an Indian woman before he married Christina, kept touch with her Barrington family. She inherited a musical talent and was an excellent pianist.[20] After Olivia's husband James worked for the railroad in Spokane for years, the Monroes relocated to Seattle.

When the Hill Barringtons returned north to riverboat life in 1925, they rented Wrangell apartments in the old Mathison Building (now the Angerman Building). Hill and Mildred lived upstairs in the back, Syd and Hazel below in the back, while the front of the building was devoted to the Barrington Transportation business[21] downstairs. Above the offices, overlooking the street, general agent Andy Smith and his wife resided.[22]

Accountant Andy Smith not only kept the books for the Barringtons, but he handled their wagers too. He fielded bets from all over—in and out of town. Syd gambled at a pool hall in Wrangell as well. Longtime resident, Leonard Campbell, as a boy, recalled his mother warning him away from the hall and told him not to even *glance* inside or he would be corrupted. Of course, this only intrigued Leonard and the other boys even more.[23]

Hazel, always a standout, dressed in ruffles and vibrant colors, walked around town with her dogs. When she returned home, she often settled in the apartment window downstairs and watched the residents go by. Mildred, described as traditional, dressed more conservatively. Both were short and well-padded. Mildred cooked excellent fudge and, on occasion, sold it to residents.[24] In such a small town as Wrangell, everyone knew everyone else. Ladies in the upper social strata opened their homes on certain days, taking calling cards,

Olivia Barrington Monroe as a woman. She married
James Monroe, and they had two daughters.
Credit: Courtesy of Peggy Darst Townsdin.

Barrington Transportation Company office and home
at the left, downtown Wrangell.
Credit: Courtesy of the Wrangell Museum, P 91.10.05.01.

serving tea, eating cucumber sandwiches. On these occasions they
wore midcalf afternoon dresses most purchased "Outside," with hats
and gloves. All the ladies waited to see what dress Mildred wore first[25]
before choosing their own. If the men were in town, they went to the
Elks.[26]

Townspeople did not schedule many activities in the summertime,
as most residents worked. The community played up the Fourth of
July and dances on Saturday night. Hazel was fond of inviting a
relative to visit Wrangell and stay with her during the summer, as she
had in Yukon days.[27]

If there had been any reticence toward the Barringtons when they
first arrived in town several years before, none existed by the 1920s.
Their affectionate and open personalities made them popular with
those around them. This was true, too, even on the physical side. As in
earlier days, the Barrington men were known "huggers." On meeting a
Barrington, a woman had the man's arms wrapped around her in a

friendly embrace and her face kissed. So much so, that females of that "show no affection in public" era, felt uncomfortable about the physicalness of such a greeting. Ed Arola, young resident at the time, remembered seeing Syd back in town for the new season. As he walked up the street, the ladies, on spotting him, scattered to avoid the bear-hugging captain and his warm greeting.[28]

While on the boats Syd sometimes gave another impression. Females, meeting him for the first time, drew back alarmed, actually afraid of Syd. After all, he stood tall and commanding, and he bellowed and swore at the crew as they worked.[29] Later Syd charmed these same ladies, capturing their hearts with his gentlemanly manner as he invited them up to the bridge and told them stories.

Once the Barringtons established a solid Stikine River business, there came a rhythm to their wild finances. Syd borrowed money to hire the spring crew in Wrangell. They painted the boats and got them ready. Halfway through the season with the money rolling in, Syd paid off his debts. Any plus after that the Barringtons spent on gambling, travel, gold investments and high living.[30]

During the season, the brothers earned $30,000 to $40,000 and more, per year, outside of any gambling wins or losses.[31] In the 2007 dollar market, that would be, roughly, over $400,000.[32] Quite a healthy amount in the 1920s.

The waterway, every sandbar, every riffle, proved Barrington's river. Besides miners, trappers, and tourists, the Barringtons transported big game hunters to the wild regions of the Canadian Cassiar. They arrived from all over the world—Germany, England—some with fancy rifles, some with gun bearers.[33] Kodak camera director George Eastman and singer Lauritz Melchoir[34] were a few of the more remembered American notables.[35] In 1925, cruise ships added a side trip up the Stikine to their advertising brochures, which attracted more visitors.[36]

Serious big-game hunters rode the *Hazel* boats into this hunting paradise of the Cassiar. Even as the vessels plied up and down the river, moose, mountain sheep and bear frequently appeared along the banks. When the Barringtons spotted an interesting animal, they used a robust bell with a code of signals—at anytime—to alert the passengers. One breakfast, as author R. M. Patterson said, "during the meal…it sounded for two bears, various seals fishing, and a bald-headed eagle floating downstream on a log. It was, you might say,

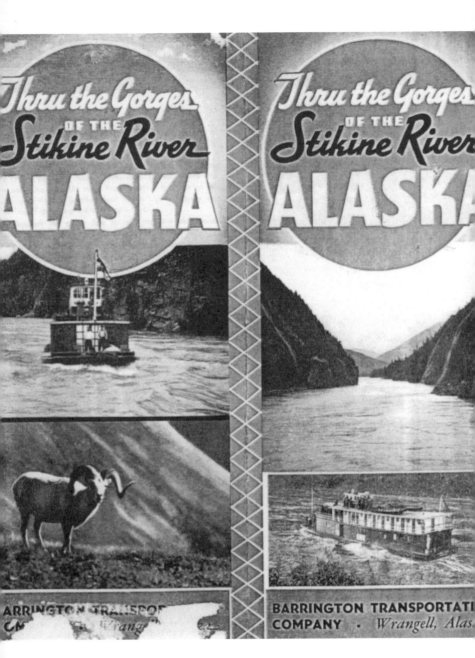

Flyer for the Barrington Transportation Company in
1930 and 1940s.
Credit: Courtesy of the Wrangell Museum.

quite a bell. What it might have done to a nervous woman with her mouth full of hot coffee I hate to think."[37]

Passengers more than enjoyed observing wild game from the deck of a *Hazel*. One reporter dryly complained it was a shame, wildlife were so prolific along the Stikine that the vessels often had to swerve to miss hitting an animal—especially out of season. "How convenient it would be during the hunting season," the reporter went on, "simply to steam up alongside prime moose and bear, tap them gently behind the ear with an oar and drag them aboard."[38]

Occasionally a passenger with an itchy trigger finger took a pot shot at a wild animal from the deck. Normally the game kept a distance and ran off, and bullets seldom found their marks.

One attempt, however, made the newspaper. On the route up the Stikine to Telegraph Creek, a Mr. Jones from Illinois spotted a huge grizzly a distance from shore. The bear prowled so far away, no one thought a kill possible. Captain Syd slowed the boat in order for Jones to take decent aim. Surprisingly to everyone, the first blast brought down the bear. Jones took the hide back home, but said no one would believe he shot an animal, regardless of the evidence.[39]

Another traveler on the *Hazel B. No. 3* was startled by the immensity of a grizzly—the size of a cow, he said—not far away on shore. The passenger remarked the boat should be equipped with a machine gun mounted on the bow "to protect itself in case of an attack."[40]

A hunting group from Wisconsin spent five weeks in the Canadian Cassiar, taking out a "bag" of brown and black bear, goat, sheep, moose, caribou and smaller game of grouse, ptarmigan, duck and coyote. One of the men stated he had often, in the past, been disappointed in a hunting area that had been highly touted. But speaking of the Cassiar region, he said, "as we leave we can truthfully say there is one sportsman's paradise that more than justifies its reputation as the greatest big game hunting ground in America."[41]

If successful hunters returned to Wrangell with game, an enterprising tanner in town processed the skins for a price. His name was Sam Jekyl, and he posted a sign on the dock which read: "Jekyl Will Tan Your Hide."[42]

Occasionally a friend from old Yukon years visited Wrangell. W.D. McLaughlin, a successful miner swapped stories of Klondike days with Syd on the *Hazel* when McLaughlin rode to the Cassiar to

Caribou antlers galore on the *Hazel B. No. 4*.
Credit: Courtesy of the Wrangell Museum, P 80.12.203.01.

look around. "Any old timer who comes this way will find Sid just the same as in the days of old," McLaughlin reported.[43]

Fellow-well-met most of the time, Syd flashed that quick and fiery temper when riled. On the flip side, it never lasted long. As mentioned, he swore at the "marking" crew and issued orders peppered with blue words. However, only two situations on the boat stirred his ill-humor toward the passengers. First, the Barringtons did not want travelers in the wheelhouse without invitation; and second, as with captains the world over, no whistling allowed on board—it was bad luck.[44]

Many years later banker Ed Rasmuson told of his blunder when he was twelve. Riding a *Hazel* boat, he whistled in the wheelhouse before the boat entered the canyon. Quickly scolded, Syd added to Hill, "If anything happens, we'll know why." Luckily they made it through without incident.[45]

• • •

1. Jean Potter, *The Flying North*. NY: The Macmillan Co., 1965, pp. 26–29.
2. "First Planes from States Arrive in Alaska Saturday." *Wrangell Sentinel,* August 19, 1920.
3. "Alaska Flying Expedition From New York to Nome Successfully Negotiates Long Journey." *The Nome Nugget,* Aug. 28, 1920.
4. Editorial: "The Air Expedition." *The Nome Nugget,* August 21, 1920.
5. "In Memory of Joseph C. Power." Untitled newspaper dated Oct. 20, 1922. Courtesy of the Coupeville Museum. Sent to author Aug. 10, 1998.
6. Copy of a letter from Bill Barrington to Peggy Darst Townsdin, Dec. 6, 1998.
7. Kent Sturgis, *Four Generations on the Yukon*. Fairbanks: Epicenter Press, 1988, p. 30.
8. "Chas. Binkley Passes Away in Seattle." *Wrangell Sentinel,* Jan. 18, 1923.
9. "School Boy Is Shot by Friend While Hunting." *Ketchikan Alaska Chronicle,* Sept. 3, 1923.
10. 1923 postcard courtesy of Peggy Darst Townsdin.
11. "President Harding Visits Wrangell." *Wrangell Sentinel,* July 12, 1923.
12. Conversation with Elna Barrington, Anchorage, August 29, 1998.
13. "Young Hunter Shot; Accident." *Alaska Daily Empire,* Sept. 5, 1923.
14. "Presidents' Biographies." *World Almanac and Book of Facts,* 1995. Mahwah, NJ: World Almanac, 1994, p. 476.
15. "Details of Death Yorke Barrington." *Petersburg Weekly Report,* Sept. 21, 1923.
16. Ibid., "School Boy Is Shot by Friend While Hunting."
17. "Death Calls Chris Fisher Wednesday." *Farm Bureau News,* May 8, 1924.
18. Peggy Darst Townsdin, *History of a Whidbey Island Family,* compiled and printed by the author, July 1994.
19. "Funeral Services for G. Barrington Jan. 14." *Farm Bureau News,* January 15, 1925.
20. Hill Sr. and Mildred Barrington tape, recorded by Eddie Barrington 9/1/1970, courtesy of relatives Marlene and Hill Barrington, III.
21. Conversation with Ken C. Mason, Wrangell, July 29, 1997.
22. Phone conversation with Bill Barrington, Anchorage, Oct. 6, 1998.
23. Phone conversation with Leonard Campbell, Wrangell with author, May 26, 1998.
24. Conversation with Ed Arola, Wrangell, Sept. 16, 1998.
25. Bill and Elna Barrington tapes, 2001–02, courtesy of relatives Marlene and Hill Barrington, III.
26. Ibid.
27. Conversation with Elna Barrington, Anchorage at her home, Aug. 29, 1998.
28. Ibid., Conversation with Ed Arola.
29. Conversation with Edith Carter and author, Juneau, Feb. 27, 1998.
30. Ibid., Hill Sr. and Mildred Barrington tapes, 9/1/1970.
31. "Seattle Man Cleans Up $150,000 on Frisco Election!" Untitled newspaper, probably a Seattle paper, undated, but most likely in 1927. Item courtesy of Peggy Darst Townsdin, Coupeville.
32. John J. McCusker, www/eh. net/hmit/ppowerusd/
33. Ibid., phone conversation with Leonard Campbell.
34. Bess Winn, "The Stikine." *Alaska Sportsman,* September 1947, p. 49.
35. "Big Game Hunters Arrive From States." *Wrangell Sentinel,* August 21, 1924.
36. "The Way We Were." *Wrangell Sentinel,* April 25, 1925.
37. R.M. Patterson, *Trail to the Interior*. NY: William Morrow & Co., Inc., 1966, p. 42.
38. Ken Neville, "Stikine and Cassiar Hotshots." *Wrangell Sentinel,* Sept. 3, 1938.
39. "Illinois Lawyer Kills Grizzly From Boat Deck." *Wrangell Sentinel,* Sept. 13, 1923.
40. "Our Trip Up the Stikine." *Wrangell Sentinel,* Sept. 13, 1917.
41. "Big Game Hunters Praise the Cassiar." *Wrangell Sentinel,* Sept. 26, 1918.
42. Anton Money, "A Voyage Up the Stikine." *Alaska Sportsman,* August 1964.
43. "M'Laughlin Enroute to the Cassiar." *The Alaska Weekly,* July 11, 1924.
44. Conversations with Betty Henning (Phoenix, 9/21/1998), Ed Arola (Wrangell, 9/16/1998), and several other people.
45. Phone conversation with Ed Rasmuson, Anchorage, Jan. 18, 1999.

15: BUILDING A NATIONAL REPUTATION

During the 1920s, one of the *Hazel*'s more permanent crews consisted of Emerson Reid[1] (who was part of the Binkley/Barrington entourage),[2] engineer; Dar (John Darwin) Smith, purser; and Jack Wilson, cook. The crew, along with whichever Barrington was captaining the boat, had a grand time. Handsome cook Jack Wilson entertained passengers with his own cache of stories. He had, after all, experienced an exciting life before signing on with the Barringtons. Besides doing a hitch with the Canadian RCMP, Wilson had been shipwrecked on a South American coast.[3] In addition, he proved an accomplished chef. Women particularly demanded his recipes—and himself, it seems. It was rumored that a number of passengers tried to lure him away to more profitable employment and more exotic lands. One lady extolled Wilson's skills in poetry:

> Our Steward was Jack Wilson
> He is a chef supreme.
> He fed us on hot apple pie
> And the best of milk and cream.[4]

Dar Smith, who grew up in Oak Harbor and took the purser's job in 1923, said no tourist went away dismayed. They asked questions, and they always received answers even if they were exaggerated or on the off side of being truthful.[5]

Years later, Alaska Historian Robert DeArmond spent time in the wheelhouse with Syd trying to record the endless, fascinating stories the captain told.[6] "I took a notebook with me," DeArmond said in a letter, "...but as soon as I started making notes, Syd stopped talking. So I put it away and didn't bring it out again."[7] No doubt Syd enjoyed building and whitewashing his stories without having them down in any concrete form.

And it was not just storytelling. The passengers found Syd fascinating to watch. He could run a boat almost automatically. Art Knutson in his book, *Sternwheels on the Yukon* (p. 63) summed it up nicely: "Since there were no microphones on the boats, a captain had to signal other ways. On watching a pilot in the wheelhouse, he would be smoking a cigarette, drinking a cup of coffee, handling the pull handles for the bells and jingles to the engine room...ringing the buzzer and gong for jack-knifing, steering the boat and telling a story, all at the same time."

Taken in hand by such unique hosts with so many tales, enthralled the passengers. "Every cabin along the banks whether hunter, trapper or deserted has a name, a pedigree and a history," one passenger said. "You get to know Chief Shakes, Dutch Charlie and Trader Larson like old friends."[8]

Leonard Campbell who grew up in Wrangell recalled, "Syd and Hill put on a real show for the passengers. When you went on the boat, you had a real experience. He [Syd] was full of baloney, spit tobacco out the window, was accomplished boatman and performer. Acted the part, put on a real show."[9] Proudly standing at the wheel, a large cigar in his mouth, he was fond of scraping a wooden match across his bottom to light it; passengers found this amusing.[10]

The yarns Syd and Hill told—or even exaggerated—thrilled the audience. A hunter said, "Our trips on the *Hazel B. 3* to and from Telegraph Creek were surely delightful and left no doubt in our minds as to why Capt. Sid Barrington's name is famous in the north."[11]

Syd, of course, stretched the truth at times, or played jokes on the passengers, just like his father. At the end of one trip, for instance, the *Hazel* drifted round a bend onto the delta area fronting Wrangell. Ahead in the early evening, only a few shore lights showed through the dusk. A passenger on the bridge told the story. "As we left the swell of the straits and picked up the first lights of Wrangell, Sid turned to his wheelhouse audience and asked, 'Anyone want to bet five bucks I can't turn on lights ashore from here?'

"We were too cagey after five days with this gambler to take him

Hill, Syd and Harry Barrington on the *Hazel B. No. 3*, Wrangell.
Credit: Winter & Pond, Alaska State Library.

up even if it looked like a good bet. Sid chuckled and yanked the whistle cord for a long blast. Immediately houses ashore lit up and one [Noland's] came ablaze, porch, windows and all.'[12]

"That's Jimmy Noland, Senator to you," Syd proudly declared.

Aside from the scenery, the animals and the storytelling, passengers trusted the Barringtons. They held a composure that comes from knowing a job inside and out, and the instincts to react instantly in a tight situation. People felt safe with them. And certainly years of experience built that self assurance.

Though riverboating was the job, gold proved the dynamic lure. As word of more enticing discoveries drifted from Canada, Syd spent less time on the river, and more time outfitting or prospecting for treasure in the Cassiar. Andy Smith managed the business from Wrangell, and Hill captained one of the fleet.

During the 1920s, the Cassiar continued as a central area for placer gold mining, seducing newcomers with newspaper headlines

Hill enjoyed the winters south, too. Here he is walking down a Seattle street.
Credit: Courtesy of Bill Barrington.

such as "Encouraging Reports From the Cassiar"[13] or "Big Gold Strike in Cassiar."[14] A hot spot in the Dease Lake district—Gold Pan Creek[15]—stirred more prospects for gold seekers. There had been a trail between Dease Lake and Telegraph Creek since 1874 when William Moore cut through.[16] Constructing a road from Telegraph Creek to Dease Lake—seventy-two miles—proved an interesting possibility. An earlier trip taking three days to cover the trail by foot could be crossed in a day by auto.[17]

Reports of "Gold!" triggered passion in everyone. On one trip up the Stikine, Syd became so enthused about what he heard that he, along with the entire *Hazel* crew, left the boat and traveled a hundred miles to stake claims.[18]

With the early growth of air transportation in Southeast, Seattle's Dease Lake Mining Company leased a Vickers Viking amphibian plane to photograph Dease gold properties for future exploration. They also arranged for the Barrington Transportation Company to haul supplies and heavy equipment up the Stikine into Canada. In addition to riverboats carrying stampeders, the plane also brought in prospecting parties during the summer.[19] This use of air travel proved one of the first in the Southeast. People speculated that permanent air travel could cut the Wrangell–Telegraph Creek run from three days to several hours.[20] Such change was bound to affect river business in the future.

The Barringtons, however, took care of "now" first. For the most part, stampeders had to use boats to ship equipment and to reach the goldfields. So sure were the brothers about the upshot in Cassiar activity, they contracted for another boat, a renumbered *Hazel B. No. 2.* Since Charles Binkley was dead, naval architect L.H. Coolidge[21] designed the new boat.

The *Wrangell Sentinel* announced the vessel would be ready in May. Syd and Hill planned on running a *Hazel* boat up river every forty-eight hours, when a rush of stampeders from all over would be flooding the Cassiar.[22] Get the business while you can, was the Barrington motto. Not only equipped for passengers and freight but, as always, the brothers added a new technology for further efficiency. They installed a Kohler electric light plant for a powerful night searchlight. Later, construction workers increased the length of the *Hazel B. No. 4,* enabling it to carry twice the freight.[23]

Because the Cassiar called loud and clear, as the next river season approached, the anxious Barringtons could not wait. They began river operations in April, a full month sooner than usual.[24] Every season it seemed, they arrived in Wrangell earlier to get a jump on the prospecting. While most of the mining interests focused on Dease Lake properties, the brothers took a gamble on another area not far away. They explored and bought on the Chutine (known locally as the Clearwater) River in British Columbia.[25] A former mining man from Nome and a friend, a Mr. Reilly, managed the property on Clearwater Creek for the men.[26]

Syd and Hill took turns prospecting.[27] Hill returned to Wrangell in October, 1926, saying: "'I have been in all of the good camps of the North and I can honestly say that I never saw a better showing in any of them than I saw on Clearwater.'"[28] The Barringtons landed their materials on the Stikine shore and then followed a trail about ten miles to their holdings. Several miles along this route, Barrington River—named after the brothers—emptied into the Chutine.[29]

Syd later told a traveler that the gold on the Chutine pocketed at bedrock and they traced it down to the pay streak. "Gold up in this country often concentrates like that," he went on, "and even though hundreds of miners have worked most of it over, there's still plenty of places where you can hit more."[30]

The main thrust for stampeders at the time, however, proved to be the Dease Lake area east of Telegraph Creek. The Canadian government, too, anticipated the rush. Though there had been no police in the Cassiar since 1892, officials decided to station Royal Canadian Mounted Police and sled dogs there for two years.[31]

Seattle's *Alaska Weekly* newspaperman Frank Cotter extolled the prospects in the Cassiar, stating 1926 as the best year since the 1880s. More men are up there than in any previous time, he wrote in an article.[32]

When one considers that Dease Creek gave up as much as fifty ounces of gold in one day with two men working with pick and shovel,[33] no wonder such news enticed miners to the area.

Like always, Syd's flamboyant instincts drove activity at the Cassiar gold diggings too. Modern equipment, that's what he needed. Efficiency, speed, keywords to success—why work with pick and shovel, when water-fed hydraulics could loosen the gold 150 times faster?[34] It worked in the Yukon. That Cassiar strike was not the same as the Klondike, but it snared those driven, career-minded miners.

After the hype of the 1926 season, Frank Cotter revised his glowing opinion to a more moderate tone. "Nothing startling has been found," he reported, "but the encouraging feature of it all is that enough has been found by practically every man who has been in the hills to take him back again next year."[35]

For those hard-core miners who spent the winter months in the mountains, they always longed for spring. "You thought you had enough [food] to go through the winter," one prospector told the *Wrangell Sentinel,* "but some long haired gent from the sticks drops in on you occasionally and by the time the snow goes off, your "cache" is empty." By March, with most of their cupboards bare as "last year's bird nest," they spent a good part of their time "sitting on a woodpile-listening for the exhaust of the *Hazel B.* Whoops, my dear, spring has CAME!"[36]

Although winter living in Seattle could not hold the kick of the Clearwater, Syd Barrington cooked up his own excitement. When off season down south, he continued as usual to gamble. A favorite haunt was *The Turf,* a card room downtown. Although Syd always fancied himself a good poker player, Edwin C. Callbreath remembered his fellow gamblers watching for Syd and always cleaning him out. Just like Nome so many years before. He never learned, and came back over and over for the slaughter.[37]

Syd and his wife were either rich or poor. Hazel proved as flamboyant as her husband. One month she would be in Seattle wearing diamond rings on every finger, all aglitter. A month later she would come back from a trip and all the gems would be out of her rings and in a pawn shop. Come money again, the jewels found their way back into their settings.[38]

If Syd could not find gold in the ground, he worked it through other sources. Election betting proved one avenue. Robert DeArmond remembered Syd telling him of making sizable wagers on one presidential election. Both Syd and Hill, as diehard Republicans, always wagered from that view.[39]

One unknown author explained Syd's procedure, and he was very systematic about taking the voting pulse of the nation.

"Sid hit upon this device [polls] as the best way to get an unbiased accurate measure of how people felt on any issue. Then he...hired a crew of trained canvassers, studied the voting results of the previous elections in the city of his choice. He then sent his men out to sample that sentiment in each precinct on the same percentage basis as the city had voted before.

"With this data compiled and analysed, Sid had a fairly good idea how the voters felt and what they would do. Then he picked his odds and laid his bets accordingly." And the author ended, "Here is a man who has covered a lot of water on the Stikine and a lot of territory all over the U.S.A."[40]

In the spring before traveling to Wrangell, Syd took bets from all over the United States that Herbert Hoover would win in November. So sure of himself, he accepted wagers well over his head. After the river season, Syd discovered Roosevelt was going to take the election by a landslide. In a wild rush of his own, the captain scurried around the country pulling his bets. In the end, he just about broke even, but it taught him a lesson: never bet the presidential elections.[41]

Seattle businessmen, however, knew Syd for his city election wagers where he won and lost many thousands.[42] The winter of 1927 Syd found a possible election pay streak in another city, San Francisco. Just political "digging" here, with pure election betting. "I never bother much with national or state politics," Syd explained, "because the average voter never gets too excited about those fights, but when it comes to city campaigns, they really get stewed up and you can get good odds."[43] He proved this statement in the Bay City.

Before going to San Francisco Syd told friend and *Alaska Weekly* editor Frank Cotter while in Seattle, "Jim Rolph is running for office, and I'm going down. If Jim says he has a chance, I'm going to string the bank roll right on his nose and after the election the missus and I may take a little swing around to New York and points east, just timing our schedule to land back here in the spring in time for the breakup."[44]

Syd gathered some advanced knowledge. "I sent my agent down here [Seattle]. He made all the preparations. I did not leave Wrangell, Alaska, my home, until October 8. Most of the work had been done by then.

"My agents came down here and at once began to make a survey of public opinion.

"We sent out some 20,000 letters to voters, seeking an expression of opinion. We did not ask them to tell us who they would vote for; we merely asked who, in their opinion, would be elected.

"I don't know how many replies we got, but we heard from at least 10,000 persons, representing every walk of life."[45]

Syd Barrington with wild mountain goat baby. (Date and location unknown.)

Credit: Courtesy of Bill and Elna Barrington.

After the Wrangell season, Syd, Harry,[46] Hazel and Boston bulldog "Dandy," and James Ketchum, and probably others, sailed to San Francisco before the voting. Syd's gambling paid off, and he cleaned up $150,000 in San Francisco that winter. Knowing Syd steamboated on the Yukon years back, and had old-time friends there, Cotter went on in a newspaper article, "The north is filled with old-timers who will be tickled to learn that Sid Barrington has taken the wise ones into camp down in Frisco. In many a log cabin on unknown creeks they will chuckle and say, 'Darn Old Sid, I knowed if he got a break, he'd clean that gang and now he's went and done it.'"

The opposition questioned Syd about gaining knowledge illegally during the voting, but he denied the assumption, and nothing was ever proven.[47] A rumor spread through the Bay area that the ballot machines had been opened during the election, so that Barrington had advanced knowledge of the results. Syd denied all allegations, easing through that difficulty with his honor still intact.

The following March, Syd and Hazel spent some of their winnings on trips to New York and other cities on the eastern seaboard.[48] Several years later, in hopes that Syd had not got the "goat" of the San Franciscans, and to prove he harbored no hard feelings, he presented a real Alaska goat to the Fliesacher Zoo in the Bay area.[49]

The popularity of the Barringtons and the Stikine River trip spread word-of-mouth by regional, national and international passengers carried on the *Hazel* boats. The spectacular scenery, the great Barrington personalities and the good food, all made the trip an outstanding experience.[50]

During the mid-1930s, Juneauites Carol and Trevor Davis took Barrett Willoughby on their boat, the *Cordelia D*, for a daytrip south of the capital city. Here she poses in front of a private, abandoned cabin in the area. Her pose, and the sign, give an idea of the independent character of Willoughby. *Credit: Courtesy of the Connie Davis Collection.*

While Hill remained an equally important figure in the Stikine operation, it was the flamboyant promoter Syd who continued as focus for most of the publicity. Several magazines printed articles about him, the *Pacific Motor Boat Magazine,* for one.[51]

During the 1920s an Alaska/California author Barrett Willoughby fashioned her own facts and fiction around the Barringtons and their Stikine operation, as well as planning a boat excursion up the river. Her enthusiasms about Syd appeared in the October 1928 issue of *American Magazine* under the title, "Champion White Water Pilot of the North." Later much of the article was reprinted in her book, *Gentlemen Unafraid,* published in 1928.

Rumor has it that in her fiction novel, *River House,* Willoughby created the hero as a Hill/Syd character. In the book, the heroine (Denise Keith) fell in love with a "reckless and daring"[52] river captain (Rev Bourne) who plied up and down the Stikine River. The book flap described Bourne as "captain and owner of the river boat, *Stikine Maid...*He was reckless and a born gambler, but he was respected and liked. He could run white water better than any river man in the North."[53]

A friendship grew between the Barringtons and Willoughby, and she visited them in Wrangell and Seattle. Petite and pretty, with daringly bobbed hair, Willoughby reveled in romance. And her independent personality had quite an impact on the Barrington females. A known flirt, Willoughby played up to Syd, and probably Hill also, which grated on Hazel. She most definitely did not like other women claiming the spotlight or her husband's attention. Because of this, Hazel did not enjoy having Willoughby around.[54]

When the book *River House* came out in 1935, no doubt Hazel read a copy. Being possessive of Syd, and knowing he was in part hero of the book, feelings of jealousy must have pricked even deeper, especially when book heroine Denny described Captain Bourne, "Yet she stood looking at the slim river man before her—insolent and powerful and sure of himself; his dark-gold hair sweeping back from his face; his eyes that could change like water under the wind; his bold nose that just escaped being predatory; his lips that held kindness and a hint of cruelty. He was ugly. He was beautiful. He was the Stikine with all its wild charm, its ruthlessness, its bounty. He was something that made life full and marvelous and intense."[55]

On the other hand, and perhaps in a secretly contrary way, Hill's wife, Mildred, in spite of her social mind set, took another view. She admired

Willoughby's confidence, her disdain for convention. At a time when skirts and pumps dressed the ladies, Willoughby wore jodhpurs and boots.

Once the author scheduled for the cruise to Telegraph Creek, the four Barringtons accompanied her. Quietly and on an impulse, Mildred bobbed her luxuriant waist-length hair. And, quite shockingly, she stepped aboard the *Hazel* outfitted in jodhpurs and boots.

Imagine Hill's reaction, seeing his steady, conservative wife, beautiful hair gone, dressed like a man! He exploded with fury. Before the trip had finished the first day, Mildred's boots and pants flew over the railing into the roiling Stikine River.[56]

Hill's instant reaction proved a temporary explosion, however. For the Hill Barrington family became great friends with Willoughby and visited her in California at her San Carlos home.[57]

Hazel may have balked from Willoughby's visits, but she did love entertaining other people in Seattle. Hill's son, young Billy Barrington remembered visiting Hazel on Queen Anne Hill. Sometimes he spent enjoyable winters with them while going to school there in later years. It was then he noticed Hazel's secret habit. She stashed little gin bottles under the cushions in the living room, in a shoebag in the bedroom, and in a vanilla bottle attached to the rubber tree in the sun room. That way she could have a secret nip whenever the urge came upon her. Once in a while, Bill admitted, he dipped into the stash himself.[58]

· · ·

1. R.M. Patterson, *Trail to the Interior,* NY: William Morrow and Co., 1966, p. 222.
2. Kent Sturgis, *Four Generations on the Yukon.* Fairbanks: Epicenter Press, 1988, p. 28.
3. "Jack Wilson Passes Away in Seattle." *Wrangell Sentinel,* June 1, 1962.
4. "Cassiar Prospector Writes From Gold Pan Creek." *Wrangell Sentinel,* Aug. 19, 1932.
5. Phone conversation with Darlynne Gendreau, Dar's daughter, Sept. 10, 1998, Ketchikan.
6. Bob DeArmond, "Riverboat Journey up Stikine with Capt. Barrington Like Nothing Else in This World." *Alaska Weekly* reprinted from the *Wrangell Sentinel* July 23, August 6, 1954.
7. DeArmond letter from Sitka to the author, March 14, 1998.
8. Author unknown. "Sid Barrington." Written about 1952. Letter given to the author from Robert DeArmond, March 1998.
9. Phone conversation with Leonard Campbell, Wrangell, with the author, May 26, 1998.
10. Phone conversation with Edwin Callbreath, Seattle, with the author, July 15, 1998.
11. "Big Game Hunters Praise the Cassiar." *Wrangell Sentinel,* Sept. 26, 1918.
12. Ibid., author unknown. "Sid Barrington."
13. "Encouraging Report From the Cassiar." *Wrangell Sentinel,* July 30, 1924.
14. "Big Gold Strike in Cassiar." *Wrangell Sentinel,* Sept. 11, 1924.
15. "S. Barrington Builds for Gold Rush Trade." *Farm Bureau News,* Feb. 19, 1925.
16. *The Stikine River.* Anchorage: Alaska Geographic Society, 1979, p. 29.
17. "Much Activity in the Cassiar." *Wrangell Sentinel,* May 15, 1924.
18. "Big Gold Strike in Cassiar." *Wrangell Sentinel,* Sept. 11, 1924.
19. Jim Ruotsala, *Pilots of the Panhandle.* Juneau: Seadrome Press, 1997, pp. 24–25.

20. "Wrangell a Probable Base." *Alaska Weekly,* June 1, 1928.
21. "Magnificent New Boat for the Stikine River." *Wrangell Sentinel,* Jan. 29, 1925.
22. Ibid.
23. "More Travel Is Anticipated." *Alaska Weekly,* April 20, 1928.
24. "Stikine River Navigation Records Broken." *Wrangell Sentinel,* April 22, 1926.
25. "Capt. Hill Barrington is Enthusiastic Over Clearwater Prospects." *Wrangell Sentinel,* October 7, 1926.
26. "George Ball of the Cassiar, Comes South." *Alaska Weekly,* May 18, 1928.
27. Conversation with Bill Barrington, Anchorage April 11, 1998.
28. Ibid., "Capt. Hill Barrington is Enthusiastic Over Clearwater Prospects."
29. "Lower Stikine River Recreation Map." British Columbia Ministry of Forests, Dec. 1997.
30. Ibid., author unknown. "Sid Barrington."
31. "Royal Canadian Mounted Police for the Cassiar." *Wrangell Sentinel,* June 17, 1926.
32. "Latest News From the Cassiar Goldfields." *Wrangell Sentinel,* June 17, 1926.
33. Ibid., "Much Activity in the Cassiar."
34. Ibid.
35. "Frank J. Cotter, Returning from the Cassiar District, Is Optimistic As Ever About Camp." *Alaska Weekly,* October 15, 1926.
36. "Navigation on Stikine Opens This Week." *Wrangell Sentinel,* May 12, 1927.
37. Phone conversation with Edwin C. Callbreath of Seattle, July 15, 1998.
38. Conversation with Bill Barrington, Anchorage, April 11, 1998.
39. Phone conversation with Ed Rasmuson, Anchorage, Jan. 18, 1999.
40. Ibid., author unknown. "Sid Barrington."
41. Letter from Bob DeArmond in Sitka to author, March 14, 1998.
42. "$150,000 Won Betting on Election." *Seattle Post-Intelligencer,* Nov. 17, 1927.
43. Ibid., author unknown. "Sid Barrington."
44. Frank Cotter, "Meet Sid!" No newspaper title, probably *Alaska Weekly,* Nov. 27, 1927.
45. "Seattle Man Cleans Up $150,000 on Frisco Election!" No newspaper title, probably a San Francisco paper, undated, probably November, 1927.
46. "San de Fuca Notes." *Island County Times,* Jan. 6, 1928.
47. "Barrington Wins Big Bet San Francisco Election." *Wrangell Sentinel,* Nov. 24, 1927.
48. Untitled article. *Alaska Weekly,* March 9, 1928.
49. "Sid Barrington Recovers His Goat." *The Alaska Weekly,* June 24, 1932.
50. Untitled article. *Alaska Sportsman,* March 9, 1928. It is interesting to note that one cook on the river baked only layer cakes. Since the boat rolled, the cook could match the finished thin side from the layer pan with the thick side from the other layer pan for a perfect looking cake when decorated.
51. "Capt. Barrington of the Stikine is Subject of Magazine Article." *Pacific Motor Boat Magazine,* January 1933.
52. Nancy Warren Ferrell, *Barrett Willoughby: Alaska's Forgotten Lady.* Fairbanks: U. of Alaska Press, 1994.
53. Barrett Willoughby, *River House.* NY: Triangle Books, 1935, 1936, book flap.
54. Ibid., conversation with Bill Barrington.
55. Ibid., Barrett Willoughby, p. 388.
56. Conversation with Elna Barrington, Anchorage, August 29, 1998.
57. Phone conversation with Bill Barrington, Anchorage, Oct. 6, 1998.
58. Interview with Bill Barrington, Anchorage, April 11, 1998.

16: LURE OF THE CASSIAR

The Barrington business had long been a faithful transport company, keeping a constant schedule on the Stikine. Hill ran one vessel of the *Hazel* fleet, while Captain Ed Kalkins[1] commanded another. An accident in February 1932, turned out to be an opportunity instead of a tragedy.[2]

A mysterious fire outside Wrangell[3] destroyed the *Hazel B. No 2*. No one seemed to know the cause. Since the *No. 2* was the largest, best equipped of the vessels, the first thought was to replace it. And replace it they did, but certainly not "as was."

Anyone close by could almost hear the Barringtons rubbing their hands together in anticipation. Upgrading, the joy of boat owners. Here was the excuse…er, the need…to fill a void with the very latest in boat advancements. The brothers took a breath, cast a fond thought to Binkley and arranged for the new boat. The Seattle Marine Construction Company built the modern renumbered *Hazel B. No. 2* vessel, which slid off the ways in mid-May.[4] This was the Barringtons' new toy.

Top of the line, the riverboat reflected all the great improvements devised over the years, everything literally from bow to stern. Even the engine room glowed with pride. A passenger remarked, "The motors are incased to void fumes and odor, and the engine room floor laid with patterned linoleum. The engine room is as cool and neat appearing as any other part of the ship."

One-hundred feet in length overall, two 135-horsepower engines[5] powered the boat—the first oil-generated diesels in the *Hazel* fleet.[6] At the shipyards, the boat received special attention, for Syd designed it to

Spanking clean engine room of the *Hazel B. No. 2* (renumbered). On the left is Emerson Reid, and next to him is Ken Neville. (Location and date unknown.)
Credit: Bill and Elna Barrington Collection.

Hazel B. No. 2 in the harbor. Syd and Hill are at the wheelhouse.
Credit: Courtesy of the Wrangell Museum P 80.112.03.72.

The Hazel B. No. 3 at Jackson's Landing on the Stikine River. That's Syd leaning on the wheelhouse door. Photo taken in the fall of 1926.
Credit: Courtesy of Peggy Darst Townsdin.

contain all the innovations developed in his thirty-some years of battling white water rivers.[7] "She is a darlin," stated Syd. "She'll go over sand bars like an eel.[8] I never held a wheel on a ship that handled like this one…She's got the speed of a caribou calf, and from the way she sits on the water I think I could take her overland on a heavy dew."[9]

Supervising every step, Syd remained in Seattle until workers finished the vessel. Imagine his pride when he ran up the coast and sailed into San de Fuca where his eighty-four-year-old mother and relatives waited. A rejoicing crowd met the *Hazel,* and the gathering ate dinner at Christina's house soon after. Catching the tide, the boat slid away from port at three o'clock in the morning for the final leg to Alaska.[10] No record of this ocean trip exists, but there might have been some challenges for Syd as he navigated a flat-bottomed vessel through saltwater seas of the Inside Passage.

With Hill captaining one of the boats on the Stikine, Syd and often Harry focused on developing their gold properties in British Columbia.

Sister Sibbie Fisher traveled north to Wrangell in 1934 and cooked for the men mining Barrington diggings in the Cassiar.
Credit: Courtesy of Peggy Darst Townsdin.

There was always new, up-to-date equipment. The latest was a caterpillar dragline scraper powered by a diesel engine. Ten men kept the work going.[11] Even sister Sibbie Fisher took part, as she cooked one summer for the mining men on the Clearwater property.[12] With a crew doing the actual labor, Hazel and Syd, he now fifty-seven, took more time to sail south during the summertime.[13] Not to laze around, but to promote. Wheel and deal. Keep an eye out for opportunities—distant gold strikes as well.

Into the 1920s and 1930s the seasonal aspect of the job continued to offer time to explore other regions for gold. When the Stikine opened in the spring, the brothers arrived. Come winter and a frozen river, they often headed for other properties. All told, the Barringtons owned gold claim holdings in Alaska, the Yukon, British Columbia and California.[14]

Syd continued traveling the west coast on various projects. First priority, keeping his gold "antennae" tuned to any new strikes. For example, a University of Southern California mining graduate uncovered a secret gold deposit while digging on Soledad Mountain near the Mohave Desert in California. When word leaked out the following months, it ignited a 1935 stampede. Syd caught the rumor, took action immediately, and put men on the ground driving a tunnel.[15]

The *Alaska Weekly* later reported on the venture. "Sure, [Barrington said] I took in that stampede as long as I was down there. Lots of stories of big purchases and I grabbed off a bunch of volcanic rock along with the rest of them and spent the winter trying to locate pay ore, but I didn't lay up much money. Guess I've been too long in the North to ever be a good 'desert rat.'

"Some of the boys down there have some pretty good showings, but they sure earn what they get. I staked some ground and drove some

Syd mining in the Cassiar up the Stikine River.
Credit: Courtesy of Peggy Darst Townsdin.

tunnels, but we didn't connect up with the pay, so I figured that the water would be running in the Stikine pretty soon, and I know a country up North that has all of California lashed to the mast..."[16]

Without question, a mutual love existed between Barrington and the Cassiar. Ever the prospector and gambler, Syd held high hopes for northern diggings, especially with the new, higher gold prices.[17] Whereas gold topped at about $20 per ounce into the 1920s, the rate sprang to $35 in the 1930s, pointing added focus to gold exploration.[18]

Headquarters for the family in the south, remained in San de Fuca where Christina lived—Auntie Chris as most people called her. Grandson Bill remembered her at home, her gray hair woven into a long braid down her back, reclining on a Victorian settee with an afghan thrown over her legs.[19] Though still active, reports of her periodic illnesses appeared in San de Fuca newspaper items.[20]

It was clear from notes in the Whidbey *Island County Times* newspaper, that even the wandering Barringtons spent more time in Washington than in previous years. The brothers, still rugged, felt age

Possibly Syd driving, with Harry next to him,
enjoying the Seattle scene.
Credit: Courtesy of Peggy Darst Townsdin.

creeping up on them. Harry, with his wife Kate,[21] made their home in
San de Fuca, near their mother. Perhaps because he was oldest, he felt
responsible for the family, as he spent more time down south than the
other brothers.[22] Besides running boats up the Stikine and prospecting
on the Clearwater, Harry piloted boats in the Puget Sound area. Active
in the San de Fuca community, Kate Barrington frequently hosted or
attended dinner parties, bridge parties, the Thimble Club and other
activities. In the mid-1930s, however, Kate passed away.

Always considerate, Harry occupied each day during the winters
after that caring for his widow friends by hauling their groceries,
filling their wood boxes or driving them on errands. When asked about
his health in later years, he always said, "I'm damn near dead."[23] But
he certainly proved himself not "dead" enough to remain a widower.
Several years after the passing of his first wife, Harry wedded Dora
Grasser Arnold.[24]

Though Hill traveled to California at times, he still spent many winter months in Oak Harbor. Hill, more settled than Syd, felt comfortable there, and of course young Bill attended school. With a mere five miles between his home and San de Fuca on Whidbey, Hill, Mildred and Billy often visited between the two towns. There breathed in Hill a streak of gypsy, as he always rented, never bought a house in any community.[25]

When in Seattle, Syd and Hazel enjoyed their lovely Queen Anne home, continuing to welcome out-of-town and Seattle friends. It was a setting for socializing, for talking business. At one New Year's Eve party, more than 100 guests attended, entertained by a live orchestra in an alcove just off the living room. Jack Wilson, chef on one of the *Hazel* boats,[26] supervised a supper in the solarium during the evening.

The Stikine out of Wrangell, however, still held the main business focus for the Barringtons. Along with the goldfields nearby. Occasionally the Cassiar gave up a surprise, as it did for Alice and Vern Shea.

Late in the Wrangell River season 1937, Hill Barrington captained the *Hazel B. No. 3* running down from Telegraph Creek. On board, coming out from their diggings on Muddy River rode the Sheas. No doubt broad smiles stamped their faces, for in their possession—and they enjoyed showing it around—was a gold nugget weighing fifty-three ounces. Nearly three and one-half pounds! Almost $1,900 at the time, in one, lone chunk (worth about $45,000 in today's gold market). A *Wrangell Sentinel* reporter described the nugget as over seven inches in length, four inches in width and about one and one-half inches thick. Something like a small book, but irregular in shape.

Hill Barrington's mouth dropped open on seeing the slab—no one could believe the size. The nugget had slid around, been stepped on, seen but unseen, among rocks on the creek bank within six feet of Sheas' sluice boxes. "I had walked over and around it for weeks," Shea told the reporter. "It lay exposed on the gravel, but on account of its size escaped notice for it did not look real. All the rocks of the creek bed glisten and shine and the nugget seemed just like one of the many colored rocks."[27] What secret clue urged Vern to examine the "rock" closer can only be imagined.

The Sheas weren't the only ones who made a strike. During the same period, miner Percy Peacock panned out $7,000 with pick and shovel[28] also from the Boulder Creek area. The news drew prospectors and fired up Syd Barrington. No real stampede into the country, the *Alaska Weekly* stated, but quite a number of experienced men worked the district.[29]

The new gold value and the heavy pay sacks surfacing from the

Cassiar urged Syd Barrington to buy more claims. Partnered with Joseph Walsh,[30] Syd added placer leases in the McDames area of the Cassiar to his properties, paying $85,000. Then, as was his habit, he hauled in seventy-five tons of mining equipment,[31] some shifted from his Clearwater properties.[32] He was willing to gamble on any place that showed color.

Syd raved to a Seattle reporter about his plans for the 1938 summer season, his very words vibrating excitement: "You're liable to see a big mining camp spring up there in the next year, and if it does, this is one place where I am going to be in on the ground floor...I'm taking in a good, big diesel powered 'cat' equipped with a bulldozer and that's the 'baby' to move dirt with in there...I'm also taking in a portable sawmill—we have lots of timber there, and I want to cut plenty for sluice boxes, flumes and camp buildings. I'm taking a short wave radio to keep communication with the Outside...we can ship perishables and mail by plane..."[33]

As always, Syd drew upon the latest in technology, communication and transportation. He figured if you could pile up money with simple handmade methods, you could amass a lot more using up-to-date machinery.

Hiring others to help captain the Barrington fleet[34] along with Hill,[35] Syd took personal charge of the claims. He sent a pack train of sixty-two horses ahead, and then he and three other men left for Boulder Creek in May.[36] Finally running back down to Wrangell the end of August, a tired Syd sprouted a fiery beard like his father's.[37] In time, the Barringtons proved the Boulder site excellent ground.

It was at this time a global issue came into play. For twenty years, developers had talked of the United States building an International Highway from the States through Canada to Alaska. For national security reasons, Canada pushed away the idea.[38] However, because of a possible European war and continued rumors of Japanese interest in the U.S. West Coast, pro-and-con voices grew in volume. Finally there seemed no choice. The highway had to go through. With that in mind, engineers from both countries hiked east of the Cassiar in British Columbia,[39] and completed preliminary survey work. The end plan, eventually to connect up a series of civilian air fields linking the U.S., Canada and throughout the Northwest.[40]

While these military/civilian plans took form, aviation in a commercial sense affected Barrington business. At first airplanes from

Hazel B. No. 2 under power.
Credit: Courtesy of Wrangell Museum, P80.12.03.78.

Atlin, Canada added traffic to Stikine river movement,[41] carrying in men and equipment to the Boulder/Muddy River sections of the Cassiar. The Barringtons knew these changes were taking place.[42] After all, aircraft now delivered mail, transported prospectors into Cassiar country and big-game hunters into the wilderness. Without a doubt, the swiftness of planes drew passenger and cargo service from slower river travel.

The Barringtons, nonetheless, continued making money as the riverboats chugged up the Stikine with heavy equipment not handled by lighter aircraft. Many passengers and tourists, too, were not ready to give up the scenery or the experience of a *Hazel* ride, whether the trip took longer or not. If the brothers groused about air competition, no one recorded it. For when necessary, they used air travel themselves.

A surprise awaited bookkeeper A.W.H. Smith in July when he was belatedly awarded the Military Cross for his outstanding service during World War I. Aboard the Canadian Pacific liner *Princess Alice* in Wrangell harbor, with Hazel, Mildred, Hill and Louise Smith looking on, Canadian legislative officials presented the cross in military fashion, "in the name of the King." Officials had tried to present the medal years sooner, but time and opportunities had passed by.[43]

Harry Barrington mining in the Cassiar.
Credit: Courtesy of Peggy Darst Townsdin.

A proud Syd Barrington displays 50 ounces of gold nuggets from his Boulder Creek property, fall of 1939.
Credit: Courtesy of Alaska Magazine.

Meanwhile, that summer of 1938 Whidbey Island citizens honored the Barrington matriarch, Christina Power, who had resided on Whidbey longer than any other living person.[44] Festivity planners organized a skit, a wedding reenactment, and a white elephant sale presided over by Harry Barrington.[45]

The timing for Christina's spotlight proved fortunate. A few months later, on December 16, 1938, after a short illness, this pioneer passed away at her home in San de Fuca. Her death occurred only a few days shy of her ninety-first birthday on Christmas. Interment took place in the family plot of Lake View Cemetery in Seattle. Thought of as "The First Lady of Whidbey Island,"[46] Christina experienced, the *Island County Times* reported, the Puget Sound area growth from a wilderness with canoe transportation to the present state.[47]

Sibella carried on in her mother's spirit after Christina's death.

Delighted with entertaining, the Fisher house often reverberated with laughter and debates as the family gathered in San de Fuca. Great-granddaughter, Peggy Darst Townsdin, remembered her dad speaking of "Bucket-of-Blood" evenings, the fond name applied to Sibella's home during her famous bean dinner entertainments.[48] As in Christina's time, the relatives enjoyed a good squabble—arguing loudly and often, which they all considered good fun. When the evening was over, each forgot any differences and left in the warmest humor.

The brothers returned north the following spring. Low water in the Stikine proved a problem, as one of the *Hazels* had to line nineteen times in a two-mile stretch.[49] The son of an old friend arrived in Wrangell during the 1939 season. Young Charles "Jim" Binkley, traveled up from California and helped crew—and party—with Hill for a summer.[50]

In spite of Cassiar excitement, not all were miners and heavy loads the summer of 1939, for Hill also carried lighthearted sightseers on the *Hazel B. No. 2.* While the ship was "loaded to the guards with freight," as one reporter stated, "and headed across the salt chuck for the mouth of the Stikine River like a hog going to war," it also carried "distinguished representatives of pulchritude and conviviality"—of whom Mildred Barrington, Andy Smith's wife Louise, and Doris Barnes (later to become an Alaska senator) were three. Meeting the boat at Telegraph Creek, going out, were "Capt. Harry Barrington and Ed Merrifield, with gold in their teeth and pockets, returning to civilization to enjoy the fruits of their labors."[51]

While they kept the river boats running on the Stikine, again Syd and Harry[52] concentrated on mining operations, keeping the high gold price in mind.[53] Besides prospectors, government men also headed up the Stikine—some to explore Boulder Creek, others to complete preliminary survey work for the international highway.[54]

What excitement in August! Imagine the astonishment when the Wrangell post office received a placer gold shipment *mailed* from the Barrington/Walsh Boulder operation. The sack, sent as registered mail with stamps at $36, headed for the Canadian mint at Vancouver. Valued at $18,000, the postmaster thought it best to secure the shipment in the Bank of Wrangell until a steamer sailed south after the weekend.[55] Just in case.

A proud, exhilarated Syd Barrington followed the gold shipment down the Stikine a month later. On arrival, he displayed a pan with fifty ounces of gold nuggets, which eventually sat in the Wrangell Bank front window.[56] Value of the nuggets ranged from $5 to $75 each. All told, Syd took out $70,000 in nuggets from Boulder Creek during the season.[57] In today's gold market that would be roughly $1.7 million.[58]

The riches did not come easy. Syd told the *Wrangell Sentinel* the operating schedule Barrington and Walsh had followed at the claim, and the paper reported, "Since last July they have worked a crew of 14 men, including two cooks, in two shifts, work beginning at 4 o'clock in the morning and the last men turning in at 10 o'clock at night. Sundays and all.

"The weather in the high mountain valley...has been unpleasant. After cleanup on Tuesday of last week when icicles four feet long hung off the wash machine, the sun began shining."[59] Barrington said they could have continued operations, but the mining machines needed rest and maintenance—and so did the exhausted crew.

Perhaps Syd's sixty-odd-year-old frame pressed down more heavily on his bones just then. For instead of swooping up his wife, traveling during the winter months and spending his money, all Syd could think about at that point was rest.

After slaving all winter and summer, what was he planning for the long months in Seattle? Nothing much, he told a reporter, except sit by the fireplace and talk to his wife. It would be a stay-at-home winter, with none of the usual trips.[60] At least that's what he said just then.

But this easy winter living on the West Coast did not reflect the troubles stirring in the rest of the world. About the same time Syd headed south, far across the continent and the Atlantic Ocean, German soldiers invaded Poland. Although Wrangell held a far corner from this crisis, the invasion soon meant more contracts for the brothers and added work up the Stikine. Defense projects would presently infuse the Barrington Transportation Company and the waning river industry with energy.

• • •

1. Phone conversation with Carolyn Steele in Oklahoma with author, July 1, 1999.
2. "Fire Destroys Stikine River Boat, Hazel B." *Wrangell Sentinel,* Feb. 5, 1932.
3. "107 Years of Stikine Riverboating." *The Stikine River.* Anchorage: Alaska Geographic Society, 1979, p. 59.
4. "Barrington Has New Boat for Stikine Travel." Petersburg Press, May 28, 1932.
5. Gordon Newell (Ed.), *The H.W. McCurdy Marine History of the Pacific Northwest.* Seattle: The Superior Publishing Co., 1966, p. 417.
6. "*Hazel B. No. 2* Heading for White Water." *Alaska Weekly,* May 20, 1932.
7. "Barringtons Close 19th Season on Stikine Riv." *Wrangell Sentinel,* Oct. 26, 1934.
8. "Capt. Barrington of the Stikine Is Subject of Magazine Article." *Wrangell Sentinel,* Feb. 10, 1933.
9. Ibid., "*Hazel B. No. 2* Heading for White Water."
10. "Barrington Sails *Hazel B.* to San de Fuca." *Island County Times,* May 20, 1932.
11. "Barringtons Will Work Clearwater Placers." *Wrangell Sentinel,* April 21, 1933.
12. Alaska Picturesque Souvenir Book, mailed from Wrangell Oct. 13, 1934. Courtesy of Peggy Darst Townsdin, Coupeville.

13. "San de Fuca Notes." *Island County Times,* July 1, 1932.
14. Lancaster Pollard, *A History of the State of Washington: Vol. III.* NY: The American Historical Society, Inc., 1937, p. 66.
15. "Barrington Is Interested in Mojave Strike." *Alaska Weekly,* Dec. 13, 1934.
16. "Sid Barrington No 'Desert Rat.'" *Alaska Weekly,* April 12,1935.
17. Ibid.
18. Kitco Inc.-Historical London PM Gold Fix, 1833 - Present. Kitco Inc., database. August 10, 1998.
19. Copy of letter from Bill Barrington to Peggy Darst Townsdin, Dec. 6, 1998.
20. "San de Fuca Notes." *Island County Times,* Oct. 21, 1937.
21. Ibid., Alaska Picturesque Souvenir Book.
22. Conversation with Bill Barrington, Anchorage, April 11, 1998.
23. Copy of letter to Peggy Darst Townsdin, Dec. 6, 1998.
24. Phone conversation with Bill Barrington, Anchorage, Dec. 16, 1998.
25. Conversation with Bill Barrington, Anchorage, April 11, 1998.
26. "Barringtons Entertain At New Year's Eve Party." *Alaska Weekly,* Jan. 6, 1933.
27. "Vern Shea Finds 53 Ounce Nugget in Gold Discovery on Alice Creek." *Wrangell Sentinel,* Sept. 24, 1937.
28. "Captain Barrington Takes Modern Outfit to Boulder." *Alaska Weekly,* April 8, 1938.
29. "Barrington Takes Outfit Into Boulder." *Alaska Weekly,* June 17, 1938.
30. "Fourteen Passengers Leave for Telegraph." *Wrangell Sentinel,* June 9, 1939.
31. Gold and Galena. Mayo, Yukon: Mayo Historical Society, 1990, p. 465–66.
32. "Barrington and Walsh Buy Placer Lease from Peacock, Wheaton." *Wrangell Sentinel,* August 26, 1938.
33. Ibid., "Captain Barrington Takes Modern Outfit to Boulder."
34. "Navigation on Stikine Opens Soon." *Wrangell Sentinel,* May 5, 1939.
35. "Captain Barrington Says First Trip 'Not Too Bad.'" *Wrangell Sentinel,* May 19, 1939.
36. "Largest Pack Train in Years Leaves Telegraph for Muddy R." *Wrangell Sentinel,* June 10, 1938.
37. Ken Neville, "Stikine and Cassiar Hotshots." *Wrangell Sentinel,* August 26, 1938.
38. Stephen Haycox, *Alaska: An American Colony.* Seattle: U. of Washington Press, 2002, p. 263.
39. "Wrangell May Profit If Big Road Is Built." *Wrangell Sentinel,* Sept. 27, 1940.
40. Ken Coates, *North to Alaska.* Fairbanks: University of Alaska Press, 1992, p. 28.
41. "Barrington Takes Outfit into Boulder." *Alaska Weekly,* June 17, 1938.
42. "Cambron Says Peacock-Wheaton Ground on Boulder Is Real Mine." *Wrangell Sentinel.* Oct. 21, 1938. "Old time miner Ben Cambron took a pack train from Dease Lake into Boulder which covered a week's time. After returning to the lake, a Fairchild plane flew in from Atlin, on the way to Boulder. When Mr. Cambron found he could make the round trip in one and one-half hours at a cost of $50.00, he promptly embarked on his first plane trip."
43. "War Medal Awarded to A.W.H. Smith." *Wrangell Sentinel,* July 29, 1938.
44. "Mrs. Christina Power to be Honored Guest in Oak Harbor Event." *Island County Times,* June 9, 1938.
45. "Daughters of Pioneers Re-Enact First Wedding." *Island County Times,* June 30, 1938.
46. Island County Historical Society of Coupeville, Wash., Sails, Steamboats and Sea Captains. 1993. [E-mail from Peggy Darst Townsdin, August 11, 2000]
47. "Rites Held for Christina Power, Whidbey Pioneer." *Island County Times,* Dec. 24, 1938.
48. Peggy Darst Townsdin, *History of a Whidbey Island Family.* Coupeville, WA: Printed by the author, July, 1994, p. 37.
49. Ibid., "Captain Barrington Says First Trip 'Not Too Bad.'"
50. Kent Sturgis, *Four Generations on the Yukon.* Fairbanks: Epicenter Press, 1988, p. 31.
51. Ibid., Ken Neville, August 25, 1939.
52. Ibid.
53. "Capt. Barrington In With Poke of Gold from Boulder; War Stymies Development." *Wrangell Sentinel,* July 26, 1940.
54. "Fourteen Passengers Leave for Telegraph." *Wrangell Sentinel,* June 9, 1939.
55. "Gold Shipped to Mint Thru Wrangell P.O." *Wrangell Sentinel,* August 25, 1939.
56. "The Sluice Box." *Alaska Sportsman,* December 1939, p. 32.
57. Barrington and Walsh Take out $70,000 Placer Gold Short Season." *Wrangell Sentinel,* Sept. 29, 1939.
58. www.eh.net/hmit/ppowersd/ – John J. McCusker, monetary comparisons.
59. Ibid.
60. Ibid.

17: THE WAR YEARS

The 1940 Wrangell River business started off at its usual tempo—with a slight diversion on the way up the Inside Passage.

Hill arrived in Wrangell the beginning of April, and Syd brought the rest of the family two weeks later. This time Hazel trailed a maid in tow.

The only family member lost along the journey was Princess, Syd's pet dog. While boarding the *Princess Norah* in Vancouver, it seems the dog slipped her leash and decided to be a tourist herself. Syd alerted the Canadian police and offered a reward. The Barrington clan continued their cruise to Wrangell on the *Norah,* "but," the *Sentinel* reported, "like the red-coated 'Mounties' get their man, the Vancouver prowl-car officers found the wandering 'Princess,'"[1] and shipped her north on the next boat. Princess, however, refused to give up the spotlight that spring, as did Hazel Barrington. A month later, with Princess attending, all Wrangell celebrated the colorful Potlatch Dance. The celebration combined modern days with the spirit of historic times. Rallying at the Alaska Native Brotherhood (ANB) Hall, 109 people donned their "potlatch blouses." The dance drew a large crowd, in part because of the notices proclaimed beforehand, "Hitler can go to Brussels, the British can go to Berlin, Queen Wilhelmina can go to London, but everybody in Wrangell is going to the Potlatch party tomorrow night at the ANB hall."[2]

The Grand March, led by former dancehall queen Hazel Barrington in bright potlatch costume, highlighted the evening. She strutted in her glory. From her arm dangled the leash of Princess, who wore a potlatch blanket. Though Hazel did not win the grand door prize, the paper stated that Princess "was awarded a special prize of dog biscuit for her poise and style."[3] "It's 'Dos-a-Dos' And Swing Your Partners At Colorful Potlatch Dance On May 18." *Wrangell Sentinel* announced May 10, 1940. What an evening! Other parties, too, followed that season, lightening the more serious business activities up river.

The 1940 season in the Dease Lake[4] area of the Cassiar, nonetheless, proved profitable for the Barringtons. In July, Syd *flew*—not sailed!—into Wrangell from Boulder Creek, hefting a poke of $12,000 in gold. "The war has put a decided damper on mining activity in Canada," the *Sentinel* reported Syd saying, "and there are few outfits operating in his section of the country, men and money being summoned to the colors."[5]

Hazel Barrington clowning around at a local party in Wrangell.
Credit: Courtesy of Betty Henning.

Rising transportation costs—$1.25 for a gallon of gas—also checked mining activity. Fewer miners prospected in the Cassiar, especially Canadians, who enlisted in the military. Canadian government money, too, marched in that direction. Syd, however, had one thing on his mind right then. Once flushed with gold, he headed back for the hills. A month later he landed back in Wrangell, another $12,000 in his poke.

The money energized Syd. He cut the season short, gathered his gear and, with Hazel, boarded the steamer *Alaska,* south. From there they traveled to New York.[6] Wheeling, dealing and gambling on the East Coast, making contacts with all that Cassiar money in his pocket, had to be high for Syd, the promoter. Winter months meant rest, travel and often business. And big-time money making—really serious money—was afoot.

Always aware of events beyond the Northwest, you can be sure the Barringtons followed every battle fought in Europe during World

Hazel Barrington and "Princess" at the Wrangell Potlatch Dance,
summer of 1940. Princess earned a Friskies cookie.
Credit: Courtesy of Betty Henning.

War II. As businessmen, too, they envisioned American military eyes
shifting to the Pacific arena. The brothers knew of increased U.S.
Navy activity along the West Coast. They, of course, were more than
watchful of the Cassiar as highway plans proceeded, not to mention
the airfield construction in northwest Alaska. They were also sure they
could tap into these good works—and the profits—someway.

The prospector side of Syd Barrington encouraged highway
activity in Canada. As a result, development would bring more men
and companies to the region, and possibly open up rich mining fields,
he told a reporter.[7] Certainly that was Syd's "now" viewpoint.

In the long run, that vision, river-wise, proved shortsighted. The
Alaskan-Canadian Highway eventually turned into a main artery for

Syd with "Bobo" the dog and one of the crews and passengers on *Hazel B. No. 4*.
Credit: Courtesy of the Wrangell Museum.

shipments in and out of the Cassiar.[8] Eventually it bypassed the Stikine River, and thus reduced waterway use in future years.

Not only that, the flavor of travel itself had shifted. By the early 1940s, beginning commercial air services flew throughout Southeast Alaska, mainly carrying mail and passengers. Larger airlines like Pan American operated on longer flights,[9] while smaller shuttle craft served between close communities like Wrangell and Petersburg.[10] During this time in Wrangell history, these air flights caused a downturn in the Barrington's Stikine activities. Not so noticeable, perhaps, because of revved up military construction.

As World War II months flew by, the U.S. and Canadian government officials focused on constructing air bases in British Columbia. These airfields, in turn, established the groundwork for building the proposed Alcan Highway, as well as possible defense for the continent if needs be. Yet freighting thousands of tons of supplies to build landing fields through a trackless wilderness proved a major problem.

Finally, Canadian officials approached the Barringtons. The

One of Hazel and Syd Barrington's favorite dogs doing some advertising for the Stikine River business.

Credit: Courtesy of Peggy Darst Townsdin.

shipping route, they said, would proceed up the Stikine to Telegraph Creek, on to Dease Lake, down the Dease and Liard Rivers and follow through to Watson Lake.[11] Could the Barringtons haul the immense amount of supplies and machinery needed?[12]

"Sure, we can do it," the brothers answered confidently. It was just the huge contract the Barringtons had been working for.

Privately, they wondered. Anxious as to whether the *Hazel B. No. 2* or *Hazel B. No. 3* could actually manage heavy burdens from Wrangell to Telegraph Creek without grounding, the brothers deliberated. They put their river knowledge together with chief engineer, Emmy Reid, who had worked as an airplane inspector during World War I.[13] A Barrington friend might well imagine the eagerness with which the three brainstormed ideas and concepts. Eventually they conceived and built the new renumbered *Hazel B. No. 1,* a shallow-draft vessel that could haul heavy loads without hitting every snag along the route.

The vessel shaped up rapidly. Especially constructed at Wrangell, this small, sturdy boat fit the bill. In the spring of 1941, the *Hazel B. No. 1* slid down the Anderson marine ways and began hauling everything from toothbrushes to oversize steam shovels.[14] The plan called for the boat to run upriver, pushing truck laden barges to Telegraph Creek. Workers then trucked materials to Dease Lake, towed them down the lake and trucked them again to Watson Lake.[15]

Wrangell hummed with the added Canadian airfield activity, resident Ken Mason remembered. "There were barrels and barrels of asphalt then, stored over by the light plant. A few barrels got to leaking. Anyway, they rolled the barrels aboard a *Hazel* barge, and up the river they went."[16]

Hill captained the first trip aboard the new *Hazel.* Lacking a radio on board, no word of progress filtered back to Wrangell, and residents worried whether the small craft could manage its heavy freight. On the third day, finally, a Telegraph Creek official wired Wrangell that the struggling *Hazel* had been spotted twelve miles down river. Hours later, Hill and the *Hazel* made port.[17] For this important beginning of the war effort, the Barringtons had done their part—and collected a packet in the bargain.

With the Japanese attack on Pearl Harbor in December 1941, an urgency to be fast and efficient vibrated along the coast at the time. The Barringtons felt this pressure, too. The task of transferring 3,500 tons of materials seemed impossible. Normally, the number of runs needed to shift that much freight could not be squeezed into a river season between breakup and freeze up. The brothers, nevertheless, kept their boats constantly on the go and finished the job in the specified time.[18]

The speed with which the Alcan Highway was completed proved astonishing. Begun in March of 1942, construction workers hacked a course through the wilderness. Engineering workers, one-third African-American soldiers, chopped and laid a 1,522-mile road in eight months.[19] The Barringtons constantly brought load after load up the Stikine, keeping the water churning to Telegraph Creek. They hauled workers and supplies to Canada as the highway tracked its muddy trail to Whitehorse and beyond.

In spite of the hectic time schedules, Stikine passenger service continued on the *Hazel* boats. Just because the Barrington boats hauled critical, heavy freight, did not mean the atmosphere had to be stodgy. There were lighter moments, too. Reporter Winifred Williams took a vacation trip to Telegraph Creek, describing the scenery, extolling the virtues of Hill Barrington and crew, who were characterizing the passengers, and narrating events aboard.

A mock wedding highlighted Williams' trip. One female passenger donned britches, fashioned a mustache of rope and became the "gloom." A 200-pound male passenger was the bride, complete with green mosquito-netting veil. Captain Hill turned his collar around and presided as minister. Acting as best man and dressed appropriately in men's clothing, Dar Smith's sister, Sue, "led the groom to the wedding bower on top deck by a rope around his (her) neck."[20] Cook Jack Wilson baked a "wedding" cake, and by the time festivities ended, the passengers lost their breath from so much laughing.

While in Wrangell itself, an actual wedding brightened the winter of '43–44. After courting a local Wrangell girl, Hill's son Bill married

Wedding photo of Bill and Elna Barrington, Wrangell, Alaska, January 23, 1944.
Credit: Bill and Elna Barrington Collection

Elna Arola on Jan. 23, 1944. Elna had known Bill Barrington in younger school years, for he spent the summers in Wrangell. Elna went away to beauty school in San Francisco after high school, but she, too, traveled to Wrangell in the summer. At the time, Bill worked for the Barrington Transportation Company as an assistant bookkeeper under Andy Smith.[21] The young couple dated over a period of several years, but Bill knew he was going to marry Elna in spite her not getting along with Mildred: It seems Elna either spoke up too much or not enough to the older future mother-in-law.[22]

When it came time for the wedding in the winter of 1944, mother Mildred was not happy her Billy was leaving her. She fussed a bit, but young love conquered all. Still Mildred made her protest. She came down with the "vapors" and attended the wedding in a wheelchair, wearing a black veil.[23] The newlyweds honeymooned on the steamer, *Princess Nora,* on their way to Skagway for Bill's U.S. Customs Service employment.[24]

Several changes occurred in the Barrington business over the winter. No records exist as to why, but several reasons might be suspected. First, the brothers were taking on added years, both into their sixties by 1940—the innards of their wheelhouses might still bubble with activity, but the hulls were losing their strength. Second, although Hill's son had worked for the river company, Bill had set his sights in another direction. And third, except for the war effort, river traffic was dying when competing with faster air travel. But there was a chance of making one more bundle, and the Barringtons went for it.

In February Syd sold a number of Stikine vessels to his brother Hill, Al Richie and Charles Early who formed the Barrington Richie and Early Company (BRE),[25] the new firm continuing to freight up the Stikine during the summer. The old Barrington Transportation

Company (in which Hill still retained membership)[26] under Syd and Smith[27] would not be doing Stikine River trips that year.[28] By the time of the Barrington Transportation business separation, changes had taken place in personnel, too. A.W.H. Smith had passed away,[29] and Emmy Reid took a job as engineer on a small ocean ship[30] but remained on the West Coast.[31]

After a short trip to Milwaukee, Wisconsin,[32] in the spring—possibly buying machinery—Syd traveled farther north in Alaska. Hazel remained in Seattle.

Barrington plans soon became public knowledge. Syd signed an army contract to transport equipment for the Galena, Alaska, airfield construction site west of Fairbanks during the 1944 season. Frantic military officials contracted air, railroad, highway and river transport to bulk up defense in western Alaska. The Galena airfield proved the lift off point for Soviet allies piloting U.S. bombers and fighters to Nome, across the Bering Sea, and on to Russian defense points.[33]

In support of Syd's contract, Al Richie ferried the 400-horsepower *Hazel B. No. 1* riverboat across the Gulf of Alaska in July, running into a storm which nearly sank the flat-bottom vessel. Richie lost an empty barge off Montague Island at the entrance to Prince William Sound, but by chugging "dead slow," the boat slipped into Seward safely. Finally cruising southwest through False Pass, Richie replaced the lost barge at Good News Bay,[34] and ultimately arrived on the Yukon River.

Syd did not care for flying, "although he has been up in everything but a kite."[35]

Nevertheless, he flew from Seattle to Fairbanks to save time, rather than ferry with Richie.[36] They later met on the Yukon.

Central Alaska throbbed with movement. Tons of airfield materials reached Nenana via the Alaska Railroad from Seward. A once-quiet wilderness stirred with activity as a mass of river craft flowed down the Yukon. Barges and boats arrived from as far east as Whitehorse, and as far south as the Stikine River,[37] assembling on the Tanana and Yukon Rivers. Mountains of equipment collected to clear the Galena airfield, as well as other sites on the lower Yukon.[38] There were rumors of possible future flooding at Galena, but few paid any attention. So desperate the need for water craft,[39] river men pressed scows fashioned from empty oil drums into service,[40] rafting them downstream with small kicker boats pushing them along.[41]

"The largest volume of freight in the history of interior navigation is moving down the Tanana and Yukon rivers during the current season, and the movement is expected to continue until the freeze-up," announced Fairbanks officials.[42]

Once the crew assembled, Syd then piloted the *Hazel* with Al Richie, Ted Sterling and others.[43] While in the Interior, no doubt Captain Syd Barrington renewed acquaintances with his old northern pals and exchanged gold rush memories (tall tales?). Evenings of nostalgia for sure.

Syd also met up with his friend's son, Charles "Jim" Binkley.[44] Like his father, Jim could never live far from white water. After crewing on the Stikine with Hill several years earlier, Binkley attended the University of Alaska on and off. During World War II, Jim joined the U.S. Army Air Force and was, in 1944, a sergeant in the transportation division stationed near Fairbanks. By then, a civilian captain had purchased the old *Hazel B. No. 2*, which navigated the Kuskokwin River. For use on the Galena project, the army gave *Hazel B. No. 2* a number—ST467.[45] Jim, one of the few army men who really knew riverboating, commanded this old vessel. No doubt with his warm connection to the Barringtons, Jim felt a strong nostalgia while at the wheel. After all, his father had indeed helped to design the boat. Actually, Jim brought his own spotlight to the boat when he helped save a life while in command. The incident happened in late fall.

The *Hazel B. No. 2* chugged upstream past Squaw Crossing where the Tanana flows into the Yukon, with a particularly dangerous, shifting current. The flow was so strong, "a chip will float faster than a man could run along the bank." Not only that, but the river silt hung heavy in the water, sifting into any object, weighing it down.

The *Hazel* butted a barge before it on which soldiers Heimdahl and Britz marked the depth of the channel with long sounding poles. Suddenly one pole stuck in the mud, throwing Britz into the water. He cried out once and then disappeared. Heimdahl saw the accident and knew it was suicide to dive in after Britz. Instead, he leaped aft and began struggling with a work boat lying on the barge deck, trying to launch it. But it was too heavy.

Binkley, on the *Hazel* pushing from behind, also observed the accident. He dashed down the steps, vaulted the rail and jumped to the barge deck. Together Heimdahl and Binkley launched the heavy work boat into the river and set off rowing downstream.

The drowning Britz bobbed to the surface, desperately trying to swim, but silt crept into every crevice of his clothing, weighing him down and pulling him under. Heimdahl and Binkley strained forward, grasped Britz, and hauled the exhausted man aboard the skiff. Struggling against the roiling current, it took the rescuers twenty minutes to row the heavy work boat back to the waiting *Hazel*.

Although the recovery action played out in about sixty seconds, the waterlogged, terrified Britz disagreed. A rescuer said Britz swore he battled the silt-laden current for hours—no less.[46]

At the end of autumn in 1944, most river craft based in the area wintered at Chena Slough. Barrington left the *Hazel B. No. 1* berthed at Nenana, in readiness for the following season.[47] Officials figured about 90,000 tons had been freighted between Nenana and Galena during the summer of that year.[48] Still the job was not finished.

That time up north decided Syd on one thing: he had to get Hill up there for the next season. Working with old friends on the Galena project, chewing over old memories, Hill was missing it all.

While in Southeast, Hill continued captaining the *Hazel B. No. 3* on its scheduled run to Telegraph Creek. Alaska Governor Ernest Gruening and his wife took the trip in the summer of 1944. How did Gruening like the voyage? someone asked Hill. "He's the first passenger I ever had on the river we couldn't get down off the pilot house at meal time," Hill answered. "He was so eager to miss nothing that we served him on top of the pilot house."[49] With courtesy to the Alaskan governor, Canadian officials flew the American flag next to the British emblem on Government House while the governor visited.[50]

As mentioned earlier, the Barringtons had sold their operations on the Stikine[51] to Al Richie. Together the two brothers had worked riverboats in the north for nearly fifty years. A last job was the fulfillment of the government airfield contract on the Yukon River, transporting the remaining 10,000 tons of freight.[52] Syd would go, of course, but this time Hill would be there also.

While Al Richie navigated the Stikine with the *Hazel B. No. 3,* both Syd and Hill traveled north the 1945 season. Together they would finish the Nenana/Galena army contract, an estimated forty boats expected to cargo the heavy freight.[53] The brothers leased the *Aksala,*[54] formerly the *Alaska,*[55] which a Canadian engineer had skippered from Whitehorse.

Jim Binkley remembered those months he spent with Hill and Syd on the *Aksala* that summer. While the Alaska Railroad, which

Hill Barrington on the dock in front of the *Aksala*, with the crew during a freight movement to the Nenana/Galena area during WWII, summer 1945.
Credit: Courtesy of Peggy Darst Townsdin.

contracted for many of the boats, was not as interested in making a profit, Syd as a private operator, was. And because the government paid the captains by the ton, Syd pushed massive loads on the three barges in front of his boat—as much as 400 tons on each. Wild, heavy loads, much more than any other captain. But, Jim said, "Syd always played the odds, and ran his riverboats the same way."[56]

The possible flood rumored for the Galena area actually did occur in the spring of 1945, literally wiping out most of the project. A massive ice dam jammed below Galena backing up the river for over twenty-four hours. It took bombs—actual bombs—from a squadron of B-17 bombers to burst the ice dam and thus drain the Galena area.[57] The disaster only temporarily halted Army construction; workers completed the job before freeze up. Although the surge of army building slowed when World War II ended August 14, 1945,[58] the conflict served as a wake-up call to Alaska's geographical importance.[59]

Completing the Galena project proved an emotional climax for the Barrington family. While the brothers finished up north, Hill's son Bill traveled to Eagle, Alaska, taking a job as customs inspector for three months. Elna and Mildred met him in Eagle,[60] and when the job was over in fall, Syd, Hill, Mildred, Elna and Bill took a boat to Dawson where they spent several days visiting old friends. It is easy to imagine what memories flooded back of those raucous Klondike days almost fifty years earlier. The sandbars, the gambling, the laughter, the fears and disasters, the wild scrambling for gold, the disappointments, the joys—all wrapped up and shared in a few days of nostalgia.

The Barrington clan then cruised to Whitehorse, and eventually traveled down the Inside Passage. For the next nineteen years, young Bill and Elna settled in Juneau, raising four children. Hill and Mildred found the young family a good excuse to visit the north country, which they did often.[61]

Age and energy took a toll on the Barrington brothers and their river operations—but not their wills! The Yukon job proved nearly the last riverboating for Hill,[62] his years numbering sixty-eight by then. Hill figured it was time for retirement, and he and Mildred took up residence in their house on Midway Boulevard[63] in Oak Harbor, Washington. At first they opened a Boat Haven and Ferry Landing facility in Keystone Harbor south of Coupeville in May of 1948.[64] At one point Hill owned a haberdashery.[65] Later he operated the Pastime pool and card room, as well as the Pioneer Motel[66] in Oak Harbor, only a few hundred yards from his own birthplace.

Syd, an active seventy, continued piloting the *Hazel B. No. 3* for Richie, mining when time permitted and spending the winter in Seattle. Newspaper accounts conflict as to whether Syd retained Hill's interest in the Barrington Richie Early company. In all likelihood, the Barringtons sold all their Wrangell interests before 1948 as one newspaper account professes, with Richie steadily paying up his share. However, a story later circulated, remembered by Ed Rasmuson, which, knowing Syd and his outrageous wagers, might be true.

When Al Richie and Syd took the *Hazel B. No. 3* up and down the Stikine during the summer of 1948, discussions about the U.S. presidential contest between Thomas Dewey and Harry S. Truman heated up the wheelhouse. On one trip, as the story goes, Syd bet his remaining interest in the BRE business on Republican Dewey, while Al Richie backed Democrat Harry Truman. Of course, history tells us Truman won. After the election returns, old-timers said it more directly: "Al Richie went up the Stikine *owing* the business, and came down, *owning* it."[67]

Although the older Barringtons relished the northern adventure, and the country provided their livelihood, Canada and Alaska were only half their home. Each found their wives in the north, and developed lifelong friendships, but Washington continued to be their home territory where their roots and descendants lived.[68] Not so for young Bill, Elna and their family, as they stayed in Alaska, and remained the touchstone for visits from their southern relatives.

At the end of the war, between prospecting and war contracts, Syd was a millionaire. Four years later, 1949, he was broke.[69] Even at a senior age, Syd the gambler, the promoter, enjoyed the high living, the power money commanded,[70] and he spent it as fast as it jingled in his pocket.

Always keeping abreast of Yukon River activities, the Barringtons no doubt read of the Alaska Railroad's intention of abandoning the riverboat service on the Yukon River in 1949. Time was yet making another change. Alaska Railroad manager, John P. Johnson said, "Too many airplanes and too few outlying gold mines were driving the picturesque but outmoded and uneconomical stern-wheelers off the river."[71] So it was that the soft, romantic profile defining the sternwheeler sharpened to the edgier lines of more efficient transport.

Once Hill Barrington retired and settled in Oak Harbor, Syd and Hazel spent several more years in their Queen Ann home.[72] Hazel no longer commuted north during the summer season in Wrangell, but remained in Seattle.[73] In 1950[74] the Syd Barringtons sold their Seattle home, and bought a house in Oak Harbor, about a block from Hill. Closer to family. Syd played pool at the Pastime, and taught pool to some of the older boys. Closer to San de Fuca now, the elder Barringtons visited and spent holidays there.[75]

Growing older, perhaps some gray in his hair, Syd's passengers in the late 1940s and 1950s still remembered red-headed Syd standing tall at the wheel, wearing his brilliant red cap,[76] with the ever-present cigar in his mouth, his rock collection lining the bridge window sills.[77] He enjoyed chewing Star[78] tobacco in addition to his famous "1886" cigars. In his senior years, he developed diabetes and was not allowed sugar—some of which was processed in the tobacco. So, Syd cut out the tobacco and chewed the cigars instead.[79]

But when he did stand in the wheelhouse, he held court there, weaving his interesting stories, making a fascinating trip even more memorable. He always spoke of the past, but planned for the future, as if life would never end.

• • •

1. "Barrington Party Arrives Here on Princess Norah." *Wrangell Sentinel,* April 19, 1940.
2. "All Wrangell Will Dance at Big Potlatch Party Tomorrow Night at ANB." *Wrangell Sentinel,* May 17, 1940.
3. "109 Blouses At Potlatch Dance; At Least 250 Are Expected Night of June 4." *Wrangell Sentinel,* May 24, 1940.
4. "Capt. Barrington to Start Summer River Operations." *Wrangell Sentinel,* April 5, 1940.
5. "Capt. Barrington In With Poke of Gold From Boulder; War Stymies Development." *Wrangell Sentinel,* July 26, 1940.
6. "Capt. Barrington Takes Out Another 371 Ounces of Gold from Boulder Creek Property." *Wrangell Sentinel,* August 30, 1940.

7. Ibid., "Capt. Barrington In With Poke of Gold From Boulder; War Stymies Development."
8. "Famed Cassiar Gold District May Get New Asbestos Mine." *Alaska Weekly,* Oct. 5, 1951.
9. "Wrangellites Soon Can Have Lunch at Cassiar; Dinner in Seattle." *Wrangell Sentinel,* April 18, 1952. Long distance air passenger travel was becoming so common and frequent, the *Wrangell Sentinel* noted that those flyers bound for Seattle can eat at Lloyd Goodrich's Cassiar Café for lunch, and dinner in Seattle that evening.
10. "Air Shuttle Service Starts In Southeast." *Wrangell Sentinel,* June 28, 1940.
11. Bess Winn, "The Stikine." *Alaska Sportsman,* Sept. 1947, p. 14.
12. The lake itself was named after Englishman, Frank Watson, who had set out for the Klondike in 1897, but gave up and settled in the Cassiar area.
13. Richard A. Ramme, "They Rule the Stikine." *Alaska Life,* February 1942, p. 10.
14. "Photo Album: The Passing of an Era…" *Alaska Life,* April 1948, pp. 22–23.
15. Phone conversation with Leonard Campbell, Wrangell, with author May 26, 1998.
16. Conversation with Ken Mason, Wrangell, July 29, 1997.
17. Richard A. Ramme. "They Rule the Stikine." *Alaska Life,* February 1942, p. 11.
18. R.M. Patterson, *Trail to the Interior.* William Morrow & Co., Inc., 1966, pp. 222–223.
19. www.visi.com/~alcan/now/nowhome.html
20. "Mighty Stikine Offers Traveler Real Thrills: Even Veteran Gal Reporter Succumbs to Lures." *Wrangell Sentinel,* June 6, 1941.
21. "William Barrington, Jr. Is Appointed Deputy Collector, Skagway." *Island County Times,* March 9, 1944.
22. Bill and Elna Barrington tape 2001–02, courtesy of relatives Marlene and Hill Barrington, III.
23. Ibid., Bill and Elna tape 2001–02.
24. "Arola–Barrington Nuptials Last Sunday." *Wrangell Sentinel,* Jan. 28, 1944.
25. "Barrington Company Completes Season of Hauling on Yukon." *Wrangell Sentinel,* Oct. 27, 1944. Note: An early issue of the *Wrangell Sentinel,* Feb. 11, 1944 said Hill, Richie, and Early formed the new company. It is believed that Hill sold his interest to Syd. A May 10, 1945 issue of the *Island County Times* of Whidbey Island stated both brothers sold their Stikine interests to Al Richie. This is probably what happened, as Hill remained in Oak Harbor, and while Syd still worked the Stikine, he may well have been paid by owner Richie or was gaining payments at intervals.
26. "Barrington, Early, Ritchie to Operate on River This Year." *Wrangell Sentinel,* Feb. 11, 1944.
27. "Mrs. Sid Barrington Entertains for Mrs. Clements in Seattle." *Wrangell Sentinel,* June 9, 1944. Andy Smith died sometime between the February 1944 date and June of the same year. The widowed Mrs. Smith attended the Clements gathering.
28. Ibid., "Barrington, Early, Ritchie to Operate on River This Year."
29. Ibid., "Mrs. Sid Barrington Entertains for Mrs. Clements in Seattle."
30. "'Emmy' Reid Leaves River for Briny Deep." *Wrangell Sentinel,* Sept. 24, 1943.
31. Capt. Campbell Arrives with New Vessel From South for Season's Work." *Wrangell Sentinel,* July 14, 1944.
32. "Sourdoughs on the Wing." *Alaska Weekly,* March 24, 1944.
33. Barry C. Anderson, *Lifeline to the Yukon.* Seattle: Superior Pub. Co., 1983, p. 84.
34. "Barrington Once Again on Yukon." *Island County Times,* Aug. 17, 1944.
35. "Barrington Once Again on Yukon." *The Alaska Weekly,* August 11, 1944.
36. Ibid., "Barrington Once Again on Yukon." *Island County News.*
37. "Largest Freight Volume in History Is to Move Down River This Season." *Jessen's Weekly,* July 7, 1944.
38. Ibid.
39. "More River Boats Are Needed to Move Army Supplies from Nenana." *Jessen's Weekly,* July 21, 1944.
40. John E. Pegues, "More or Less News." *Jessen's Weekly,* July 28, 1944.
41. Ibid., Barry C. Anderson, p. 87.
42. "Rivers Are Now Busy Highways." *The Alaska Weekly,* August 18, 1944.
43. "Barrington Company Completes Season of Hauling on Yukon." *Wrangell Sentinel,* Oct. 27, 1944.
44. Kent Sturgis, *Four Generations on the Yukon.* Fairbanks: Epicenter Press, 1988, p. 30. Jim Binkley eventually settled in Fairbanks and developed the Discovery sternwheeler trips, plying the waters of the Chena and Tanana Rivers. He and his family ran a commercial operation beginning 1950, the business soon working into a major tourist attraction.
45. Phone conversation with Jim Binkley in Fairbanks, with author August 9, 1999.
46. "Alaskans Save Fellow Soldier From Drowning." *Jessen's Weekly,* October 6, 1944.
47. "Barrington Company Completes Season of Hauling on Yukon." *Wrangell Sentinel,* Oct. 27, 1944.
48. "Freight Movement From Nenana Down Yukon Is Ended for Current Year." *Jessen's Weekly,* October 20, 1944.
49. "Governor, First Lady Enjoy River." *Wrangell Sentinel,* July 14, 1944.
50. "Finest Trip Ever." *The Alaska Weekly,* August 11, 1944.
51. "Barringtons Leaving for Yukon River." *Island County Times,* May 10, 1945.

52. Ibid.
53. "River Boats Leave for Freighting Season on Yukon." *Jessen's Weekly,* June 22, 1945.
54. "Barrington Leases Famed *Aksala*; Will Operate on Nenana–Galena Route." *Jessen's Weekly,* April 20, 1945.
55. Arthur E. Knutson, *Sternwheels on the Yukon.* Snohomish, WA: Snohomish Publishing Co., Inc., 1979, p. 36. In gold rush years, running out of Whitehorse, the *Aksala* was called that when under Canadian Registry. When she transferred to American Registry, her name was simply spelled in reverse—the *Alaska.* Stan Cohen, in his book *Yukon River Steamboats,* states the *Aksala* was built in Whitehorse in 1913 by the American Yukon Navigation Co (AYNCo.) Name changed to *Aksala* when it was owned by the British Yukon Navigation Co. (BYNCo.).
56. Phone conversation with Jim Binkley in Fairbanks, with author August 9, 1999.
57. Ibid., Barry C. Anderson, p. 90.
58. "War Ends." *Jessen's Weekly,* August 17, 1945.
59. Claus-M Naske and Herman E. Slotnick, *Alaska: A History of the 49ᵗʰ State.* Grand Rapids, Mich.: William B. Eerdmans Publishing Co., 1979, p. 124.
60. "Casca Makes Final Voyage of Season on Upper Yukon Route." *Jessen's Weekly,* Sept. 21, 1945.
61. Conversation with Elna Barrington, Anchorage, August 29, 1998.
62. Bob Greenhagen, "Searching for Fortune on the Yukon Rivers." *Whidbey News,* April 13, 1972. Also, Lucile McDonald, "The Barringtons of Oak Harbor." *The Seattle Times,* Nov. 29, 1964, p. 2.
63. Trudy J. Sundberg, "Captains Sid and Hill Are Oldest Native Sons." *Whidbey Press Progress Edition,* p. 4, All Whidbey Section.
64. "Barringtons Establish New Business in South." *Wrangell Sentinel,* June 4, 1948.
65. Phone conversation with Bill Barrington, Anchorage, Oct. 6, 1998.
66. Lucile McDonald, "The Barringtons of Oak Harbor." *The Seattle Times,* Nov. 29, 1964.
67. Phone conversation with Ed Rasmuson, Anchorage, Jan. 18, 1999.
68. "I'm Satisfied Now." *Alaska Life,* March 1941, p. 2.
69. Phone conversation with Edwin Callbreath, Seattle, July 15, 1998.
70. Jim Binkley told of a small incident which Syd showed the power he commanded with his money. Syd was driving in Seattle with Jim as a young lad beside him. A policeman stopped the car for some infraction, and Syd told Jim as he left the car, "You stay here." After a few minutes Syd returned and started the car. "What happened?" Jim asked. "Nothing," Syd replied. "I just introduced the policeman to General Grant." Phone conversation with Binkley, August 8, 1999.
71. "Alaska Railroad Considers Abandoning Yukon Riverboat Service at End of 1949 Season." *Alaska Weekly,* April 29, 1949.
72. "Couple, Formerly of Wrangell, Entertain." *Alaska Weekly,* May 30, 1947.
73. "Mrs. Barrington Ill." *Wrangell Sentinel,* May 28, 1954.
74. "Funeral Services for Mrs. Barrington Held in Seattle." *Oak Harbor News,* June 17, 1954.
75. "San de Fuca." *Oak Harbor News,* Nov. 29, 1951.
76. "Sid Barrington." Unknown author Undated article, possibly about 1952.
77. Conversation with Amos Burg, April 7, 1985.
78. "Cassiar Prospector Writes From Gold Pan." *Wrangell Sentinel,* August 19, 1932.
79. Phone conversation with Hill Barrington, III, Tacoma, with author in Seattle, Feb. 18, 1998

18: CROSSING THE RIVER

Taking on years was not the end for the Barrington men. They did opt for a more settled life; certainly that was true for Hill. Even though Al Richie now owned the Wrangell riverboat business, Syd stayed on as pilot,[1, 2] navigating a new Richie boat, the sixty-four-foot *Judith Ann*.

With more time on their hands, Hill and Mildred visited the north country,[3] especially with son Bill Barrington and his growing family settled in Juneau. During the spring of 1953, Bill and family took a long vacation south to California. On the way home to Alaska they stopped to see relatives on Whidbey Island. The young Bill Barrington family, intending to bring only Grandma Mildred back north with them, boarded the *Princess Louise* heading up the Inside Passage. Imagine their surprise spotting Grandpa Hill waving to them on the Juneau dock, welcoming them on arrival. Secretly he had taken a job on Richie's boat, *Totem*. He would be moving freight up the Taku River to Tulsequah[4] spending the summer in Alaska's capital city.

Just as river operations tapered off, so did the older Barringtons. Over the course of years, family milestones occurred. Perhaps more than anything, Harry's death in 1952 at eighty-three years brought mortality home to the men. Big brother Harry, who had been a part of the Klondike, a part of Wrangell, who shared the mining, the boating careers and certainly who remained the male mainstay of Whidbey Island life, died March 9, 1952, at his home in San de Fuca.[5]

The Barringtons endured further loss when only two years later, older sister, Sibella Fisher, passed away in 1954. Mrs. Fisher, the *Oak*

Syd Barrington in the later years at the wheel of
the *Judith Ann*, outside Wrangell.
Credit: Edith Carter.

Harbor News said, lived a long, fruitful life, being Whidbey Island's
oldest native daughter.[6]

Called "Auntie Sibbie," Sibella lived an active fifty-eight years in
San de Fuca, continuing the home base for the Barringtons following
her mother's passing in 1938. As her own death approached, Sibella
sensed it; she went downtown and had her hair done for the occasion.[7]
At the age of eighty-six, Aunt Sibbie died quietly at the home of her
sister-in-law, Mrs. Harry (Dora) Barrington in San de Fuca.[8]

Whidbeyite Mrs. Chet Thomas wrote a "Memorial to Sibella
Fisher," published in the *Island County Times*. In the poem, Mrs.
Thomas spoke of Sibella's birth, her womanhood, marriage and senior
years. The last stanza might sum up what many of the old timers felt
about passing on during those pioneer years:

> So live your life to the fullest—
> Smile while you shed your tears,
> She is just ahead—breaking the trail—
> For the rest of the Pioneers.[9]

The *Judith Ann* on the Stikine River,
about 1954.
Credit: Edith Carter.

Only six months later, Hazel Barrington, the colorful partner of Syd, passed away on June 8, 1954, in Seattle at the age of seventy-seven. For several years, Hazel had not accompanied Syd to Wrangell for the season. In spite of feeling poorly, she decided to journey north with him that spring. Could she have sensed it would be her last opportunity? In May she grew seriously ill, and Syd flew with her to Seattle where she died at Swedish Hospital.[10] Her obituary listed no surviving relatives. Syd Barrington must have felt half his life torn away when his mate of nearly fifty-three years passed on. She provided the back-drop for his living; she nurtured his flamboyant lifestyle.

But Syd, who lived for today—as his wife always had—did not indulge in self-pity. Three days after her funeral, Syd headed to Wrangell,[11] back on the job piloting the *Judith Ann*. During one trip to Telegraph, he himself became ill. Hill rushed to Wrangell to finish the river season while Syd flew south to a Seattle hospital for a short stay.[12] He could not have been an easy patient. Sickness slowed him down and interfered with his plans. He had things to do; being bed-ridden was bound to frustrate him.

Syd and Hill Barrington on shore along the Stikine
River during a trip on the *Judith Ann*, 1954.
Credit: Courtesy of Edith Carter.

Syd followed through with one more season on the Stikine. After all, freighting on the Stikine had slowed to a trickle, and Al Richie had everything well in hand. It was time to focus on mining. Even though the body might flinch at too much activity, Syd's will did not. Prospecting required his attention.[13]

On Syd's last piloting journey upriver to Telegraph Creek—actually on his eightieth birthday in June 1955—all the residents of the small town met the boat as it docked. They presented Syd with a huge sheet cake intricately displaying the *Judith Ann*. The frosting likeness told the story: Captain Syd shouting orders to two deckhands, a lifeboat overturned on deck, the cook standing in the stern, the vessel pushing a barge ahead. Everything was detailed and colored correctly.

There might have been a party and shared dessert, but Syd refused to cut the cake. After being displayed in Wrangell's Totem Bakery, Syd had the cake sent—intact—to Hill in Oak Harbor. Syd certainly felt Hill to be an equal partner during their lives and their careers.

So it seemed, riverboat travel had nearly disappeared. Excepting the Canadian steamboat, *Klondike,* historian Robert DeArmond wrote

Hill Barrington at the age of 82 in 1959, relaxing in his
Pastime recreation center.
Credit: Courtesy of Whidbey Press.

in a 1954 *Wrangell Sentinel* article, "so far as can be learned there is today only one vessel that carries freight and passengers and mail on a regularly scheduled river route on the western slope of North America."[14] He spoke of the Alaska passenger/freight diesel riverboat—the *Judith Ann* of the Stikine.

After living for years in Seattle, half-sister Olivia Monroe moved back to Whidbey Island in the 1950s. Intelligent, alert and active at ninety-seven, she died in July of 1956[15] after falling and breaking a previously fractured hip. Thus, nearly all the Barrington children who played and romped in the wilds of early Oak Harbor had passed away. Only Syd and Hill survived.

Hill Barrington busied himself with the Pastime pool hall in Oak Harbor. Anxious to hear Hill's early-day stories,[16] women frequently visited the Pastime. A nearby naval air station supplied most of the actual pool hall business.[17] Hill never took any guff from the sailors though, and if they grew rowdy, he kicked them out.[18] Occasionally Alaska visitors journeyed to Oak Harbor to talk over old times with Syd and Hill. Doris Barnes, until then the only female Alaska senator, drove through to see her daughter in Anacortes during the spring of 1955. Another visitor to Whidbey commented on Syd's appearance, even in his eighties. "Unlike the common conception of the wrinkled, weather-beaten seafarer, Capt. Sid's face is as fair and unlined as the taut white sails of a schooner heading into the wind."[19]

Hill still traveled out and around in his seventies and kept a sharp memory. One time riding on the way to Mt. Vernon, he looked out the car window, recognized an Indian friend from long past and shouted, "Stop the car!" Hill stepped out, hurried to cross the road and purposely stopped the man. Surprised, both stared at each other. Suddenly, the Indian smiled and asked, "Is that you, Tenas (Little Devil)?"[20] Hill and his friend had spent school days together, and though they had been out of touch for decades, each recognized the other within seconds.[21]

Living so close to Syd in town, Hill strolled over and looked in on his brother every day.[22] When it finally became necessary, Mildred cared for both of them. Hill never did believe he would die, and Syd went along with the idea. Hill's son Bill said if you closed your eyes when they were talking, you'd think some guys twenty years old were dreaming about what's going to happen. "Next year's the one," Hill would say.

"We'll hit it big," Syd echoed. Both always looked forward.[23] They thought they would live forever.

Never giving up, near the end of the 1950s Syd formed the Barrington Mines, Ltd. company with local businessmen. Their plan: "To develop and mine extensive Canadian placer holdings on Thibert Creek in the Cassiar Mining District at the western side of Dease Lake." With the development of mechanical improvements such as diesel engines and water pumping plants, the outfit hoped to mine gold on a large scale as well as recover other minerals such as platinum. After workers constructed a road, the business sped into full swing the summer of 1960.[24]

A year before his death, Syd vented his frustration and anger because he could no longer backpack and hike to his Cassiar holdings. "If I could get up to that mine. They don't know how to do anything. If I could just get up there!" he often complained.[25]

Still a hardcore miner, at the age of eighty-seven Syd summoned the strength to make one last trip to the Cassiar in 1962. While there, he experienced a slight accident with the vehicle he was riding on[26] and later became ill.[27] Slowly he recovered. A year later on June 28, 1963, a few days after his eighty-eighth birthday, he died of a stroke[28] in an Oak Harbor nursing home.[29]

Perhaps Hill's easy-going style and sense of humor eased him into a longer life, for he lived ten more years in Oak Harbor. He passed away at the age of ninety-five in the Coupeville Hospital Nov. 10, 1972.[30]

After Hill's passing, Mildred lived on quietly. It soon became evident that she needed everyday care, and son Bill brought her to his Anchorage home for the next five years.

Still attractive into her eighties, Barrington relatives tell one of the last memories of Mildred. She sat like a queen, attending a party in black hat and gloves, sipping a martini, surrounded by men.[31] Mildred joined the earlier adventurers on Sept. 12, 1977, at the age of eighty-seven.[32] Thus, a steamboating era ended.

• • •

The pioneering Barrington family ran a course of riverboating through the Northwest. One hundred years earlier, Edward Barrington Sr. launched his *Eclipse* into Washington waters, and began operations on the inland sea. The Barrington family careers then—first father in Puget Sound, and later sons in Washington, the Yukon, British Columbia and Alaska—generally paralleled the span of commercial riverboating in the Northwest.

Washington State, where the Barringtons grew up, where their relatives lived and where they located during the winter months, remained their family home throughout the years. It was a time before airplanes and heavy travel, when families settled in one place all their lives and drew comfort from social companionship.

But routine pursuits did not satisfy adventurers like Edward Barrington Sr. and his sons, who reached out for something more. Certainly Sydney and Hill found their careers in Alaska and Canada, spending half a year overall for nearly fifty years in the north, riverboating and mining. While Washington supplied the strength and stability for the brothers, the north provided the excitement and challenge both craved. The combination created rich, unique and fulfilled lives.

Times of daring, times of hustle. Harking back, one can almost feel the cool air, hear the whistles, the bells, the throb and swish of the paddlewheel in tune with every pounding heart, the shouting of voices thrilling through the air, "Steamboat a' coming! Here she comes!"

And as surely as Hill's boat crossed the river and touched shore where Syd waited for him, their voices mixed with exciting plans. "Next year's the one. You bet'ya. Next year's the big one!"

Perhaps that's how they should be remembered.

· · ·

1. Untitled article. *Alaska Sportsman,* July 1954.
2. "Alaskans Here & There." *Alaska Weekly,* Dec. 14, 1951.
3. "Alaskan Waters Call Pioneer Captain Brothers." *Island County Times,* May 7, 1953.
4. "Barrington Family Will Spend the Summer in Alaska." *Daily Alaska Empire.* June 10, 1953.
5. "Death Takes Capt. Harry G. Barrington, 83." *Seattle Times,* March 10, 1952.
6. "Whidbey's Oldest Native Daughter Dies Sunday in San de Fuca at 86." *Oak Harbor News,* Jan. 21, 1954.
7. Conversation with Elna Barrington, Anchorage, August 29, 1998.
8. Ibid., "Whidbey's Oldest Native Daughter Dies Sunday in San de Fuca at 86."
9. Mrs. Chet Thomas, "Memorial to Sibella Fisher." *Oak Harbor News,* Feb. 4, 1954.
10. "End O' the Trail." *Alaska Weekly,* June 11, 1954.
11. "Funeral Services for Mrs. Barrington Held in Seattle." *Oak Harbor News,* June 17, 1954.
12. Phone conversation with Edwin Callbreath, Seattle, July 15, 1998.
14. Bob DeArmond, "Capt. Barrington Skippers *Judith Ann* on Stikine: Last Passenger and Mail Run Riverboat Operating in West." *Wrangell Sentinel,* July 4, 1954.
15. "Olivia Monroe Pioneer, Dies." Unnamed newspaper obituary, dated July 19, 1956.
16. Conversation with Bill Barrington, Anchorage, April 11, 1998.

17. *Washington Road Map*. A Gousha Travel Publication, Simon & Schuster Inc., undated.

18. Phone conversation with Hill Barrington, III, Tacoma, and author Feb. 18, 1998.

19. "Barrington History Told in Progress Edition of *Whidbey News-Times*." *Wrangell Sentinel,* July 7, 1961.

20. Dorothy Neil, "Whidbey Indians Befriended 'hyas tyee' Ed Barrington." *Whidbey News-Times,* June 17, 1995. The Indian word 'Tenas' actually means "child," but in this context, it meant "child of Red Devil," with reference to Edward Barrington Sr. Hill knew his friend meant "little devil."

21. Ibid., conversation with Bill Barrington.

22. Conversation with Elna Barrington, and author, Anchorage, August 29, 1998.

23. Ibid., conversation with Bill Barrington.

24. "Barrington Mines, Ltd." Undated, unauthored "contract."

25. Ibid., conversation with Elna Barrington.

26. Ibid.

27. "Pioneer Steamboat Man of Far North Dies at Age 88." *Juneau Empire,* July 8, 1963.

28. Washington State Department of Health, Certificate of Death #12146, issued June 28, 1963. Also, Dr. Henry Akiyama, Juneau, August 14, 1998, cause of death information.

29. "Capt. Sydney Barrington Services Set." *Seattle Post-Intelligencer,* June 29, 1963.

30. "Obituaries." *Whidbey News Times,* Nov. 16, 1972.

31. Bill and Elna Barrington interviews, 2001–02, courtesy of relatives Marlene and Hill Barrington, III.

32. "Obituaries: Mildred Barrington." *Anchorage Times,* Sept. 14, 1977.

BIBLIOGRAPHY

AGENCIES

Alaska State Historical Library, Juneau, Alaska.
Anchorage Museum of History and Art, Anchorage, Alaska.
Columbia River Maritime Museum, Astoria, Oregon.
Dawson City Museum & Historical Society, Dawson City, Yukon, Canada.
Heritage Library, Museum, Anchorage, Alaska.
Irene Ingle Public Library, Wrangell, Alaska.
Island County Historical Society, Coupeville, Washington.
Jefferson County Historical Society, Port Townsend, Washington.
King County Records, Seattle, Washington.
Maritime Museum Library, San Francisco, California.
National Archives & Records Admin., Pacific Alaska Region, Seattle, Washington.
Puget Sound Maritime Historical Society, Seattle, Washington.
San Francisco Maritime National Historical Park, San Francisco, California.
Seattle Public Library, Seattle, Washington.
University of Washington Libraries, Seattle, Washington.
University of Alaska, Fairbanks, Alaska.
Washington State Historical Society, Research Center, Tacoma, Washington.
Western Washington University, Bellingham, Washington.
Wrangell Museum, Wrangell, Alaska.
Yukon Archives, Whitehorse, Yukon, Canada.

ARTICLES

"Alaska Girl Power." *Alaska Magazine,* August 1998.
Burlingame, Virginia S. "John J. Healy's Alaskan Adventure." *Alaska Journal,* Autumn, 1978.
"Capt. Syd Barrington of the Stikine." *Pacific Motor Boat,* Jan. 1933.
"Columbian." (Steamer) *Fort Wrangel News,* 1898. (Kinky Bayers card, Ms 10, Alaska State Library)
"Comment and Controversy." *Alaska Life.* March 1941.
Commercial Age, Vol 1, # 3 Microforms A 427, Oct. 16, 1869, Alaska State Library
Vol 1, # 5 Microforms A 427, Oct. 30, 1869, Alaska State Library.
"Community Profiles, Wrangell" Alaska Economic Development internet database.
Conover, C.T. "Just Cogitating: Marine Mishaps Between Seattle, Skagway." *Seattle Times,* Jan. 8, 1956.
Darst, Madeline Fisher. "Christina McCrohan Barrington Power." *A History of a Whidbey Island Family,* undated.
Davis, Ebby. "More on Early Yukon Steamboating." *Alaska Sportsman,* July 1967.
Deane, Leslie. "The Stikine—River of Beauty." *Alaska Sportsman,* August

1937.

DeArmond, R.N. "Down Through the Years." *Alaska Journal,* Winter 1979.

DeArmond, R.N. "Riverboating on the Stikine." *Alaska Journal,* Autumn 1979.

DeArmond, Bob. "Riverboat Journey Up Stikine with Capt. Barrington Like Nothing Else in This World." *Alaska Weekly,* Aug. 6, 1954.

Dirks, Clarence, "Oak Harbor Clan Outshines Hornblower." *Seattle Post-Intelligencer,* June 18, 1952.

"End of the Trail." *Alaska Sportsman,* February 1973.

"End of the Trail." *Alaska Sportsman,* October 1963.

"Excursion to the Great Glacier." *Alaska Sportsman,* April 1963.

Findley, Rowe. "Road to Santa Fe." *National Geographic,* March 1991.

"From Cook Inlet." (Unknown paper, probably one from Whidbey Island), September 1896.

Gibbs, George S. "The Breaking Up of the Yukon." *National Geographic Magazine,* May 1906.

"Glad to be Back to the Halcyon Land." *Dawson Daily News,* May 23, 1916.

Grealey, Scoop. "Glitter of Gold Brings Back Memories for Oak Harbor Man." *The Sound,* Sept. 12, 1972.

Greenhagan, Bob. "Searching for Fortune on the Yukon River." *Whidbey News,* April 13, 1972.

Grimm, Tom. "Journey on the Stikine." *Alaska Sportsman,* May 1968.

Heckman, Edward. "I Was a Yukon Steamboat Man." *Alaska Sportsman,* November 1960; December 1960.

Holder, George, "Steamboat Stampeder." *Alaska Sportsman,* November 1958.

"In Memory of Joseph C. Power." (Unknown Washington paper) Obit: Oct. [20] 1922. (From Coupeville Museum to author, 8/10/98).

"Judith Ann Boat" (Untitled article), *Alaska Sportsman,* July 1954.

"Klondike Gold Rush" (Map and Guide). Klondike Gold Rush National Historical Park, National Park Service, undated.

"Letters, Notes and Comments—More on Early Yukon Steamboating." *Alaska Sportsman,* July 1967.

"Lower Stikine River Recreation Map." British Columbia Ministry of Forests, Dec. 1997.

Lung, Edward R. "Men Against the Ice." *Alaska Sportsman,* November 1952.

Lung, Edward R. "Racing Down the Yukon Trail." *Alaska Sportsman,* April 1951.

McDonald, Lucile. "The Barringtons of Oak Harbor." *The Seattle Times,* November 19, 1964.

Money, Anton. "A Voyage Up the Stikine." *Alaska Sportsman,* August 1964; September 1964.

Morison, Jack L. "Steamboats on the Yukon." *The Denver Westerners Roundup,* Nov–Dec. 1979.

"Mounted Police" E-mail information from Dawson City Museum, Dec. 1, 1998.

Neil, Dorothy. "Edward Barrington was an honest man." *Spindrift Magazine,* Summer 2003.

Parfit, Michael. "The Untamed Yukon River." *National Geographic,* July 1998.

"The Passing of an Era...." *Alaska Life,* April 1948.

Pearson, D.O. "Original Stories." *(The Coast) Northern Star,* May 1902. (In Morris Eldridge Scrapbook # 5, University Washington Library.)

"Perils of the Pioneer." *The Tacoma Sunday Ledger,* March 26, 1893.

"A Pioneer Passes Away." (Unknown date) Supplied by the Coupeville Museum August 1998.

"Prosecuting Boundary Survey," *Alaska–Yukon Magazine*, April 1911.

Ramme, Richard A. "They Rule the Stikine." *Alaska Life*, February 1942.

"S.S. Klondike" flyer. National Historic Site, Canadian Parks Service (undated).

Scidmore, Eliza Ruhamah. "The Stikine River in 1898." *Alaska Journal*, Autumn 1979.

"Seattle Man Cleans Up $150,000 on Frisco Election." (Untitled, undated, likely a Seattle 1927 paper) Courtesy of Peggy Darst Townsdin.

"Seattle Timeline." Seattle Public Library flyer, 1995.

"The Sluice Box." *Alaska Sportsman*, December 1939.

"Sounds Shipbuilding Industry Began with 4 Sailors in 1854." *Marine Digest*, January 13, 1940.

Strobridge, Truman R. and Dennis L. Noble. "North in the Spring, South in the Fall." *Alaska Journal*, Winter 1978.

Sundberg, Trudy. "Captains Sid and Hill Are Oldest Native Sons." *Whidbey Press*, June 1961.

"Thru the Gorge of the Alaska" flyer by Barrington Transportation Co., Wrangell, 1930s.[?]

Tower, Elizabeth A. "Hazelet's High Road to Chisana." *Alaska History*, Fall 1991.

Washington Road Map. New York: Gousha Pubs, S. & S, (undated).

Webb, Melody. "Steamboats on the Yukon River." *Alaska Journal*, Summer 1985.

"Welcome to Wrangell." *Wrangell Guide*, 1998.

"Whidbey Indians Befriend 'hyas tyee' Ed Barrington," (columnist Dorothy Neil) in *Whidbey News-Times*, June 17, 1995.

Willoughby, Barrett. "Champion White Water Pilot of the North." *American Magazine*, October 1928.

Winn, Bess. "The Stikine." *Alaska Sportsman*, September 1947.

"The Wrangler." *The Wrangell High School*, 1921.

BOOKS

Adney, Edwin Tappan. *The Klondike Stampede of 1897–1898*. Fairfield, WA: Ye Galleon Press, 1968.

The Alaska Almanac. Anchorage: Alaska Northwest Publishing Co., 1996.

Alaska Atlas & Gazetteer. Freeport, Maine: 1992 DeLorme Mapping, 1992.

Alaska Geographic, *The Lower Yukon River*. Anchorage, Alaska: Alaska Geographic Society, 1991.

Alaska Picturesque Souvenir Book. (No author listed, undated. Only stamped mail date: Oct. 13th, 1934.)

Allen, A.S. *Yukon Territory, Alaska, and Puget Sound*. Seattle: Pacific Coast Steamship Co., 1916.

Anderson, Barry C. *Lifeline to the Yukon*. Seattle: Superior Publishing Co., 1983.

Andrews, Clarence L. *Wrangell and the Gold of the Cassiar*. Seattle: Luke Tinker, Commercial Printer, 1937.

Annual Report of the Supervising Inspector-General Steamboat-Inspection Service. Washington, D.C.: Government Printing Office, 1909.

Bancroft, Hubert Howe. *History of Washington, Idaho, and Montana*. San Francisco: The History Company, Publishers, 1890.

Bayers, Lloyd G. *Mariner's Notebook # 2*, spiral bound. Juneau: AK. State Historical Library, various dates.

Berton, Pierre. *The Klondike Fever*. New York: Alfred A. Knopf, 1960.

Clark, Norman H. *Washington*. New York: W.W. Norton & Co., Inc., 1976.

Clifford, Howard. *Rails North*. Seattle,

WA: Superior Publishing Co., 1981.

Coates, Ken. *North to Alaska.* Fairbanks: University of Alaska Press, 1992.

Coates, Ken and Bill Morrison. *The Sinking of the Princess Sophia.* Toronto: Oxford University Press, 1990.

Cohen, Stan. *Yukon River Steamboats.* Missoula, Montana: Pictorial Histories Publishing Co., 1982.

Cook, Jimmie Jean. *A Particular Friend, Penn's Cove.* Coupeville, WA: Island County Historical Society, 1973.

Crowell, Edwin. *A History of Barrington Township and Vicinity, Shelburne County, Nova Scotia, 1604–1870.* Yarmouth, Nova Scotia: Edwin Crowell, Publisher, 1923.

Curtin, Walter R. *Yukon Voyage.* Caldwell, Idaho: The Caxton Printers, Ltd., 1938.

Denny, Arthur A. *Pioneer Days on Puget Sound.* Seattle: Alice Harriman Co., 1906.

Dobrowolsky, Helene and Rob Ingram. *Edge of the River: Heart of the City.* Whitehorse: Lost Moose Publishing, 1994.

Downs, Art. *Paddlewheels on the Frontier, Vol. 1 and 2.* Surrey, B.C., Canada: Foremost Publishing Co. Ltd., 1967.

Drago, Henry Sinclair. *The Steamboaters.* New York: Dodd, Mead & Co., 1967.

Duggan, William Redman. *Our Neighbors Upstairs: The Canadians.* Chicago: Nelson-Hall, 1979.

Elson, Robert T. (plus editors). *Prelude to WWII.* Alexandria, VA: Time-Life Books, 1977.

Ferrell, Ed. (Compiler, Editor) *Biographies of Alaska–Yukon Pioneers, 1850–1950, Vol. I.* Bowie, Maryland: Heritage Books, Inc., 1994.

Ferrell, Nancy Warren. *Alaska: A Land in Motion.* Fairbanks: University of Alaska Press, 1994.

Ferrell, Nancy Warren. *Barrett Willoughby: Alaska's Forgotten Lady.* Fairbanks: University of Alaska Press, 1994.

Graves, S.H. *On the "White-Pass" Payroll.* New York: Paladine Press, 1908 (reprint 1970).

Hacking, Norman R. and W. Kaye Lamb. *The Princess Story: A Century and a Half of West Coast Shipping.* Vancouver: Mitchell Press Limited, 1974.

Haycox, Stephen. *Alaska: An American Colony.* Seattle: University of Washington Press, 2002.

Henrick, Basil and Susan Savage. *Steamboats on the Chena.* Fairbanks: Epicenter Press, 1988.

Henrick, Basil and Susan Savage. *The Role of the Steamboat in the Founding and Development of Fairbanks, Alaska.* Fairbanks: Alaska Historical Commission, 1986.

Heilprin, Angelo. *Alaska and the Klondike.* New York: D. Appleton & Co., 1899.

Hutchinson, Ernest (Director: Sec. Of State). *Told By the Pioneers, Vol. II.* W.P.A. sponsored Federal Project No. 5841. Seattle 1938. (Unknown Pub.)

Janson, Lone E. *The Copper Spike.* Anchorage, AK: Alaska Northwest Publishing Co., 1975.

Juneau Telephone Directory. Juneau, Alaska, 1924–1941.

Kellogg, George Albert. *A History of Whidbey's Island.* Printed by author, 1934.

Kitchener, L.D. *Flag Over the North.* Seattle: Superior Publishing Co., 1954.

Knutson, Arthur E. *Sternwheels on the Yukon.* Snohomish, WA: Snohomish Publishing Co., Inc., 1979.

Lawrence, Guy. *40 Years on the Yukon Telegraph*. Vancouver: Mitchell Press, Ltd., 1965.

Lokke, Carl L. *Klondike Saga*. Minneapolis: Norwegian–American Historical Assoc., by University of Minnesota Press, 1965.

McBride, William D. (Also spelled MacBride) (Compiler) "Saga of Famed Packets and Other Steamboats of Mighty Yukon River." *Cariboo and Northwest Digest*, Spring 1949–Winter 1948. pp. 97–114.

McDonald, Linda E.T. and Lynette R. Bleiler (compilers). *Gold & Galena*. Mayo, Yukon: Mayo Historical Society, 1990.

Martinsen, Ella Lung. *Black Sand and Gold*. Portland, OR: Metropolitan Press, 1969.

Martinsen, Ella Lung. *Trail to North Star Gold*. Portland, OR: Metropolitan Press, 1969.

Mates, Pilots, and Engineers of Merchant Steam Vessels, Motor, Sail. Steamboat-Inspection Service. Wash. D.C.: Government Printing Office, various years. Books for years, 1895, 1899, 1902, 1903, 1904.

Mathews, Richard. *The Yukon*. New York: Holt, Rinehart and Winston, 1968.

McLain, John Scudder. *Alaska and the Klondike*. New York: McClure, Phillips, & Co., 1905.

Mighetto, Lisa & Marcia Montgomery. *Hard Drive to the Klondike*. Seattle: Northwest Interpretive Assoc. in assoc. with the U. of Washington Press, 2002.

Money, Anton. *This Was the North*. New York: Crown Publishers, Inc., 1975.

Morgan, Lael. *Good Time Girls of the Alaska–Yukon Gold Rush*. Seattle: Epicenter Press, 1998.

Morrell, W.P. *The Gold Rushes*. Chester Springs, PA: Dufour Editions, 1968.

National Geographic Road Atlas. Wash.

D.C.: GeoSystems Global Corp, National Geographic Maps and Melcher Media, Inc., 1999.

Naske, Claus-M and Herman E. Slotnick. *Alaska, a History of the 49th State*. Grand Rapids, Michigan: William B. Eerdmans Publishing Co., 1979.

Newell, Gordon (Editor). *H.W. McCurdy Marine History of the Northwest*. Seattle: Superior Publishing Co., 1966.

Newell, Gordon & Joe Williamson. *Pacific Coastal Liners*. Seattle: Superior Publishing Co., 1959.

Newell, Gordon. *Pacific Steamboats*. New York: Bonanza Books, 1958.

Newell, Gordon R. *Ships of the Inland Sea*. Portland, OR: Binfords & Mort, Publishers, 1951.

Norman, Thelma C. *Stampeder From Connecticut*. Issaquah, WA: Written and printed by the author, November 1998

Officers of Merchant Steam, Motor, and Sail Vessels. Steamboat-Inspection Service. Wash. D.C.: Government Printing Office, 1907.

Orth, Donald J. *Dictionary of Alaska Place Names*. Washington D.C.: U.S. Government Printing Office, 1967.

Patterson, R.M. *Trail to the Interior*. New York: William Morrow and Co., Inc., 1966.

Pioneers of Alaska 1907 through 1969. (Vol. 1, A–L). University of Alaska and Pioneers of Alaska Project, Jan. 1989.

Polk's Alaska Directory & Gazetteer, 1901–12; 1917–18; 1934–35 Index. Seattle: Alaska Directory Co., 1935.

Polk's Seattle City Directory, 1929; 1941. Seattle: R. L. Polk and Co., 1941.

Polk's Seattle City Directory, 1949. Seattle: R.L. Polk and Co., 1948–49.

Pollard, Lancaster and Lloyd Spencer. *A History of the State of Washington*. New York: American Historical Society, 1937. (Northwest Coll., University of Washington, Vol III.)

Potter, Jean. *The Flying North*. New York: The Macmillan Co., 1965.

Roche, W.J. (Hon. Minister of the Interior). *The Yukon Territory: Its History and Resources*. Ottawa: Ministry of the Interior, 1916.

Ruotsala, Jim. *Pilots of the Panhandle*. Juneau: Seadrome Press, 1997.

Steamboat Days on the Rivers. Portland: Oregon Historical Society, 1969.

Stefoff, Rebecca. *Washington*. New York: Marshall Cavandish, 1999.

The Stikine River. Anchorage: Alaska Geographic Society, 1979.

Stuck, Hudson. *Voyages on the Yukon and Its Tributaries*. New York: Charles Scribner's Sons, 1917.

Sturgis, Kent. *Four Generations on the Yukon*. Fairbanks: Epicenter Press, 1988.

Townsdin, Peggy Darst. *History of a Whidbey Island Family*. Compiled and printed by the author, 1994.

Urdang, Laurence (Editor) *The Timetables of American History*. New York: Simon & Schuster, Inc., 1981.

Wharton, David. *The Alaska Gold Rush*. Bloomington, IN: Indiana University Press, 1972.

Wickersham, James. *Old Yukon*. Washington, D.C.: Washington Law Book Co., 1938.

Williamson, Joe and Jim Gibbs. *Maritime Memories of Puget Sound*. Seattle: Superior Publishing Co., 1976.

Willoughby, Barrett. *Gentlemen Unafraid*. New York: G.P. Putnam's Sons, 1928.

Willoughby, Barrett. *River House*. New York: Triangle Books, 1935, 1936.

World Almanac and Book of Facts–2001. Mahwah, NJ: World Almanac Books, 2001.

Wrangell Telephone Directory–1944; 1945–57; 1958. Wrangell, various years.

Wright, Allen A. *Prelude to Bonanza*. Sidney, B.C.: Gray's Publishing, Ltd., 1976.

Wright, E.W. (Editor). *Lewis & Dryden's Marine History of the Pacific Northwest*. Seattle: Antiquarian Press, Ltd., 1967.

MISC. VITAL RECORDS, UNPUBLISHED

Application for Marriage License #906, at Dawson for Mildred Clare Ward (23) and William Hill Barrington (36), June 30, 1913.

"Barrington Mines, Ltd.," contract. Unsigned, undated, written about 1958. (Courtesy of Peggy Darst Townsdin.)

Bayers, Lloyd H. Kinky Bayer's Ms 10 Clippings. Alaska State Library, Juneau.

"Births, Marriages, and Deaths" registry, St. Mary's Church, Dawson. CM #016 (001) microfilm reel, supplied by Yukon Archives.

Certificate of Death #12146, Sydney Barrington. Washington State Dept. of Health, Vital Records, Olympia, WA.

Certificate of Marriage #6061, Sydney Charles Barrington and Hazel Delisle. Washington State Dept. of Health, Vital Records, Olympia, WA.

DeArmond, Robert. Biography card for Syd Barrington. Alaska State Library.

DeArmond, Robert. Letter to the author about personal experience with Syd Barrington. Letter dated March 1998.

Unpublished letter from Edward Barrington, Sr. from Albins Mines, Canada, to his father in England, dated May 5, 1842. (Courtesy of Peggy Darst Townsdin.)

Unpublished letter from Edward Barrington, Sr. from Oak Harbor, WA. to his brother in Cape Breton, Canada, December 1865. (Courtesy of Peggy Darst Townsdin.)

Unpublished letters from Eddie, Syd,

and Yorke during Klondike gold rush days of the 1896–1909 from Kenai, Dawson, and the Puget Sound area. (Courtesy of Peggy Darst Townsdin.)

"Masters Trip Reports to the Superintendent," 1903–27. Inventory to the White Pass & Yukon Route records. Supplied by the Yukon Archives, Whitehorse, December 1998.

Morgan, Lael. Personal typed notes on the Barrington family and relatives during their lifetime.

"The Most Unforgettable Character I've Met." Type written article about "Sid Barrington," unsigned author, undated. (Raw pages supplied courtesy of Robert DeArmond, June 1998.)

"Naturalization Papers." For Edward Barrington, Sr., Washington Territory, November 27, 1859. Supplied by Western Washington University, Bellingham.

"North West Mounted Police" records, D series 4, Misc. 1898–1951. Registered Persons inwards, December 1898–Sept. 1900. Dawson City Museum.

United States Census, Washington Territory–1880., Island County, Enumeration District #37.

University of Washington, Suselow Library, Information card. Newsletter 109, April 1959. Seattle, Washington.

Websites

Alcan Highway Home Page
British Columbia History Database
California Gold Rush
Center for the Study of the Pacific Northwest
Dollar Times Inflation Database
Filson's Pan for Gold Database
John J. McCusker, monetary comparisons
Kitco Inc. Historical London PM Gold Fix, 1833–Present. Kitco Inc., database. August 10, 1998.
Klondike Gold Hypertex Database
San Francisco Museum
Skagway Museum Database
Yukon Info Database

Personal Contact

Akiyama, Henry (Juneau). Phone conversation, August 14, 1998.

Arola, Ed (Wrangell). Personal interview September 16, 1998.

Barrington, Bill and Elna (Anchorage). Several personal interviews April and August 1998, plus numerous phone conversations and letters until their deaths in 2003 and 2004.

Barrington, Hill, Sr. and Mildred tapes, recorded by Eddie Barrington 9/1/1970, courtesy of relatives Marlene and Hill Barrington, III.

Barrington, Bill and Elna tape interviews, 2001–02, courtesy of relatives Marlene and Hill Barrington.

Barrington, Hill, III (Tacoma). Phone conversation, February 1998.

Binkley, Charles "Jim" (Fairbanks). Phone conversation, August 1999, Dec. 5, 2002. (Passed away Jan. 3/2003, 82 years old, Fairbanks.)

Burg, Amos (Juneau). Personal interview, April 1985. (Now deceased)

Callbreath, Daisy (Wrangell). Phone conversation, September 1998.

Callbreath, Edwin C. (Seattle). Phone conversation July 1998.

Campbell, Leonard (Wrangell). Phone conversation, May 1998.

Carter, Edith (Juneau). Personal conversation, June 1985.

DeArmond, Bob (Sitka). Correspondence, March 1998.

Ellis, David and Jean (Petersburg). Phone conversations September and October 1998.

Ferrell, Nancy Warren, trip up the

Stikine River to Boundary by jet boat, summer 1998.

Gendreau, Darlynne (Ketchikan). Phone conversation and correspondence, September 1998.

Henning, (Betty) Marion (Sun City, Arizona). Several phone conversations and letters, winter 1998–1999.

Jabusch, Kay (Wrangell). Director, Irene Ingle Public Library 1998–

Kaer, Cathy (Wrangell). Personal conversation, September 1998.

Kaer, Verna (Wrangell). Phone conversation September 1998.

Mason, Ken (Wrangell). Personal interview, July 1997.

Neal, Patricia (Portland, OR). E-mail conversation, September 1998.

Otteson, Dorothy (Wrangell). Phone conversation September 1998.

Rasmuson, Ed (Anchorage). Phone conversation, January 1999. (Now deceased)

Seimears, Margaret Rose (Wrangell). Phone conversation, January 1999.

Steele, Carolyn (Oklahoma). Phone conversation, July 1999.

Townsdin, Peggy Darst (Coupeville, WA). Numerous phone conversations and correspondence, 1998–present.

Newspapers

Numerous and various issues of the following newspapers:

Alaska Daily Empire (Juneau)
Alaska Daily Guide (Skagway)
Alaska Times (Cordova)
Alaska Forum (Rampart)
Alaska Weekly (Seattle)
Alaskan (Skagway)
Anchorage Daily Times
Anchorage Times
Cook Inlet Pioneer
Daily Alaska Dispatch (Juneau)
Daily Alaska Empire (Juneau)

Daily Klondike Nugget (Dawson)
Daily Alaskan (Skagway)
Daily Colonist (Victoria, BC)
Daily Evening Star (Whitehorse)
Daily Morning Alaskan (Skagway)
Dawson Daily News
Dawson Morning Sun
Dawson Record
Fairbanks Daily News-Miner
Fairbanks Weekly Times
Farm Bureau News (Oak Harbor)
Intelligencer (Seattle)
Island County Times (Whidbey Is.)
Jessen's Weekly (Fairbanks)
Juneau Empire
Ketchikan Alaska Chronicle
Ketchikan Dispatch
Klondike Nugget (Dawson)
Mining Journal (Ketchikan)
Morning Sun (Dawson)
Nome Gold Digger
Nome Nugget
Oak Harbor News
Petersburg Press
Petersburg Weekly Report
Seattle Post-Intelligencer
Seattle Daily Times
Seattle Times
Semi-Weekly Nugget (Dawson)
Semi-Weekly Star (White Horse)
Sound (Washington)
Stikeen River Journal (Wrangell)
Tacoma Sunday Ledger
Vancouver Province
Weekly Star (Whitehorse)
Whidbey Press Progress Edition
Whidbey News-Times
Whidby News
White Horse Star
Wrangell Sentinel
Yukon Daily Morning World (Dawson)
Yukon Midnight Sun (Dawson)
Yukon Morning Sun (Dawson)
Yukon Sun (Dawson)
Yukon World (Dawson)

INDEX

103, 115; renumbered 180

Hazel B. No. 2, 107, 115, 124; renumbered, 163; photos of renumbered vessel, 164

Hazel B. No. 3, 115, conquers canyon 119, 124-125, 128, 130; photo of, 165

Hazel B. No. 4, 115; launched in 1919, 131; used for hunting, 148

Healy, Captain John, 52

Henderson, Bob, prospector, 84

Henderson, Scow, 51

Heney, Michael J., 23

Henning, Betty, 6

Henning, Bob, 6

Hootalinqua River (now Teslin), 53, 75, 100

Hoover, Herbert, 140, 157

Hudson Bay Company, 115, 125

Humboldt, 39

hunting, 67, 94 (with photo), 115, 120, 130, 139, 141, 147

hydraulic mining, 72, 131, 155

- I -

ice breakup on Yukon River, 24, 26, 27 (photo), 65, 75, 81, 87-88; 101; early breakup of 1913, 103

ice cream, 118

influenza, 130

Inside Passage, 19, 39, 65, 101

insurance, 83

international boundary, 118. See also American Boundary Survey.

International Highway discussed, 170

Irving, see *Willie Irving.*

Iskut, largest tributary of Stikine, 118, 128

Iskut district, opened for mineral exploration, 128

- J -

Jackman, Captain, 67

James, Dennis, friend of Yorke

Barrington, 139

James Domville, steamer, 37; photo of wreck, 40

James Lee, Captain, 39

Jekyl, Sam, tanner in Wrangell, 147

John C. Barr, steamer, 52

Johnson, Liisa Barrington, 6

Jordan, Captain Ernest, 53-54

Judith Ann, 191-192

Juneau, 8, 191. See also Inside Passage.

- K -

Kalkins, Captain Ed., pilot of *Hazel* vessel, 163

Klootchman's Canyon, gorge, 119

Klondike Gold Rush, 10, 17, 24, 34, 60, 115, 120

Klondike River, 96

Kluane diggings, 66, 73

Koyukuk River strike west of Fairbanks, 51

Kustika-a, bad spirit, 128

- L -

La France, steamer purchased by Syd and associates, 72, photo of 76, photo of 82

Lake Bennett, 20, 31, 57

Lake Lebarge, 20, 28, 38, 65, 72, 75; opens for navigation in spring of 1911, 79; 87; spring of 1914, 102.

Lake View Cemetery, Seattle, 105

lava beds, 121

Llewellyn Glacier, 23

Long Beach, California, 137

Lowe, Robert, engineer on *La France,* 73-74

- M -

Macmillan River strike, 84

mail delivery, 87, 170

Malstrom, Mrs. Harold, sister of Christine Anderson Barrington, 84

Marconi project (telegraph line), 51

Martin, Captain Steve, cousin to Barrington family by marriage, 73; 82